SAA AND UNIX

IBM'S OPEN SYSTEMS STRATEGY

IBM Series

K. BOSLER • *CLIST Programming* 0-07-006551-9

H. MURPHY • *Assembler for COBOL Programmers: MVS, VM* 0-07-044129-4

H. BOOKMAN • *COBOL II* 0-07-006533-0

P. MCGREW, W. MCDANIEL • *In-House Publishing in a Mainframe Environment, Second Edition* 0-07-046271-2

J. RANADE • *DB2: Concepts, Programming, and Design* 0-07-051265-5

J. SANCHEZ • *IBM Microcomputers Handbook* 0-07-054594-4

M. ARONSON • *SAS: A Programmer's Guide* 0-07-002467-7

J. AZEVEDO • *ISPF: The Strategic Dialog Manager* 0-07-002673-4

K. BRATHWAITE • *System Design in a Database Environment* 0-07-007250-7

M. CARATHANASSIS • *Expert MVS/XA JCL: A Complete Guide to Advanced Techniques* 0-07-009816-6

M. D'ALLEYRAND • *Image Storage and Retrieval Systems* 0-07-015231-4

R. DAYTON • *Integrating Digital Services* 0-07-016188-7

P. DONOFRIO • *CICS: Debugging, Dump Reading, and Problem Determination* 0-07-017606-X

T. EDDOLLS • *VM Performance Management* 0-07-018966-8

P. KAVANAGH • *VS COBOL II for COBOL Programmers* 0-07-033571-0

T. MARTYN • *DB2/SQL: A Professional Programmer's Guide* 0-07-040666-9

S. PIGGOTT • *CICS: A Practical Guide to System Fine Tuning* 0-07-050054-1

N. PRASAD • *IBM Mainframes: Architecture and Design* 0-07-050686-8

J. RANADE • *Introduction to SNA Networking: A Guide to VTAM/NCP* 0-07-051144-6

J. RANADE • *Advanced SNA Networking: A Professional's Guide for Using VTAM/NCP* 0-07-051143-8

J. TOWNER • *CASE* 0-07-065086-1

S. SAMSON • *MVS: Performance Management* 0-07-054528-6

B. JOHNSON • *MVS: Concepts and Facilities* 0-07-032673-8

P. MCGREW • *On-Line Text Management: Hypertext* 0-07-046263-1

L. TOWNER • *IDMS/R* 0-07-065087-X

A. WIPFLER • *Distributed Processing in the CICS Environment* 0-07-071136-4

A. WIPFLER • *CICS Application Development Programming* 0-07-071139-9

J. RANADE • *VSAM: Concepts, Programming, and Design, Second Edition* 0-07-051244-2

J. RANADE • *VSAM: Performance, Design, and Fine Tuning, Second Edition* 0-07-051245-0

M. KILLEN • *SAA: Image Processing* 0-07-034609-7

M. KILLEN • *SAA: Managing Distributed Data* 0-07-034608-9

SAA AND UNIX

IBM'S OPEN SYSTEMS STRATEGY

Michael Killen

McGraw-Hill, Inc.

New York   St. Louis   San Francisco   Auckland   Bogotá
Caracas   Hamburg   Lisbon   London   Madrid
Mexico   Milan   Montreal   New Delhi   Paris
San Juan   São Paulo   Singapore
Sydney   Tokyo   Toronto

Library of Congress Cataloging-in-Publication Data

Killen, Michael.
    SAA and Unix : IBM's open systems strategy / Michael Killen.
       p.   cm.
    Includes index.
    ISBN 0-07-034607-0
    1. IBM Systems Application Architecture.   2. UNIX (Computer file)
  I.   Title.
    QA76.9.A73K54   1992
    004.2'2--dc20   91-44104
                                                  CIP

1 2 3 4 5 6 7 8 9

ISBN   0-07-034607-0

The sponsoring editor for this book was Jeanne Glasser.

Printed and bound by R. R. Donnelley & Sons.

Subscription information to BYTE Magazine: Call 1-800-257-9402 or write Circulation Dept., One Phoenix Mill Lane, Peterborough NH 03458.

I dedicate this book to my lovely wife Josephine, who helps me understand another aspect of computing.

Contents

Acknowledgments

Many people have contributed to my understanding of Systems Application Architecture and UNIX and the roles they will play in customers' future information systems.

First, I would like to thank all the people who participated in two television series produced by Charlie Class and myself for our business technology talk show "High Technology with Killen & Class." They are Robert Kavner, president of the Data Systems Group of AT&T; David Tory, president of the Open Software Foundation; Peter Cunningham, president of UNIX International; Geoff Morris, president and CEO of X/Open; Scott McNealy, president and CEO of Sun Microsystems, Inc.; Wim Roelandts, group vice president of Hewlett-Packard; Don McInnis, formerly of Digital Equipment Corporation; L. Robert Libutti, programming systems director of Marketing Strategy, IBM; David Liddell, manager of Market Plans for Image Processing, IBM; Jack Hancock, executive vice president of Technology for Pacific Bell; Jon D'Alessio, staff vice president and CIO of McKesson Corporation; Jim Bellmaier, vice president of Mips Computer; and Roger Sippl, CEO of Informix, Inc.

I would also like to thank Allan Krowe, former executive vice president of IBM; Larry Lytle, executive director of Interactive Multimedia Association; and Earl Wheeler, IBM vice president and general manager of Programming Systems; who graciously gave of their time and knowledge.

S. S. (Tim) Tyler, partner of the System Consulting Consortium, Inc., whom I cannot thank enough, has been a continuing source of inspiration and knowledge.

Thanks go also to Charles C. C. Brett, managing director of The SAA Spectrum, for his insight.

And last but not least, I thank Edie Gaertner, director of Technical Publications for Killen & Associates, Inc., for her dogged oversight of this project from beginning to end.

Trademarks

Altos Computer is a registered trademark of Acer America Corporation.

Amdahl and UTS are registered trademarks of Amdahl Corporation.

Apple, Apple II, Appleworks, and ProDos are registered trademarks of Apple Computer, Inc.

Macintosh is a trademark licensed to Apple Computer, Inc.

Apollo and NCS are trademarks of Apollo Computer, Inc.

UNIX, 5ESS, System V, 3B, SVID, 6383 Work Group System, AT&T Data Systems Group, and USO are registered trademarks of AT&T Co.

Businessland is a registered trademark of JWP Businessland, Inc.

CDC is a registered trademark of Control Data Corporation.

Claris is a registered trademark of Claris Corporation.

Compaq is a registered trademark of Compaq Computer Corporation.

CompuServe is a registered trademark of CompuServe Incorporated.

Computer Associates is a registered trademark of Computer Associates International, Inc.

Data General is a registered trademark of Data General Corporation.

DEC, VAX, and VAX/VMS are registered trademarks and DECnet is a trademark of Digital Equipment Corporation.

Dell is a registered trademark of Dell Computer Corporation.

EDS is a registered trademark of Electronic Data Systems Corporation.

Federal Express is a registered trademark of Federal Express Corporation.

Fujitsu is a registered trademark of Fujitsu America, Inc.

GE is a registered trademark of General Electric.

HP is a registered trademark of Hewlett-Packard Company.

Hitachi is a registered trademark of Hitachi America, Inc.

AIX, Application System/400, IBM, PS/2, OS/2, and RT are registered trademarks of International Business Machines Corporation. AS/400, DB2, ES/9370, ImagePlus, Micro Channel, NetView, OS/400, RISC System/6000, SQL, System/360, System/370, MVS/ESA, SAA, and Systems Application Architecture are trademarks of International Business Machines Corporation.

Intel is a trademark of Intel Corporation.

Intergraph is a registered trademark of Intergraph Corporation.

MCI is a registered trademark of MCI Communications Corporation.

McKesson is a registered service mark of McKesson Corporation.

Memorex/Telex is a registered trademark of Memorex/Telex N.V.

Microsoft, MS-DOS, and XENIX are registered trademarks and MS Windows is a trademark of Microsoft Corporation.

Mips Computer Systems is a registered trademark of Mips Computer Systems, Inc.

Motorola is a registered trademark of Motorola Corporation.

NEC is a registered trademark of NEC Corporation.

NCR and NCR Comten are registered trademarks of NCR Corporation.

OSF and OSF/MOTIF are trademarks of the Open Software Foundation.

Pacific Bell is a registered trademark of Pacific Telesis Group.

POSIX is a trademark of IEEE (The Institute of Electrical and Electronic Engineers).

Prime Computer is a registered trademark of Prime Computer, Inc.

PRODIGY is a registered service mark and trademark of Prodigy Services Company, a partnership of IBM and Sears.

RCA is a registered trademark of Radio Corporation of America.

ROLM is a trademark of ROLM Company.

SCO is a trademark of Santa Cruz Operation, Inc.

Siemens is a registered trademark of Siemens Aktiengesellschaft of Berlin and Munich, Germany.

Silicon Graphics is a registered trademark of Silicon Graphics Inc.

Software AG is a registered trademark of Software AG, Inc.

Sony is a registered trademark of Sony Corporation.

StorageTek is a registered trademark of Storage Technology Corporation.

Sun, SunOS, SPARC, NFS, X.11/NeWs, and RFS are registered trademarks of Sun Microsystems, Inc.

Tandem is a registered trademark of Tandem Computers, Inc.

Ungermann-Bass is a registered trademark of Ungermann-Bass, Inc.

UniForum is a registered trademark of UniForum Association.

Unisoft is a registered trademark of Unisoft Corporation.

Unisys is a trademark of Unisys Corporation.

UNIX International is a registered trademark of UNIX International, Inc.

Vion is a registered trademark of Vion Corporation.

VPL Research is a registered trademark of VPL Research, Inc.

Wang is a registered trademark of Wang Laboratories, Inc.

Wyse Technology is a registered trademark of Wyse Technology.

Xerox and ETHERNET are registered trademarks of Xerox Corporation.

X/Open is a registered trademark of X/Open Company, Ltd.

SAA AND UNIX

IBM'S OPEN SYSTEMS STRATEGY

1
Introduction

Jack Hancock, executive vice president of Technology for Pacific Bell, recently discussed with me the great challenge that managers of information systems development projects face. Hancock's responsibilities include, among others, Pac Bell's billion-dollar computer-communications infrastructure and 3000 programmers. According to Hancock, "We have entered the most competitive decade businesses have ever faced. Everyone in IS must apply new thinking to assist their corporations to gain ground in the 1990s."

Hancock expresses the concerns of business leaders everywhere. Many chief executive officers (CEOs) are less sure than ever that they can hold ground in the 1990s, much less gain ground. The demanding forces of competition that spur us all on will continue to build in the 1990s and will strike from everywhere. Top executives do not know what actions to take to get the competitive advantage that enables them to get business ahead of their competitors.

These business leaders recognize the growing force of competition and want the men and women of information systems departments to take a leadership position in providing the enterprise with the systems that make not only a contribution, but a significant contribution. They must enable the corporation to improve the bottom line.

In large corporations, or even in small companies, it is difficult to determine what will make the greatest contribution to the enterprise. Half of the art of knowing what to work on is possessing all the relevant information about the situation, which, of course, is impossible. The other half is viewing

1

the situation through a flawless body of principles—recommendations on how to determine the best course to take. This, also, is problematic. Then, what is someone to do?

Hancock, a former U.S. Army major general, holds that we may never be able to make the optimum decision for any situation, but if we concentrate on gathering the right information and on developing the right thought patterns, we can improve our decision making. "Once you determine the 'best' objective—having taken into consideration what resources you have to attain objectives—and formulate your strategy, you have to wisely manage your resources in the pursuit of those objectives. In the pursuit of the development of information systems that enable the enterprise to increase performance, we have only three resources—information systems technology, management thought, and the human element—and they are all complex and difficult forces to manage."

In this book, I have tried to assist information systems professionals to increase their understanding of part of one of these three resources—information systems technology, specifically IBM's Systems Application Architecture (SAA) and "open software systems" strategy. It is beyond the scope of this book to address the role that important management thought, such as the Taylor school of scientific management, the mechanization school, the living and "intelligent" systems schools of thought, or even project management plays in our information systems development decisions. Neither do I address the significant role the human element—you and I—plays in this process. Sorting out the role of IBM's SAA and open software systems is in itself a large topic.

You will note that when I used the term "open software systems," I placed it in quotes. That is because it is a term that means different things to different people. Computer vendors have spent billions of dollars to educate us to their parochial and proprietary meanings.

Scott McNealy, president and CEO of Sun Microsystems, states that "Open computer systems are systems where no one supplier controls the operating systems."

Earl Wheeler, IBM vice president and general manager of Programming Systems (and the driving force behind IBM's SAA strategy), considers IBM's SAA "open"—"Every time IBM provides the customers a standard software interface across the SAA operating environments, IBM's four main line operating systems become more open. You can more easily migrate your investment forward."

Jon d'Alessio, staff vice president and chief information officer (CIO) of McKesson Corporation, holds the view that IBM's proprietary operating systems are, in a way, more open than UNIX systems are. "The fact that IBM systems are so numerous, and that a well-developed infrastructure exists to support those systems, give those main line IBM proprietary systems a quality of openness that can't presently be matched."

In my opinion, "open software systems" is a term that denotes a computing environment where the customer can, more easily than in any other computing environment, move their investment in software, data, and skills to another computing operating environment.

I wrote this book using a UNIX workstation produced by one of the most ardent promoters of open software systems. Yes, it provides a degree of openness; I can easily migrate my investment in software, data, and skills to my present supplier's next system. However, it is difficult to migrate those investments to a competitor's UNIX system. As a result, I am more locked into that particular UNIX supplier than I would like to be. Thus, the quotes around "open software systems."

The information I present here that encompasses SAA, IBM's AIX (Advanced Interactive Executive operating system) and open systems strategy, and open software systems in no way addresses all of the important issues. It is a large topic. However, I hope that those who read this book will improve their understanding of IBM's approaches to information systems and their knowledge of the history surrounding the development of open systems.

The approach I have taken in presenting the information in this book is atypical of technical books. In an attempt to enliven the role of technological issues and to keep you from putting the book down, I have written the first, mainly historical, chapters in novel style rather than technical computer style. However, the remaining chapters return to the style you would expect for a book of this genre. The two approaches, I hope, bring you greater interest and value.

2

Moment of Truth

If you had attended the February 18, 1987 IBM Management Committee (MC) meeting you would have heard IBM's top executives planning the announcement of IBM's most important software strategy, Systems Application Architecture (SAA). As a way of introducing the key concepts of SAA, I am including an excerpt here from my book on SAA—*IBM: The Making of the Common View*, in which IBM executives outline SAA to the IBM Management Committee.

•••••••••••

A few minutes before 1:00 P.M., Peter Dance, accompanied by John Friedline, drove over to the Armonk parking lot. Ten minutes later, Earl Wheeler arrived with Morris Taradalsky seated next to him and Don Casey in the back seat. Dick Hanrahan and Mike Saranga drove their own vehicles.

At the reception desk, Dance and Friedline signed into the IBM Employee Guest Book, once called the Visitors Book. After the popular TV series V aired about "visitors"—creatures and reptiles from outer space that invaded Earth for "people food"—someone in IBM thought it was distasteful for guests or IBM employees to be labeled "Visitors." Hence, the name of the guest register was changed to something less ghoulish.

Dance and Friedline walked directly to a door that separates the atrium from the rest of the building. The receptionist pressed a button, causing the door to open. Dance and Friedline took two quick steps

5

through it, then turned sharply right again and found themselves facing the elevator that would take them upstairs.

When the elevator doors opened, the men stepped in and Dance pressed the third-floor button. In a couple of seconds the elevator, which could hold no more than five people comfortably, moved upward. After what seemed to be a long time, the elevator opened onto the third-floor reception area. An attractive middle-aged woman greeted them from a desk. Dance stopped to tell her who they were.

Meanwhile, Friedline began looking about the room. As he wandered, he turned his head to his left and then suddenly stepped forward as if to dodge an oncoming person or object. Through the corner of his left eye, he glimpsed the outline of a man's face and shoulder. As he turned around, he laughed. There was John Opel, John Akers' predecessor, not walking toward him or standing next to the wall, but suspended on the wall. On the left wall, flush with the elevator door, an oil painting of Opel gazed out into the room at Friedline. The painting isn't noticed unless a guest takes a few steps into the reception area and turns around or looks backward. John laughed and said to himself, "Well, Opel still keeps me hopping."

Moments later he heard Dance say, "Hey John, there's Learson, and Cary, and over there is Watson Senior. Watson Junior's over there—all IBM Chairmen."

"Hey, Pete, who is that woman over there in the white formal?" Of all the likenesses hanging on the walls, only one was a woman.

"I think that is Watson Senior's wife."

Then John asked, "Where's Akers?"

"I think you don't get hung here until you're a retired IBM Chairman," Peter replied.

The receptionist interrupted, saying, "That's not completely correct." She pointed to a blank space on the wall and explained that it was usually filled with a rotating exhibit of other works.

Dance, beginning to think about what he was going to say to the MC, distractedly murmured, "That's great, that's just great."

With that, Dance and Friedline took seats on the orange sectional chairs. Within minutes, a train of attendees began to flow by. Krowe, Kuehler, Akers, and Paul Rizzo walked in. Everyone nodded, smiled, or otherwise briefly acknowledged each others' presence. Akers recognized Dance, but not John Friedline. A few minutes later, the rest of the MC and some assistants filed in and briskly entered the MC conference room, closing the door behind them.

Just as the conference room door closed, the elevator doors on the opposite side of the reception area opened and someone within said, "You go first."

"No, after you."

Finally, saying "Okay, I'm getting out," Mike Saranga burst into the room. The other development executives trailed behind him.

"Hi, Pete. John."

Dance said, "Glad you all decided to come. I wouldn't want to do this alone."

"You needn't worry about that," Saranga replied.

Zero Hour Approaches

As the guests seated themselves, the reception room suddenly quieted. Some participants began to look over notes. Others stared distractedly at open magazines and newspapers while thinking about their presentations. Some just sat. No one admitted to stage jitters.

About 1:25 P.M., the conference room door opened. More than one of the presenters suddenly recalled the feeling they had had as children when the dentist's nurse walked into the reception area. But it was the Administrative Assistant (AA) who had worried so much about Crawford's speech, the Raleigh storm, and Don Casey's whereabouts who stepped into the reception area.

The AA walked over to Earl Wheeler, greeted him formally, and asked whether his party was ready.

"The name's Earl. Please call me Earl. Yes, we're ready."

"Great. Ah, can we just go over a few things to make sure everything goes smoothly?"

"Sure. Peter, Mike, won't you come over here, please?"

"First, how many of you will be going in?"

Earl replied, "Speaking just for the developers and myself, there will be five. Peter?"

Dance then said, "From the Field, I will be the only one." No reference was made to Friedline.

The AA said, "That makes six; okay."

Then the AA, Wheeler, and the other presenters worked out the logistics—who would speak first, where everyone would sit, and how long the presentations might take. As soon as everyone understood the game plan, the AA excused himself, quietly reopened the door to the conference room, and disappeared behind it. A minute or two later, a light flashed on the reception's phone. As soon as she put the receiver down, she glanced at Wheeler and said, "Mr. Wheeler, you and your party may go in now."

As Wheeler and the others walked toward the door, one of them nervously joked, "Wheeler party of six, your table's ready." Another warned, "Smile as you go by them [the MC members]—look like you're happy to see them." A third took a deep breath: "I'll be glad when this is over."

Hanrahan, Saranga, Taradalsky, Casey, and Dance, followed by Wheeler, entered the conference room at the right front corner. They felt like nervous college students walking into a lecture hall in front of the professor's podium as they filed in past the MC members. The four development executives and Peter Dance took seats in the second row and along the sides of the room. Earl Wheeler remained standing between the podium and the wall on the right.

The AA briefly introduced Wheeler, who then stepped to the podium. As Wheeler took charge of the lectern, he handed the AA a folder of transparencies. Within 20 minutes, Wheeler and everyone else in the room would regret that action.

The AA took the folder and walked across the room to the overhead projector. He was pleased that Wheeler had brought overheads—the MC prefers them. When 35-mm slides are used, the lights have to be dimmed, thus obscuring the very revealing facial expressions of the presenters.

Wheeler Speaks

Wheeler cleared his throat in the shushed room several times. He lowered his eyes to a second manila folder containing his notes. For a moment he thought, "What an insignificant, plain, simple cover. This unpretentious scrap of cardboard holds the contents of SAA—a powerful, immense architecture that holds the key to future computing, perhaps the key to IBM's future." SAA was like a crucible into which the lives, souls, will, and minds of these men had been poured. How unfitting and unjust a container for so important a task was this innocuous folder. How true of life. Returning from this stream of consciousness to the room, Wheeler lifted his eyes to meet those facing him.

"I'm pleased to see all of you again," he said, and he meant it. Akers and a few others in the front row nodded, smiled, or otherwise acknowledged him. This was about the eighth time in the last year that

Wheeler had reported on the status of what eventually became SAA. Today was the most important of all the meetings.

Wheeler opened with an overview: "Today, I will briefly review why customers need SAA and some of the key benefits of SAA. I will also introduce the heads of the development team, who will each speak about their areas of technology and responsibility.

"I can categorically state that we can announce SAA on March 17 and that it is in our power to make SAA a reality in the marketplace within 2 years." As he said that, the AA placed the first transparency on the projector. It stated simply, *Systems Application Architecture*.

"I'll briefly set the stage to lead in to why customers need Systems Application Architecture." With that statement, he took a quick sip of water.

"To begin, the first computer systems available were hardware. Then, computer systems contained hardware, operating system, and applications software. Today, customers are talking about applications in an interconnected environment. That's what a computer system is today." Wheeler paused and said, "The essence of computing today is applications in an interconnected environment."

Everyone in the room knew exactly what Wheeler meant when he used the term *applications*—programs that are specific to the particular roles that a given computer performs within a given organization and that directly contribute to performing those roles. He also knew they understood what he meant by *interconnected*—multiple hardware and software systems distributed and connected throughout an enterprise. But Wheeler decided to elaborate.

"By interconnected applications, I mean applications that the user invokes that may say 'I need data,' and the system will be smart enough to say, 'Do I have the data, or is it somewhere else; if it's somewhere else, where is it throughout the multiple other systems? Bring back that data, join it, present it to the application.'

"What's important is that the user never need know that the system went a thousand miles away across many computer interconnections to get the data and present it to the application, which in turn presents it to the end user. The end user hasn't seen any effect, the application hasn't seen any effect, and the system has let the enterprise (the person who's managing the enterprise) decide where the data should be placed.

"Where an enterprise wants to place data today is not necessarily where they will want to place it tomorrow, so the enterprise should be able to build in that flexibility. The enterprise should decide where they want to do their network management and how they want to interconnect these things. Interconnected applications enable users to stop creating unique solutions that connect A to B but cannot connect C to B. Interconnected applications will eliminate that problem." Wheeler knew that he had rambled somewhat.

"This brings me to the integrated enterprise. We all know this is what the customers will want. Interconnected applications of course imply interconnected or distributed data bases. Our next major thrust will be the integrated enterprise system. And it's not a system that just takes copper or fiber optics and strings hardware together. We have to do it with software and do it in a way that's easy for us, easy for software companies, and easy for the ultimate customer.

"That means we have to offer customers a fully heterogeneous interconnect. You can truly interchange the operating systems as you form a very complex mesh network—a fully heterogeneous interconnect.

"But there's a lot we need to do to offer the customers integrated enterprise systems. A lot of problems need to be solved."

He paused, adjusted his notes, and then continued. "For a long time now, the scope and range of the IBM product line have demanded multiple hardware systems and multiple operating systems." They knew he meant the 370, 36, 38, and the PCs and their operating systems. At this point, one of the MC members interrupted to ask Wheeler to speak a little louder.

Slightly louder, he continued, "Each of these products has its own unique architecture. The individual performance of the various architectures that we have has been outstanding." He probably said that to disarm the member of the MC who had spent their professional careers helping to make the 370, 36, 38, or PC architectures a success.

At this point, Wheeler looked to his right and nodded to the AA, who placed on the overhead projector the transparency shown in Figure 2.1.

"We plan to interconnect four operating systems that support three hardware families." Pointing to the screen on his right he said, "We need to, in effect, interconnect the OS/2, the operating system of the follow-on 3X product, and the MVS [multiple virtual storage] and VM [virtual machine] operating systems. If we do that, it will enable our customers to really start moving toward implementing integrated applications and integrated enterprise solutions."

At this point, Akers raised his hand and asked, "It will enable the customers to more quickly and easily cut through their applications backlog, won't it?" Akers knew the answer, of course. He may just have wanted to be sure that everyone in the room appreciated the pragmatic quality of what Wheeler was presenting.

For a moment Wheeler paused. Then he answered, "Sure, but we've got to do a lot of work to make that happen. But that brings me to the interfaces." Again, Wheeler turned his head to the right and nodded to the AA working the projector. The AA placed a slide that looked very much like Figure 2.2 on the projector.

Then Wheeler said, "We think that four different software interfaces hold the key to making it easier than ever for customers to cut their application backlog down and to build interconnected applications and integrated enterprises. We need a common user, application, programming,

---

- OS/2, 3X Follow-on OS, MVS, and VM Operating Systems

- PS/2, 3X Follow-on, and 370 Hardware Environments

Figure 2.1 – The Scope of Systems Application Architecture

Interfaces:
- Common User Access
- Common Applications
- Common Programming
- Common Communications Support

Scope:
- PS/2, 3X Follow-on, and 370 Hardware Environments
- OS/2, 3X Follow-on OS, MVS, and VM Operating Systems

Figure 2.2 – Systems Application Architecture Interfaces

and communication support interface across the four operating systems and three hardware environments. With those interfaces, users and programmers can leverage their knowledge and tools. These interfaces will be supported across OS/2, the 3X's operating system, and the two most important 370 operating systems, MVS and VM."

At this point, Allen Krowe interrupted. "You're leaving the RT PC (IBM's workstation product) out of this?"

"Yes, at this time. But we may be able to add it in later," said Wheeler.

"Fine, sorry to have interrupted you."

"Sure."

Someone else asked, "Mmm, how do you think the customers will take it when they hear we don't plan to include the original PC with its PC-DOS operating system and the 370 with the VSE (Virtual Storage Extended) operating system?"

"Well, I don't think it's going to be a problem. We may have to explain to the PC-DOS and VSE customer base that those two operating systems lack the functions needed to participate in an SAA environment. When they realize this, I don't think we'll have a problem."

"Besides," interjected Akers, "we want customers to buy new technology and products anyway."

Another MC member asked, "What about UNIX?"

"What about it?" Wheeler shot back. "If the customers demand UNIX, we can add it to the list of operating systems that we support across the three hardware families. Technically, it's certainly possible. It's a marketing decision. It's a business decision."

Akers then added, "We have a task force studying what our UNIX business strategy should be. We can address that issue at a later date."

Wheeler continued, "This brings me to my second point—the benefits of Systems Application Architecture." He looked down at this notes and said, "Now, it's time to bring the 370, 3X, and PCs within a consistent framework to provide better productivity for customers and to improve ease of use. That is what Systems Application Architecture will do." He paused for a moment.

"Systems Application Architecture makes that new requirement of a computing system—interconnected applications—feasible." After he said that, he asked whether anyone had any questions. No one responded.

"We also believe we could do a better job of presenting those systems to the end users and to the people who write programs for them."

When he said *systems* they again all knew that he meant the three hardware families and the four operating systems. Then he said, "Systems Application Architecture will provide a single, consistent presentation."

From the audience, someone again asked Wheeler to speak louder. Wheeler is very soft-spoken—he must almost always be reminded to raise his voice when giving a speech. Today was no exception.

Wheeler again signaled for the next transparency, saying, "If applications functioning in an interconnected environment are what customers need, and I think they are, SAA provides the means to meet that challenge." Just as he said that, he heard the shishing sound of a half-dozen transparencies falling to the floor and a barely audible "God dammit."

Somehow, the AA had dropped the rest of Wheeler's slides. All eyes focussed on the AA as he struggled to gather them up. They could not hear the AA saying under his breath, "Dammit! That does it. They'll probably offer me Jackson Hole or Teheran as a sales territory after this screw up."

While the AA frantically collected the slides, Wheeler fielded a few questions. Then he signaled the AA for the next transparency. However, just as Wheeler started to say, "SAA provides . . .," he stopped. His words had no relationship to the words now projected on the screen.

"Ah, can you put up the transparency that has the SAA Benefits on it?" Wheeler requested.

Three seconds later, another group of words appeared on the screen and the AA said, "This is the one, isn't it?"

Wheeler said, "No, it's the one that says *Benefits* at the top and ah, I believe, ah, it has *Cooperative Processing* and *Enterprise Processing* on it." The AA tried another. At this point, Wheeler apologized to the audience and quickly walked across the front of the room to help the AA find the right transparency.

After inspecting three or four overheads, he told the AA to forget it. He'd finish his presentation without the transparencies—he knew what he needed to say. At least at that moment in time, he thought he did.

As Wheeler slowly returned to the podium, he stopped at the center of the room and looked out at this audience. He started, "The real benefits of SAA are . . . ." He paused. He began the same sentence again, and again paused. He apparently could not find the words to complete his thought.

Something was obviously wrong. Besides not being able to finish the sentence, he looked troubled and surprised.

As Wheeler continued to gaze straight ahead, his eyes focused on John Akers, who sat in his line of sight.

Still staring straight ahead, Wheeler tried again, "The real benefits of SAA are . . .," and again, he stopped. The people in the room began looking along Wheeler's line of sight to see what absorbed his attention. From where Wheeler stood at the center of the room, he could see straight in front of him not only Akers, the present keeper of the great IBM company and its institutions, but also Thomas Watson Senior, the patriarch of the company.

Perhaps this powerful view of Akers and the portrait of Watson behind him made Wheeler reflect on a larger view of his proposal. What Wheeler was proposing was not just another plan to build a computer product—like Eagle in Tracy Kidder's *The Soul of A New Machine*—this went way beyond that. Wheeler's proposal would alter the way millions of people would use computers and think about computing. It would also force hundreds of thousands of IBMers to change their thinking and method of operation. It would change the state of computing.

Momentarily, Wheeler, still staring straight at Akers and Watson said, "It's the view." What did he mean? Had that view of Akers with Watson majestically looming over him triggered something else deep in his mind? Did *view* have special meaning to Wheeler?

Wheeler searched to discover why the work *view* came to the forefront of his mind and his lips. Perhaps it was from the beliefs he had learned at Union College. No, not "to gather and evaluate information," or "to think coherently," or "to form aesthetic judgments," but the one that states "to view a time and place from a perspective of knowledge." Ah, that's the phrase now circling in his head—to view a time and place from a perspective of knowledge. And it influenced what he was trying to say.

Wheeler groped—trying to clarify the perception that it takes great knowledge of computer users, programmers, system analysts, software companies, IBM employees, and others to envision the problems in time and place that they faced, using computers. Mentally, he viewed the multiplicity of people and the problems each of them faced and he tried to formulate a simple and all-inclusive statement for what SAA would do for all of them.

The word *common* kept resurfacing, too. Perhaps it was because it permeated so many discussions and elements of SAA—a common user interface, common programming environment, common communications.

View—common. Common—view. Common view.

Was this what he was looking for? Were these the words that hit the mark? Was this the essence of Systems Application Architecture—a common view?

It must have all come together, because Wheeler suddenly said, "The benefits of Systems Application Architecture is that it creates a common view. No, not a single common view for everyone, but a different common view, depending on who you are and what your perspective is. Looking from each perspective, there's a common view."

With more confidence he continued, "SAA provides" (he paused briefly to do some quick arithmetic) "six or perhaps seven different types of people with a common view."

Dance, Morris, the other VPs, and all the members of the MC listened closely. Something had inspired Earl Wheeler.

"SAA enables users of our future line of PCs and midrange products, and of the 370 system, to see a common view. The common user interface makes that possible.

"SAA enables systems analysts planning multisystem implementations to see a common view of communication services across the four operating environments."

In the back of the room, Dance leaned over to Dick Hanrahan and whispered, "I like the sound of it."

When Wheeler paused for a moment, Jack Kuehler said, "And I can see how SAA will give all our employees a common view. It gives them a new focus. They know where to concentrate their resources."

Krowe said, "I can see how SAA can give our competitors one hell of a common view." With that the room filled with laughter. Krowe continued, "It gives them the broadest line of, in a way, homogeneous products to compete against."

Paul Rizzo said, "Yeah, it's like the days when we had a single family of 360s. One common view of that product."

Earl Wheeler took the floor again. "SAA will provide a spectrum of common views depending on who you are and how and where you look."

Wheeler walked back to the podium. The AA followed and handed him the transparency. Wheeler smiled a bit and told the AA it was okay. To himself he thought that had there not been a slipup, he might never have stumbled onto these insights.

After that dynamic experience, there wasn't much more for Wheeler to say. He finished by passing the podium on, stating that the development executives and the marketing representative, to whom they all owed a big debt of thanks for the tremendous job they had done on this project, would each speak on the status of his own area of responsibility in regard to SAA. A vote of thanks was also due the committee, Wheeler said, especially Messrs. Krowe, Akers, and Kuehler, for its support of this project. He then retired to the back of the room, and the AA introduced, one after another, the four development VPs and Peter Dance.

Each of the VPs spoke for no more than 15 minutes. Mike Saranga told a joke to lighten up his topic, Morris Taradalsky demonstrated his deep understanding of all the technical challenges, Hanrahan demonstrated the depth of his control of every aspect of his project, and Casey self-assuredly presented communications support. They were all ready to launch SAA. Peter Dance told the committee that the field and the team players were ready to kick off SAA on March 17.

After putting a few questions to team members, John Akers and members of the MC seemed satisfied. Akers nodded to Wheeler and thanked them all for their excellent work. With that, the Wheeler party left the MC meeting as they had come—through the door at the right front of the room.

The receptionist watched the six presenters and Friedline congratulate each other in the reception area. Wheeler made a point to tell each of them in a different way that the team could not have accomplished what it did without their specific contributions. But they, too, knew how important Wheeler's role was and would continue to be. Without him, this project might never have happened.

It never dawned on them that the MC had not really given a formal okay; at least no precise words had been spoken. But then, they hadn't gone to that meeting for a yea or nay. They went because they knew they had everything worked out.

Amid the handshaking and back clapping, Dance and Friedline extricated themselves and prepared to head for the parking lot. They told Wheeler they wanted to rush over to Ryebrook (headquarters of the field sales and marketing division) to break the news to Larry Ford and his boss, Ed Lucente, who headed the field organization. The field had no more than a month to prepare for the Saint Patrick's Day announcement. Dance wanted to get the troops moving right away. Wheeler certainly understood.

The rest of them—Mike Saranga, Dick Hanrahan, Morris Taradalsky, Don Casey, and Earl Wheeler—began to unwind. Eventually, they, too, walked to their cars. But as they drove down Old Orchard Road past the apple trees on the right and the guard station on the left, they all could feel the high of participating in a major event. Today marked the end of one phase of this project and one intense period in their lives. It foretold the beginning of an even more monumental one—implementation of the Systems Application Architecture strategy.

Later in the day as the sky darkened, Jack Kuehler, Allen Krowe, Paul Rizzo, and other members of the MC headed home. Wheeler's SAA strategy, to them, held the promise of revitalizing IBM, its people, and its marketplace. It could be the spark that would set off a renaissance in this somewhat lethargic, but still great computer company.

Akers, the former Navy pilot from Oakland, California, was the last to leave. He was thoughtful as he headed down Old Orchard Road. Any of a hundred thoughts could have been running through his mind: "It's decisive . . . . It concentrates our resources . . . . We have to make it happen fast." He may also have thought that the sooner customers, IBM employees, and the software companies would see the common view, the happier he would be.

One of the next things he would have to do would be to bring the 3X follow-on—Silverlake—to the market.

3

AT&T's Involvement in the Open Software Environment

The customers and the computer industry have AT&T, more than any other company, to thank or blame (depending on where you sit on the playing field) for the development of open software systems. AT&T, a company that, to date, has always lost money in computing, must be credited for transforming computing and the computer industry. Now that AT&T owns NCR, maybe it will also make money.

To understand open software systems, we must understand the pivotal role AT&T has played in it. This chapter reviews AT&T's role in shaping the open software systems technology, market, and industry.

3.1 THE EARLY DAYS

Charles Brown, former AT&T Chairman, first made public AT&T's desire to enter the computer market on January 7, 1982, when he participated in an announcement stating that the United States Department of Justice (DOJ) and AT&T had discovered a way to end the *U.S. vs. AT&T* case, which later resulted in the divestiture of AT&T. At that gathering, Brown stated that AT&T was now free to enter the computer marketplace—I doubt that he knew just how difficult that would be.

I met with Charles Brown in 1990 to discuss various topics. In that meeting, it became clear that when he had stated that AT&T "was now free to enter the computer market" he was under the impression that IBM would remain encumbered by the *U.S. vs. IBM* antitrust suit that had then entered its thirteenth year. I suspect he would have been less optimistic about entering the computer business if he had known that 5 hours later the DOJ would tell Judge David Edelstein that the government was abandoning the *U.S. vs. IBM* case.

AT&T was convinced it wanted to participate in the already large and rapidly growing computer market and it needed to be well positioned for the emerging "computer-communications" market. (Some of these same reasons led John Opel, former IBM chairman, to increase IBM's efforts to participate in the telecommunications market.)

In March 1984, AT&T announced the 3B line of products, which used Bell Labs' developed UNIX operating system. AT&T offered UNIX because Bell Labs had been using and enhancing that software technology since the 1970s, also because the company had no other suitable alternative operating system technology, and the operating system adequately matched the class of machine—the minicomputer. About the time that AT&T announced the 3B line, the thought of creating a UNIX standard and "open" systems began to jell.

In 1985, Jim Edwards, president of AT&T's Computer Systems line of business, and Jack Scanlon, vice president of what is now the Data Systems Group, defined a computer strategy for AT&T. Its goals were (1) to make UNIX System V an industry standard and (2) to capture a significant share of the UNIX computer market. Since 1985, two AT&T Data Systems presidents, Vittorio Cassoni and Robert Kavner, have reaffirmed these goals.

The thinking behind both goals was that creating a standard UNIX would "open" the computer market, take a decisive advantage away from IBM, Digital Equipment Corporation, and others, and provide AT&T a level playing field on which to compete. Once the field was leveled, AT&T's advantages of scale would come into play and AT&T would move briskly into the computer market. AT&T continues to work toward both goals.

As the months and years have passed, AT&T has developed a clear vision of an "open systems" environment. It's a vision, in my opinion, of an environment where standards exist for all major layers of computing—hardware platform, operating system, application enabling, user interface platform— and where all participants in the process, including customers and vendors, benefit from the use of standards. However, in this "open systems" environment vision, AT&T "owns" the operating system standard.

3.2   MAKING UNIX A STANDARD

AT&T attempted to make UNIX an "open" operating system standard because it was the only identifiable way to create a decisive advantage. The standardization of a technology like UNIX is based on the fundamental desire to use the advantages that standards setting yields—advantages of a "pull-through" force, product quality, and timing.

A "pull-through" force is that combination of external forces that helps pull a product into the market. An appropriate example of the pull-through force is the effect that shrink-wrapped software had on the sale of IBM PC clones. Because IBM made the hardware interface available to the industry (including Microsoft), all IBM-compatible PCs conformed to that specification. That enabled software developers to prepare programs for a common target machine(s) so that when the shrink-wrap was taken off the software package, the programs were ready to run.

Within a year or so after the announcement of the PC, a plethora of IBM PC-compatible software was available and helped to "pull through" millions of dollars in sales for IBM and the PC look-alikes.

AT&T has attempted, with some degree of success, to use a pull-through force for its UNIX operating system technology and computer systems. Through the licensing of System V Release 3, it attempted to force all licensees to offer systems that adhered to what AT&T defined as the "standard" UNIX implementation.

If a critical mass signed up to license Release 3 and built systems to it, a user base of systems with improved interoperability and software portability could be created, which, in turn, would create an attractive, large market for software developers. As the software developers wrote software for this market, AT&T and other UNIX system vendors would be pulled into that market. This pull-through force has developed to an extent, but not to the degree where it can be considered a success. To be considered successful, it would have to recoup the cost of creating that force.

Another relevant example of this involves IBM and the Open Software Foundation (OSF). A member of the Project Seneca team [the follow-on to the Hamilton group (a group of vendors who began to meet in response to AT&T's plans to "redistribute the wealth"), and predecessor to the OSF] placed a phone call to IBM to interest it in joining their group. Several weeks later, OSF purchased the rights to IBM's AIX operating system. In this case, the force and reputation of IBM created a pull-through that made it easy for IBM to sell its AIX technology to the fledgling OSF organization.

The creation of a standard usually gives the standard "owner" an advantage of product quality. This advantage is most noticeable when the controlling company enhances the technology that is the standard and does so in a way that improves its own product above that of its competitors. Listing a

UNIX command for a 3B system as a user-friendly mnemonic and a UNIX command for a competitive VAX (Virtual Address Extension) system as a hexadecimal is one such example.

The creation of a standard also usually gives its "owner" an opportunity to use the element of timing to its advantage. Timing advantage includes being able to execute actions, across many areas, at an optimal time; the result—outdoing the competition. A timing advantage in this case could provide AT&T the opportunity to implement the next UNIX release on its own or on a friend's hardware ahead of other licensees, or to introduce future UNIX releases when market conditions are better suited for sales of AT&T systems than for sales of other licensees' systems.

AT&T's Jim Edwards and Jack Scanlon (credited with being the first person to clearly articulate AT&T's computer objectives) identified several steps that needed to be attained to make UNIX a standard. They included

- Unifying the three major versions of UNIX
- Expanding the base of microprocessor hardware products and their infrastructure to support AT&T's UNIX software platform
- Educating potential customers about the existence of AT&T's UNIX operating system and the benefits of "open systems"
- Motivating software developers to pursue the emerging "open systems" market

Edwards' administration made some progress toward the above objectives. Vittorio Cassoni's administration restated many of the objectives and also made some progress, but during Cassoni's tenure, actions were taken by AT&T and others that would make it more difficult, if not impossible, for AT&T to attain its objectives in the foreseeable future.

To create a bandwagon behind its technology, AT&T set out to advance the UNIX technology to make it more attractive to computer systems suppliers. Most of the improvements focused on improving portability, scalability, and extensibility—all of which were necessary to achieve the desired bandwagon effect.

Making UNIX more portable encourages many computer systems suppliers to implement AT&T's operating system, as opposed to a proprietary operating system or a non-AT&T-supported version of UNIX, on the hardware platform of their choice.

By improving scalability, AT&T can offer UNIX at each of the three main price-performance points—intelligent workstations, minicomputers, and mainframes—and can ensure that applications can easily migrate along the three-tier environment. Various strains of AT&T's licensed UNIX are already offered on each of the three tiers—Microsoft's XENIX on Altos computers, AT&T's System V on Unisys computers, and Amdahl's UTS running in a native mode on Amdahl's mainframes. However, much work is needed to make it possible for applications to easily scale the three environments.

The company has also worked to improve extensibility—the facility to add features and capabilities to UNIX. Over the last few years the company has added many features (such as networking and the user interface) to the UNIX "base."

3.3 LOOKING TOWARD A UNIFIED UNIX

AT&T's wants a "unified" UNIX, but the problem is nontrivial, even if all the companies involved wanted to go along with AT&T's plans. This objective has two aspects:

1. The need to converge the three main strains of UNIX into a compatible product offering

2. The need to migrate the computer companies that market UNIX systems to the "standard" version

In 1985, AT&T began talking to both Microsoft and Sun Microsystems about eliminating the differences in their UNIX versions. Microsoft supports UNIX for the low-end market, PCs, and small multiuser systems; Sun Microsystems supports development of the Berkeley version of UNIX for high-performance technical workstations. It took several years before AT&T, Microsoft, and Sun Microsystems all agreed to merge the three versions of UNIX. When and if that is accomplished, AT&T will have made a significant step toward creating a common environment.

Persuading computer vendors to agree to AT&T's proposal to unify UNIX has not met with much success. When you consider that some suppliers use Berkeley technology as a base and add System V features as enhancements; some build systems on System V and add Berkeley enhancements; others license System V Release 2 and refuse to license System V Release 3; and there are other permutations, including an outright refusal by some companies to embrace any more AT&T technology if it means becoming further dependent on the son of Ma Bell, the situation is understandable.

Besides selling companies on the benefits of creating a unified industry and the benefits of using AT&T's advanced technology, to really unify UNIX, AT&T also had to sell the industry on licensing.

To corral all the various mutations of UNIX, AT&T began to make licensing requirements more restrictive. They introduced the System V Interface Definition (SVID), which describes the base UNIX and extensions of UNIX. SVID also defined the "standard" UNIX version that AT&T wanted everyone to offer, and SVID releases were linked to UNIX licensing contracts. With each SVID release, AT&T progressively tightened the licensing requirements to the point where licensees were required to implement all SVID features. Failure to comply with this requirement could result in revocation of a company's license. AT&T hoped this gambit would work to its advantage.

3.4   CAUSE AND EFFECT

In late October 1987, AT&T made an announcement restating many of its objectives and explaining how it planned to attain them. That announcement triggered a reaction in the industry, and several companies began the process that ultimately led to the creation of the Open Software Foundation in May 1988.

3.5   AT&T'S STATEMENT OF DIRECTION

AT&T made three important announcements in 1987 that provide insights into its strategy—the February, September, and October, 1987 announcements.

The February announcement disclosed that Microsoft and AT&T would work together to merge XENIX and System V. The September announcement gave AT&T's sales organization some new products to sell, but more importantly, it provided a framework that reveals how AT&T thinks about some aspects of computing. The historic October announcement unveiled a plan that, if executed properly, could potentially "redistribute the wealth of the computer industry" from "closed" operating systems vendors to "open" standards.

The October 17 announcement provoked such great controversy throughout the computer industry that I will comment extensively on it and quote from a telegram that was sent to AT&T by many computer industry executives who wanted clarification of AT&T's intentions.

3.6   FEBRUARY 1987 ANNOUNCEMENT

As I mentioned earlier, AT&T and Microsoft had conducted informal discussions on merging the XENIX and UNIX System V operating systems back in 1985. But according to AT&T officials, even though much had been written in the press about an agreement, no formal agreement existed until February of 1987. The agreement is significant in that a convergence of SVID and XENIX would eliminate some of the incompatibilities that make it difficult for programmers to port applications across two UNIX operating environments.

3.7   SEPTEMBER 1987 ANNOUNCEMENT

On September 2, AT&T announced an array of computer products, a statement of its direction, and its Application Operating Environment strategy.

- Products

Of the 40 or so computer products AT&T announced, the most significant may have been the 6386. The 6386 Work Group System merges the MS-DOS and UNIX operating systems. UNIX, serving as a bridge between PC products and minicomputer products, begins to play a new role.

- Statement of Direction—Operating Systems and Chips

AT&T recommitted itself to the support of two operating environments—MS-DOS and DOS derivatives, which obviously includes OS/2, and UNIX System V. AT&T pointed out that the market demanded that it provide competitive systems for the MS-DOS environment.

AT&T also reconfirmed its commitment to the Intel hardware platforms that support the MS-DOS environment. The company stated that great value had developed in the MS-DOS market, that value will remain there for a very long time, that AT&T's current machines based on the 80086, 80286, and 80386 technologies derive a lot of their value from that environment, and that AT&T will continue to ride that technology as long as it makes sense to do so.

- Application Operating Environment

AT&T introduced and defined its Application Operating Environment, a framework devised around AT&T's six elements of computing:

1. Operating Systems—master programs that interact with the hardware and control the execution of all other programs
2. Programming Languages—the programming languages and tools that make it possible to create useful applications

3. Data Management Software—software used to manage databases and teleprocessing applications

4. Networking Software—software that allows computers to exchange information and/or share processing tasks

5. Communications Software—protocols and software that facilitate communications between computers

6. Windowing—the video display and software that allow the screen to be divided into multiple "windows"

These six elements describe the layers of computing above the hardware platform.

There certainly is nothing flawed in AT&T's approach to segmenting the elements of computing. For contrast, IBM's SAA model consists of Applications, User Interface, Application Enabling, and Communications on top of hardware. The main structural difference is that IBM lumps development tools (languages, etc.) with data management to create the Application Enabling category.

In other differences between the two vendors, Application Operating Environment is based on an operating systems platform consisting of two "open" operating systems—System V and MS-DOS and its derivatives— whereas IBM's SAA platform sits on the "closed" operating systems of Operating System/2 (OS/2), Operating System/400 (OS/400), VM, and MVS. And AT&T's Application Operating Environment uses "closed" (proprietary) Intel 80XXX, Motorola 68XXX, and AT&T 32100 and 32200 chips; the IBM hardware platform sits on the Intel and IBM's own proprietary processors.

3.8   OCTOBER 1987 ANNOUNCEMENT

As previously mentioned, the October 19, 1987, announcement—"the shot heard around the world"—was broad and complex. There has been much debate about who said what when, and what it meant. I will attempt to present a fair and accurate account of the announcement and to stay above the conflict.

To begin with, AT&T announced the establishment of a computer platform that would redistribute the wealth of the industry away from suppliers of closed systems and shift the values of the industry to a standard operating environment. This strategy would "accelerate the advance of the price-performance curve and provide great benefits to users."

3.8.1 The "World of Computing" According to AT&T

AT&T shared its view of the "World of Computing" (Figure 3.1) in which the next 2 years would show a consolidation around four computing platforms—those of IBM, Digital, DOS (Disk Operating System) and OS/2, and UNIX System V.

The IBM platform consists of a closed architecture that spans a very broad range of power from microcomputer to mainframe products.

The Digital platform, based on the VMS operating system, spans not as broad a range of computing power as IBM's does, but it is coherent and consistent within itself. Again, it is a closed architecture and owned by the vendor who controls it.

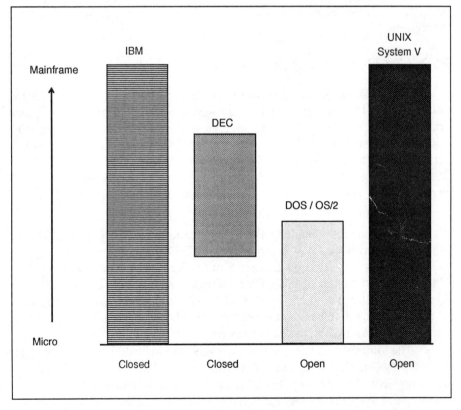

Figure 3.1 – AT&T's Vision of the "World of Computing" (*Source: AT&T*)

The third environment, DOS and OS/2, is defined by AT&T as an "open" environment but one limited by the Intel chip base of technology. (According to AT&T's definition of "open," a product must not be controlled by one vendor. Since you can only obtain Intel chips from Intel and because it does not license source code for this platform, it could be argued that DOS and its derivatives are built on "closed" or "semiclosed" systems.)

The fourth platform, AT&T's UNIX System V, spans the same range of powers as the IBM platform, and, in addition, is transportable across different architectural bases. However, UNIX is fragmented by many vendors who have used UNIX source to build different operating systems and operating environments that are not necessarily compatible with each other.

AT&T's vision of the "world of computing" seems to be a reasonable one. These are the operating systems we are stuck with for a while. But some people might argue that the fourth platform, AT&T's UNIX System V, should be labeled "closed" also, since only one vendor controls the System V operating system.

3.8.2 AT&T's New Computer Platform

AT&T announced a new computer platform consisting of three major components: (1) an alliance with a very aggressive and successful computer company, Sun Microsystems, to converge Berkeley 4.2 UNIX and Sun OS with UNIX System V; (2) the addition of a new "open systems" hardware platform based on Sun Microsystems' SPARC (Scalable Processor Architecture); and (3) the development of the "standard" Application Binary Interface (ABI) to drive binary compatibility across vendor product lines.

- Alliance to Unify UNIX

AT&T and Sun detailed a three-phase program to merge UNIX System V, Sun OS, and Berkeley 4.2 into a "single UNIX operating system" (Figure 3.2). Phase I would release a merged Sun OS Release 4.1 and UNIX System V in the second quarter of 1988. Phase II makes ABI and the enhanced UNIX System V available with NFS and X.11/NeWS in mid-1989. The third phase of the program will release a new version of UNIX incorporating the latest advances in operating system and networking technologies.

The joint software development on ABI was to be done in Summit (NJ); Sun engineers in California under the technical development of Bill Joy, Sun's vice president of R&D, were to do the hardware work. (Although no mention was made at the press conference that other members of the UNIX community would participate in this work, other AT&T press releases have mentioned it.)

It is worth pointing out here that the other computer companies were greatly concerned about "the whale and the bathtub shark" (AT&T and Sun) teaming up so closely to develop the next generation of System V, while they have to stay out of the water. AT&T, obviously, thought it had nothing to fear.

- New Architecture Based on the Sun SPARC Technology

AT&T also announced the adoption of the RISC microprocessor architecture (SPARC) developed by Sun. SPARC will be used in the development of AT&T's own midrange computers; and 3B and 6368 customers will be able to migrate easily to AT&T System V SPARC-based products in the future.

Adopting SPARC allows AT&T to drive "openness" all the way down to the hardware platforms that underpin UNIX technology, reducing its closed nature. These plans probably made more than a few semiconductor manufacturers and customers take notice.

Another point to be made here is that building a family of AT&T UNIX computers based on SPARC could provide a competitive advantage over closed and open systems based on complex instruction set computer (CISC) technology and at least level the playing field when competing against other restricted instruction set computer (RISC) vendors such as HP, Sun, and DEC. AT&T stated that Sun's RISC technology would provide a 4-to-1 price-performance advantage over traditional complex instruction set systems (CISC) products. No comparisons to other RISC-based systems were provided.

AT&T and Sun promoted RISC technology so heavily at the announcement that it was clear AT&T expected RISC, especially Sun's SPARC, to be-

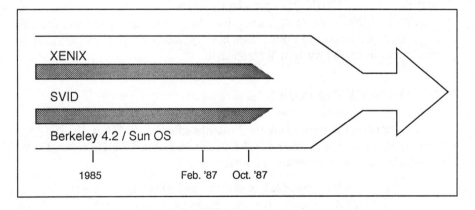

Figure 3.2 – UNIX Systems Consolidation (*Source: AT&T*)

come the AT&T UNIX platform of choice. Many of the two companies' competitors were concerned that AT&T would tune a future version of System V to the SPARC platform long before it ported that version to other hardware platforms, or that AT&T would work with Sun to merge UNIX to some specification that only the two knew about.

• The Application Binary Interface

The third element of AT&T's computer platform staggered the competition. AT&T announced that it would build upon the first two components and then attack the problem, making a common application environment difficult. The result is Application Binary Interface (ABI), and AT&T will encourage all UNIX vendors to comply with it.

ABI is a "complete" technology encompassing a multitasking operating system, NFS and RFS networking protocols, C compiler, X.11/NeWS windowing, and a user interface that operates on top of X.11/NeWS. ABI would also be based on SPARC. The benefit to the industry would be that application software written to this specification would run on all systems that comply to the UNIX/SPARC application standard in the same way that application software written for DOS has always run on PCs—you rip off the shrink-wrap, load the binaries, and the system is ready to run.

If the first two components of this plan (which were very important) warranted industry concern over the close relationship of AT&T and Sun, then surely the ABI announcement (which given its difficulty takes some time to comprehend) totally convinced the industry as it became more familiar with ABI that another governing body, other than AT&T, was needed to manage the development of UNIX. This plan had great potential impact on the industry and market. Needless to say, and, thankfully, for some vendors, the creation of the Open Software Foundation has given computer manufacturers an alternative to licensing System V Release 4.

3.9   INDUSTRY RESPONSE

On January 15, 1988, roughly 3 months after the October 19, 1987 announcement, a group of concerned UNIX licensees sent AT&T's James Olson and Vittorio Cassoni a telegram. I quote:

> As licensees of AT&T software and supporters of an open UNIX standard, we are concerned about recent announcements between AT&T and Sun Microsystems.

These announcements have created concern within our companies and our customers regarding the future of UNIX as an open standard.

We feel it is important to get a better understanding of these issues before the upcoming UniForum conference and we request a meeting between our corporate managers responsible for UNIX strategy and Mr. Cassoni during the week of January 25, 1988.

The telegram was sent under the combined names of none other than Tom Vanderslice, chairman of Apollo; Ward MacKenzie, vice president of Data General; Don McInnis, vice president of DEC; Patrick Richard, president of Gould; John Young, president of Hewlett-Packard; Jim Meadlock, president of Intergraph; John McNulty, president of Integrated Solutions; Robert Miller, chairman of Mips Computer Systems; Edward Staiano, executive vice president of Motorola; Tom Tang, vice president of NCR; Joe Henson, president of Prime Computer; Edward McCracken, president of Silicon Graphics; James Trebig, president of Tandem Computer; Donal O'Shea, president of Unisoft; and William Seymour, vice president of Wyse Technology.

The signing of this telegram by so many of the world computer industry's executives indicates the tremendous level of industry involvement AT&T triggered by its actions.

Signers of the telegram wanted clarification on some or all of the following issues:

- What did AT&T mean by "redistribute the wealth of the industry?"
- Was System V Release 4/SPARC the only planned ABI?
- Could companies besides AT&T and Sun participate in rewriting the UNIX kernel?
- Would all licensees receive System V Release 4 specifications at the same time, or would Sun and AT&T have them ahead of others?
- Who gave Sun and AT&T the right to rewrite the Berkeley UNIX technology?

In mid-May 1988, Vittorio Cassoni, president of AT&T Data Systems Group and the man credited with creating AT&T's strategy, especially the plan presented at the October 19 press conference, left AT&T and returned to Olivetti. Robert Kavner, AT&T Corporation's chief financial officer, became president of the AT&T Data Systems Group. Cassoni eventually left Olivetti. Kavner, having helped AT&T acquire NCR, a well-managed company with valuable products and people, moved on to try and make AT&T's premises telecommunications products profitable.

4

The Open Software Foundation

On March 17, 1987, IBM announced Systems Application Architecture (SAA), the center of its mainline software strategy for the foreseeable future. In later chapters of this book I will return to SAA. For now, I want to focus on the Open Software Foundation (OSF), a cornerstone of IBM's open software systems strategy and a force that shapes the open software systems landscape.

This chapter allows representatives of the seven founding members of the OSF, one of whom is John Akers of IBM, to state in their own words why they founded the organization. They address almost all the important technical concepts of open software systems. They also tell us why open software and what they are doing are good for their customers.

On May 17, 1988, 150 analysts and members of the press gathered in an auditorium in New York City. Only a handful had been briefed the evening before on what to expect. The rest only knew that a group of suppliers planned to make a major announcement.

What follows here is a transcription of that announcement (which was chaired by John Young, CEO of Hewlett-Packard) and my comments.

4.1 MAY 17, 1988—ANNOUNCEMENT OF THE OPEN SOFTWARE FOUNDATION

Well, good morning, my name is John Young. I am president and chief executive officer of the Hewlett-Packard Company. It is my pleasure to serve as moderator for today's press conference. I would like to welcome all of you here today and also extend a warm welcome to our international audience which is viewing this announcement live via satellite in Geneva.

Well, this is a first for me and for this industry. Apollo, Digital, Groupe Bull, IBM, Nixdorf, and Siemens—it's not every day that we find so many heavyweights in the ring at the same time. You might ask yourselves what's important enough to get this cast of characters together at the same time. Well, there's a simple answer to that question, and it demonstrates quite clearly that the real power in our industry resides not on the stage but with our customers. We are here today because of a shared commitment to put customer demands for a standard operating environment ahead of our own proprietary interests.

To make this rather noble sounding purpose very real, we've all agreed to redefine the roles of the next round of battle—a much more competitive round for each of us, but one where our customers are assured of winning. As a broad base of the international computing industry, then we are here today to announce a whole new approach to computing. Our vision of a new, more level playing field is as broad as our base. To show our commitment, we have founded and funded a new nonprofit organization called an Open Software Foundation, with funding in excess of $90 million. The OSF will develop and provide a new software environment that will make it much easier for our customers to mix and match computers and applications from many different sources.

This new environment will result from the cooperative efforts of private industry, universities, and many other participants, all under the direction of the OSF. It will include applications interfaces, advanced systems extensions, and a new open operating system using POSIX definitions as a starting point. Now POSIX, which stands for portable operating systems for computer environments, is an operating system standard

closely related to the UNIX system that specifies how
software should be written to run on computers from
different vendors. This announcement we expect will
make computer users around the world very happy.

Let me walk you through today's agenda. Jacques
Stern is chairman and chief executive officer of Groupe
Bull and chairman of Honeywell Bull Incorporated.
He'll describe some of the user needs to which we're
responding. Ken Olsen is president of Digital Equipment Corporation. Mr. Olsen will describe what we
mean by open systems and some of the benefits they
provide.

John Doyle, chairman of the board of the Open Software Foundation, will talk about OSF's goals and plans
and especially the open process which is unique in the
industry. Tom Vanderslice, chief executive officer and
chairman of the board of Apollo Computer Incorporated, will talk about the support the Foundation will be
receiving from industry.

And Dr. Claus Kessler is executive vice president,
Communications and Information Systems group at Siemens, and he'll discuss the Open Software Foundation's Research Institute.

Klaus Luft is chairman of the executive board for
Nixdorf Computer. He'll show us how OSF is truly
international. And finally, John Akers, president, CEO,
and chairman of the board of IBM, will wrap up with
some comments to summarize and put the Foundation
in perspective.

Now, one additional housekeeping issue—I'd like
you to hold your questions until we begin our formal
Q&A period at the end, and that will run until an
eleven o'clock cutoff time. Also, to our photographers,
we will make ourselves available to you for a few minutes after the Q&A, so I'd like to ask that there be no
photographing during the presentations.

And now to begin our program, I'd like to call on
Jacques Stern, chairman and CEO for Groupe Bull, to

talk about that very key starting point in any enterprise—that is, real user needs.

Author's Comments: John Young knew that there was another more compelling reason they brought them all together (selfish interest); however, he planned not to mention that reason. He planned to stay on the high road—the best interest of the customers.

I am also not convinced that, at this time, the customers, the majority of them, knowingly or unknowingly demanded a standard operating environment. I think the customers had increasingly become disenchanted with what all suppliers, those pushing proprietary and so-called open software systems, were offering. It probably would have been more accurate to say that the customers were demanding computing systems that made a greater contribution to their bottom line.

Did he and the other executives on the stage have trepidations that they, the suppliers, might not win as a result of what they were doing? They knew the computer market was already an extremely competitive business. None of them wanted to face a more competitive environment. They were really forced to make some changes.

Young's reference to adjusting the playing field no doubt referred to repositioning competitors vis-à-vis each other. He represented a group of suppliers that were going to tilt the playing field in their own favor and at the expense of other competitors.

One week before this announcement, Tom Vanderslice of Apollo, Bill Kay of HP, Jack Smith of Digital, and Allan Krowe of IBM traveled to Basking Ridge (NJ) to talk to Robert Allen, CEO and chairman of AT&T. They intended to discuss the group's plans to create the OSF and to ask AT&T to join. Jack Smith had been elected spokesperson, but before he got far into his pitch, Allen lost his temper.

Allen reportedly said something to the effect that "You (all that were present or the founding members of the OSF) had destroyed my chances for success in the computer industry." Bob Kavner, who was at that meeting and who shortly thereafter became president of AT&T's computer line of business, told me *it was not true* that Allen had said "You rape me and then expect me to help you," which was bandied about the industry.

But Allen's comment speaks volumes to what was really behind Young's words about "a more even playing field." Allen knew that the main intent of creating the OSF was to take a major advantage away from AT&T, and Allen wanted nothing to do with it.

The development of a new open operating system by the OSF made it clear that the OSF members had decided to wrest control of the open software market from AT&T. You can imagine how AT&T's chairman felt when he realized that after years of developing the UNIX and open software systems market, the eight companies on the stage planned to usurp AT&T. They wanted to harvest the fruits of AT&T's work. This practice has happened many times before. Xerox invested heavily in developing the concept for an icon-based workstation technology; however, it was Apple that made billions of dollars selling an icon-based personal computer. Xerox developed Ethernet and educated the industry to the need for local area networks in hopes of becoming a leader in office automation. However, Apple, IBM, Sun Microsystems, and hundreds of other companies took the desktop markets. Xerox obtained little benefit for its effort.

Regarding the OSF's funding, the members who contributed to the $90 million, a good amount of money, considered their share a small amount to pay, if the OSF accomplished what it hoped to.

The mixing and matching of computers Young mentioned is something all users want to be able to do, of course. The IBM SAA announcement of less than a year before promised to enable customers to more easily mix and match IBM's mainline computers and applications that were written for the IBM environments. What the OSF announcement now promised was to enable the customer to do the same in the non-IBM and in other supplier's proprietary environments. You could say that the OSF was announcing an "SAA" for some parts of the open software systems environments.

Some 3 years after this announcement was made and as I am writing this chapter, I confess I must disagree with Young—I still do not know of a single computer user anywhere in the world who was made "happy" by the OSF announcement.

> **Jacques Stern**: Thank you, John. Our customers have many needs. And, of course, it is our responsibility to find the best way to respond to their needs. And today, I would like just to highlight four of them—four things that are important and four needs that show that our market is becoming, today, mature.
>
> First, our customers want the ability to easily use application software on computers from multiple ven-

dors. They want to be able to migrate their existing applications. They want to be able to select from a wide variety of new applications without being dependent on a particular vendor. No single vendor today can pretend to offer complete solutions for every problem. Customers want to be able to mix and match, as John said, their computing resources. It's a fact of life. And to do all of that requires consistent interfaces on which application software can be built. What our customers need is portable software. And the existence of standard application interface, of this consistent interface running on a variety of computers from a variety of vendors, means that there will be much more applications to choose from available on the market. Independent software houses will be encouraged to develop new applications since they can address the much broader marketplace.

Second, customers want the ability to integrate and unify their applications and their systems in the distributed environment. Distributed environment with different systems and different vendors and systems spread out across the world. This means making it easy for different applications to work with different computers from different vendors in different parts of the world, independently of the geographical location. In computer jargon, we call that interoperability. Interoperability may be not the most listener-friendly word, but it is today the technological frontier that this Foundation will have to explore. It involves many things, since, like communications standards, the uniform administration management for both system and network, it includes the ability to implement distributed applications, to remote-access services, uniform protection and validation of distributed information, and data through networks.

Third, customers want to be able to use the same operating system in many classes, many sizes of computers, from the personal workstation, to minicomputer, large systems, to supercomputers. They want to be able

to have room to grow. They want to move to more
powerful computers without having to discard their
existing applications. And finally, customers around the
world want a voice in the formation of standards and
so do independent software houses of computer vendors. Users and software suppliers want to be able to
provide input on their requirements. Users and independent suppliers want their future needs taken into
account as research projects take shape. They want to
be able to monitor, to have a say in the development of
international standards. This Open Software Foundation
will address all these needs by specifying a new open
applications environment. Both the specification and
the environment will be open because the openness is,
today, a strong requirement. And the process leading to
their creation will be also an open process.

So what we are doing today, in a way, is announcing a new era of responsiveness and responsibility for
the computer industry worldwide. Today, all these
needs that we . . . for long times, our . . . dreams, we
know their feasibility and so do our users.

And now, here is Ken Olsen, president of Digital, to
describe what we mean by open systems and what benefit they will provide to our customers.

Author's Comments: Stern is correct, of course, that customers want
application software that is free of the operating environment; however,
how much freedom they can ever obtain is debatable. Also, I suspect that
when customers have the freedom to easily move a particular application
to another vendor's system they may not want to because of changing
requirements and/or because the cost to reengineer the application software won't be competitive with purchasing different application software.

What was not said here is that although the market for application
software has increased, the number of vendors competing might also
increase, making the software markets a more competitive place.

Ken Olsen: We're very excited by the announcement
today. It's the result of a lot of work. The only disappointment we have is that AT&T isn't sitting here with
us. We truly look forward to them joining us the next

time we have a public announcement. What we are, in spite of what you may read, what we are doing here is not in competition with AT&T, we are doing something beyond what AT&T has to offer, and we are complementing them and we look forward to working with them in the future.

The subject we are talking about today is not UNIX; UNIX is related in part of it. What we are talking about is what goes beyond UNIX and what makes it possible to do truly transportable software systems. Much of the success of the computer industry today, to date, has come about because of the enormous effort in standards. Manufacturers and users have invested a large amount of money, a large amount of manpower, and a lot of patience in many standards organizations in many parts of the world, and the success we've had in computers today is, to a large degree, the result of all of this work. Most of this is in open standards where everybody can take part. The decisions are made democratically, and the results are open to everyone afterward on an equal basis.

There are open standards today by the very formal standards groups that cover all sorts of things from networking communications, which include the signal levels, the technologies, and the protocols; the graphics, which include the windows and the mouses and the keyboards and other devices; the protocols and disciplines necessary to transfer letters and documents and pictures. There are a number of local area network systems. There are data base standards and standards for access of data base. There are proposed standards for security, and there are many standards we've had for tying peripherals to the systems. It is the purpose of the Foundation to standardize on a set of these standards, so that when software systems are written, they will have a set of standards even outside the software operating system that will make it work.

It is not uncommon, when asking people about the problems of transferring software, for them to say (that) transferring software from one computer to another, or cvcn one operating system to another, is small compared to the problems involved in all of these other standards. If there's no discipline in these other standards, if they're not defined, it is a frustrating job of making it transportable.

The operating system for the computer, and the computer architecture itself, are traditionally proprietary. They are built together by a manufacturer; the enormous investment in these is justified only by them being proprietary, and they fit together and are often not separable.

The languages which the application, in which the applications are written, are traditionally open, formal, public, and disciplined, and documented and supported by a very formal, public group.

Theoretically, if the software writer follows the language carefully, and if the people who wrote the operating system follow the rules of the language, applications written in these languages should be transportable between different systems, if they all met the rules. However, software writers invariably go beyond the standards of the language and exploit features of the operating system. This means that the applications quickly become not exactly transportable.

Now, it is the goal of the Foundation to specify the interface standards, those lines between the application and the operating system, so that if people write to the language standards, which are already formal, and follow these standards, which will be specified in detail— in general, the POSIX standards—then most software, or software with very little effort, will be transportable from system to system.

Most customers want to buy a whole system from one manufacturer; give him the complete responsibility. They want him to supply everything and guarantee it'll

work. For those customers, these standards will be a
big advantage because there will be much more software available, readily available to any of these systems, even if they're proprietary, because of the standards. For those customers who want to buy hardware
and software from many manufacturers and they take
the responsibility to supervise the hardware and software, make sure that it's truly transportable, and to
maintain and discipline the system, the Foundation will
offer a very formal and very disciplined Foundation on
which they can build and accomplish this goal.

We see that open systems is really a public trust,
something that is very important to our society, and the
Foundation has set about to carry out this trust and to
fulfill its obligations.

We'll now hear from John Doyle, who is chairman
of the Foundation part-time, sometimes executive vice
president of Hewlett-Packard, and for now working
largely on the Foundation.

Author's Comments: Ken Olsen has often spoken out against foolish statements about the pros and cons of proprietary systems and open
software systems. Many people have misunderstood this man, who knows
what he is talking about. Some considered him the "anti-Christ" of open
software systems.

Olsen was right that creating the OSF was the result of a lot of
work. For about 3 months, teams from Apollo, HP, and his company had
worked to determine how they could cooperate to field a viable approach
to open software systems. After the three companies had developed much
of the structure of what would become the OSF, and after they realized
they needed IBM to make the OSF a success, they invited IBM to join.

Approximately 2 years before, Olsen had become concerned about
the "democratic" process of setting standards. AT&T was setting open
software standards, and it was already hurting DEC's sales. Olsen ordered
DEC's personnel to be more active in all organizations that set open software systems standards.

Olsen has been accused of being insincere when he said "The only
disappointment we have is that AT&T isn't sitting here with us." That can
be interpreted in two ways. If it was a sincere statement, if an AT&T exec-

utive was present on that stage, it would probably mean that AT&T had abandoned its UNIX operations, and Olsen (and the others) would probably be sincerely delighted. AT&T's efforts to establish UNIX as a standard and to sell computers had hurt DEC's business more than most of the computer companies. With AT&T in the fold, so to speak, Olsen would have to worry less about them in the future.

John Doyle: Thank you, Ken. It's very exciting to be here as my first public act on behalf of the Foundation, on behalf of its three goals, its seven principles, and the seven sponsors who you see before you.

Open systems have captured the imagination of users, of software developers, and of hardware proprietors. Truly open systems require software built with an open decision and development process. The Open Software Foundation was created to meet those essential needs. It is an independent, international Foundation, created to define specifications, develop leadership software, and promote an open portable application environment. It will be run by a president and staff just as a software company would be run. The impetus behind the first discussions leading to the formation of this Foundation was widespread and deep concern about the future of open operating systems. But in getting together to explore our options, a bigger idea emerged, as often happens when truly important issues get discussed with great intensity by people with a lot at stake. The bigger idea goes well beyond a common open operating system. Our customers' needs also call for a new level of openness, and standards for data management, applications interface, graphics and user interfaces, and system and network administration. Our efforts will make it easier for users to mix and match computers and software from different vendors.

The Open Software Foundation is taking on a challenge that has never been met in the computer industry. The need for a uniform applications environment has become increasingly apparent, and it's something that computer users worldwide are now demanding. The specifications and products developed by the Open Software Foundation will meet all of the needs identified by the earlier speakers.

As we look at the commitment to user needs, first we must discuss application portability. Applications written for the OSF applications environment specification can move without modification from one system conforming to the specification to any other conforming to that specification. This will encourage people to write more applications because they have a broader market to address and will enable users to protect their application software investment.

Second, the software we develop will make it easier to integrate distributed applications and resources across systems from different vendors worldwide. The information our customers need is increasingly distributed. It is located in different places, on different systems, from different suppliers. And in order to solve the complex tasks they face, users need to assemble the cooperative efforts of as many systems on the network as are needed. These user needs lead us to the technical vision that was referred to earlier as interoperability. This vision includes a common and open operating system, applications interface, data management and networking specification, plus interfaces for proprietary systems. It combines the best of both worlds—a common open applications environment and the capability of adding proprietary systems when those are the best way to address specialized customer needs.

Third, the Foundation software will run on a wide range of processors, from personal workstations to supercomputers. This will allow users to select a hardware platform that meets their current needs and at the same time know that their applications will run on the more powerful machines that they'll need in the future.

Fourth, the Open Software Foundation will live up to its name. What is unique about OSF compared to other approaches is the open and vendor-neutral process by which we will pursue our technical vision. It will be truly open, and let me substantiate that by sharing with you the principles that will define that process.

OSF will serve as a neutral party in the computer industry competition. Its founders believe that the achievement of an open software platform is a task that is best accomplished by a joint effort. There are seven guiding principles that ensure the Foundation's software and decision making will be open.

The first three define the input part of the Foundation's process:

1. The Foundation will seek the best technologies and ideas from a wide range of sources. Its membership is open to any profit or nonprofit organization, no matter in which country that organization exists. All members will be able to provide inputs on their needs, specifications developed, and features in the new software that we bring to the computer industry.

2. Second, the Foundation will ensure openness by supporting accepted international industry standards. We'll build on existing standards rather than start from scratch. The POSIX definition will be the starting point for the operating system. The bolder X/Open specifications will be used also. As new standards emerge, we will bring our software into conformance. The press kit has a list of the standards that will be supported. It's too long to read here, but I can tell you that it includes standards for operating systems, languages, graphics, libraries, user interface, networking services, and data base management. If there are no appropriate standards in an area of interest, the Foundation will work with the international standards bodies to ensure that standards are adopted in a timely manner.

3. Third, we will be working closely with university and industry research organizations worldwide to

obtain innovative technologies, and we have established a research institute to fund and oversee research that advances the Foundation's technology. In a few minutes, you'll hear more details of that research institute.

4. In the middle of our list of principles, and also central to this Foundation's distinctiveness, is the decision-making process. This process will be completely visible to Foundation members; they will be regularly informed of our activities, they will be able to participate in international Foundation forums, and at various times during the specification process, we will poll them on issues under consideration. As specifications evolve, they will be available to all members. When those specs have been finalized, they'll be publicly available. And as we turn those ideas into actual offerings, all members will have equal access to OSF's output.

The next three principles describe the Foundation's openness in this regard.

5. At various stages of the development process, licensees will have timely access to source code for ease in designing their own applications for porting the OSF system onto their hardware.

6. Next we will have consistent and straightforward procedures for licensing source code. Non-members may also obtain source code license.

7. The final principle is really the ultimate test of openness—our offerings will not favor any given hardware architecture but will be adaptable to many different architectures.

These guidelines are the distinctive contribution that OSF will make to the international computer industry. We will create truly open software systems, and now let's move on to what those will include.

The Foundation's offerings will be phased in a manner that will give lead time to applications developers.

The first offering, the OSF application environment specification, shown in yellow on this slide, will clearly delineate the software profile. Applications written to conform with this specification will work with all future OSF products. Level 0 of the OSF application environment specification is being released today. It includes specifications such as POSIX, the X/Open portability guide, and the X Window System. Full details are enclosed in your press kit. These are well-accepted standards, and they provide the basis for people who want to code portable applications today. Level I of the OSF application environment specification will expand to such areas as interoperability and user interface.

In addition to specifications, OSF will produce an operating system consistent with the Level I specifications. Users will find it easy to migrate their applications from many current UNIX system-based products. But even prior to the full operating system release, the Foundation will release portions or subsystems of the operating system for our licensees to incorporate with their own offerings. Subsystems that address areas such as interoperability and user interface will be available shortly. All OSF software will be hardware-independent and vendor-neutral. Licensees can adapt it to their own hardware. OSF will provide validation test suites for members or their customers to verify conformance with the Foundation's specifications.

There will be a lot more to come beyond the first operating system. Standards will continue to evolve and members will continue to respond to their changing customer needs. And OSF will expand the application environment and software offerings to meet these needs. Members will work closely with us and our ongoing research will contribute even more to open systems in the future. So the future will be very interesting and very exciting, indeed.

Now let's hear from Dr. Tom Vanderslice, CEO and chairman of Apollo, on the funding and support for OSF.

Author's Comments: As I look at Doyle's third point (about the range of processors OSF's software will run on), I wonder how the OSF thinks it can develop one fundamental operating system that can span such an incredible range of requirements. How can anyone design one operating system optimized to meet the needs of a single networked user and also do what MVS/ESA (Enterprise System Architecture) does?

I also take issue with Doyle's statement that the OSF will serve as a neutral party in the computer industry competition. By definition, the founders of the OSF are not a neutral body in the computer industry. The computer industry is made up of computer systems manufacturers, software developers, and services suppliers. The OSF represents the interest of seven powerful members of the computer systems manufacturers segment of the industry. It does not represent the interest of the other segments of the industry.

Dr. Tom Vanderslice: Thank you, John. You know I can almost hear the sceptics among you asking yourselves, "Well, it's a great idea, but can they pull it off?" I think that's a reasonable question to which we think we have more than a reasonable answer. This is a very viable, international organization. First, it already has more than $90 million in initial funding, and membership fees will provide additional support if it's needed. Fees for profit-making organizations for membership are $25,000 annually, and nonprofit organizations may join for $5,000 a year.

Yesterday, we sent out hundreds of invitations worldwide to hardware suppliers, software vendors, users, and universities. Membership is open to everyone who is committed to the objectives and goals of OSF. We feel quite confident that we'll get an enthusiastic response, because an Open Software Foundation is an idea whose time has come.

As a matter of fact, last evening we received a telegram from Philips: "Philips has been committed to the UNIX world since 1983, and has played a very active role in promoting this software environment in different activities like X/Open. Consequently, we appreciate the initiative of the Open Software Foundation and we have committed ourselves to actively support and sponsor this Foundation."

Additionally, OSF will receive licensing fees from companies who choose to adopt its software. In short, then, we feel quite confident that the Foundation has the financial resources it needs to being fine software offerings to the industry.

There's another kind of resource that we expect to have in abundance, and that's the management and technical know-how. We're beginning operations with some experts we borrowed from our sponsoring organizations. And the Foundation is hiring right now. You can expect it to attract the best and the brightest because it will be a very interesting place to work. We're pushing new frontiers for the computing industry and the people who work for the Foundation will know that what they do meets the needs of millions of users.

Finally, the OSF has access to some assets of its members—technological assets. This Foundation will base its development efforts on its own research as well as on technologies which will be selected and licensed from member offerings. The Foundation is already starting with some developed and partially developed products of the members.

The Foundation is not starting with a blank piece of paper and an empty room. Technologies which are being considered by the Foundation include Siemens' OSI protocol support, and Apollo's network computing system or NCS, and Bull's UNIX-based multiprocessor architectures, and Digital's user interface toolkit and Stylesguides for the X Window System, and Nixdorf's relational data base technology, and Hewlett-Packard's National Language Support or NLS.

And to provide a clear and easy migration path for application developers and end users, the Foundation's system will include features to support current System V and Berkeley-based UNIX applications. The operating system will use core technology from a future version, unannounced, of IBM's AIX as a developmental base.

To summarize, there's a tremendous need in the industry and the Software Foundation has the resources and the commitment to meet it. We have adequate funding, good initial staffing, and base technologies from the contributing companies. These are essential ingredients for any successful startup, so today we think you're looking at the launching of a winner.

And now Claus Kessler will share with you some information on our Research Institute.

Claus Kessler: Thank you, Tom. University research has always played the key role in the advancement of open systems software technology. In the academic environment, the pressures and constraints of the business world do not apply. Researchers can investigate new areas of technology with a truly vendor-neutral view. The results have been impressive.

Over the years, university contributions have been extensive. Contributions in the same area that OSF will be working on such as MIT's work in the area of user interfaces with X Windows; Berkeley's contributions of the Berkeley standard distribution advancing utilities, tools, and virtual memory for UNIX; the University of Karlsbad's work on OSI and large networks; and the University of Wisconsin's communications contributions in the areas of TCP-IP and OSI, just to name a few—international research that has contributed to a furthering of international standards.

OSF also shares the same vendor-neutral approach that allows for unconstrained research. OSF is interested in advancing open systems technologies. OSF wants to gain access to the results of future research as well. OSF has recognized the value of research and is making a strong commitment to its support. The commitment will be in the areas of funding and direction.

OSF will sponsor research of open software and technology that contributes to meet the stated goals of the organization. Universities will develop technology that advances the state of the art in open systems. OSF will take advantage of the technology in future offerings.

OSF will create a Research Institute to build relations and interfaces with universities and research organizations worldwide. The Institute will be structured by a formation committee consisting of academic and industry research leaders.

We are proud to announce that several distinquished individuals have already agreed to join the Research Institute formation committee. These first members include: Dr. Lynn Conway from the University of Michigan, Professor Michael Dertouzos from MIT, Dean James F. Gibbons from Stanford University, Dr. Gilles Kahn from INRA, Sofia Intitopolis, Professor Roger Needham from Cambridge University, Dr. Raj Reddy from Carnegie-Mellon University, and Professor George Turin from the University of California at Berkeley.

All OSF activities are conceived on an international basis and will have worldwide representation. This is just the beginning for OSF. OSF recognizes the need for a strong research involvement from the very start to solve the difficult technical problems of the future.

I am sure you'll hear much more about the Research Institute in the near future, but now let's hear from my colleague and friend from Germany, Klaus Luft, who'll discuss how OSF is an international organization. Thank you.

Klaus Luft: By almost any standards, OSF is an unusual startup company because of its unique set of sponsors, its unique outlook, and its substantial funding. Most startups begin operating in one particular place. Right from the start, OSF will be launched worldwide. That's important. In fact, it's an essential ingredient in OSF's success.

For one, the computer business today is rapidly growing worldwide business. There is no such thing as a standard, a true standard, which is not an international standard. No open system can be generally described as open if it's not open worldwide. All of the world's major computer vendors are international companies, but more important is the fact that many of our customers operate internationally and they are on the front line of those who need information systems with portability, interoperability, and scalability, whatever they operate, whatever vendor they choose.

OSF's worldwide dimension is likewise a crucial ingredient in the effort to provide the Foundation with the best research-and-development minds, the best technologies available, wherever in the world they may exist. And what better way to encourage the development of new and better applications software than to ensure developers that their efforts can be quickly and easily used for their customers on a wide range of computer systems. And I think this is really the new dimension which OSF brings to the market. Let me just take a minute to review with you why I am convinced that OSF is a profoundly international endeavor.

OSF is committed to international standards. OSF's operating system will conform right from the start to specifications defined by X/Open, a recognized international body established in 1984. For future development in areas where no standards have yet been defined, OSF will work very closely with X/Open and ISO and other standardizing bodies to advance new standards. And these standards are much more than operating systems. We talk about application environment specifications. And even so, until today, we have standardizing bodies, there was nobody like OSF implementing, on a neutral basis, standards. And that's the new point of time we have, the startup we have today.

OSF is open to sponsors and members worldwide. Today, invitations were sent to prospective sponsors and members around the world. OSF development will be carried out on an international basis. It is OSF's intent to do worldwide development to access the widest possible range of talents and technology.

This will be done in a variety of ways and includes research centers in the United States and in Europe. OSF will work closely with universities and research laboratories throughout the world. The Advisory Committee for the Foundation, for the Foundation's Research Institute, will include members from many countries. The OSF management team will be an international team, tapping into the best talent available in the world providing insight into a wide variety of cultures and customer needs.

I have tried to demonstrate the fundamentally international nature of OSF. Permit me to close with one last reflection. A worldwide dimension is absolutely necessary if any system is to be accurately described as open. The creation and promotion of a truly open system will help ensure truly open markets.

Open markets mean open, vigorous, healthy competition. By the way, competition keeps us young. And this will be a boon to us all—customers, application developers, and vendors alike.

Now let's hear from our last speaker, John Akers, who will put into perspective some of the key points covered this morning.

John Akers: Good morning, ladies and gentlemen. I've been looking forward to taking part in today's announcement, and I'd like to try to put into perspective what we've heard this morning.

Through the years, the companies in our industry have developed a wealth of unique technologies along with our own architectures and software environments to take advantage of them. Our industry has grown and our companies have prospered because these products satisfy a wide range of customer needs. And we expect they will continue to serve customers well, now, and into the foreseeable future.

But we need to continue to be responsive to many different customer requirements. In particular, those customers currently using systems based on UNIX have told us they are looking toward a future where they will have the ability to select from a wide range of application software and to use that application software on a variety of systems from different companies, and the ability to choose hardware and software that meets their needs and solves their problems with the expectation that it will all work together, and the ability to choose a software environment that spans a wide range of processors; in short, an open software environment.

Each of our companies has had to consider how best to respond to these users. And we've concluded that these customers can be best served if an independent body, beholden to no one vendor but benefiting from the expertise and support of many, can create a common set of standards for a POSIX- and X/Open-based software environment, a standard that makes it possible to develop applications that can run on systems from many different manufacturers.

The Open Software Foundation is the result. The Foundation will enhance and extend its software through its own efforts and the creative contributions of its members, as well as the academic community, as we work toward providing what customers have told us they expect.

While the Foundation's offerings will be significant, so is its charter in the process it will follow. In its work, the Foundation will be truly open—in its membership, in reaching out for input and ideas from all over the world, in its decision making, in providing equal access to specifications and developments, and in its relationships with standards bodies.

Long-term, the Foundation's work holds the promise of a completely open software environment with no limits on its creative growth. We believe it will complement the many unique architectures our industry will continue to offer and that customers will be the winners.

Will our companies continue to compete with each other? Of course, we will. We are all in a race for customer preference and customer loyalty, and we will all be adding value to differentiate our products. But our customers and the industry can only benefit by the Foundation's work. This is quite an eventful day and I believe a good one for the customers of our industry and the companies in it.

And I thank you for joining us for this beginning. And now I will return the meeting to John Young, who will moderate the question and answer session.

Author's Comments: In 1988 the UNIX market was about a $6 or $7 billion market. Akers' staff had told him they expected the UNIX market to grow rapidly, so the company was beginning to move in that direction.

IBM had also begun transforming itself into more of a software business and less of a hardware company and had started investing in software companies.

In terms of how best to respond to users, IBM's approach had been to license an early and limited release of AT&T's UNIX, build upon that technology, and offer systems to the customers. However, IBM decided not to license any of the later versions of AT&T's UNIX because it feared becoming dependent on AT&T and its technology. Instead, the company invested heavily in developing its own UNIX, AIX.

One of the main reasons Akers decided to go the OSF route was because it had become too risky for IBM to build AIX alone. The IBM

AIX development organization in Austin, Texas, required increasing resources to keep up with competitor's UNIX development efforts. Also, Akers' advisors had concluded that IBM's open software systems window of opportunity to go it alone was already shut. The AT&T faction shut down part of the opportunity. The OSF faction headed by DEC and HP shut down the rest.

Akers clearly hoped that the open software systems would complement IBM's unique architectures and not undermine them. Akers sees IBM's unique architecture—SAA—as the mountain in the middle of the commercial customers' information systems; open software belongs around the periphery of that mountain.

It was, indeed, an eventful day for all computer manufacturers worldwide that had a stake in the open software market. I am sure that Akers, and every other presenter on that stage, knew that the race for customers was about to go into high speed. AT&T's hold on the UNIX technology and the market would soon be cut in half. Software developers chasing the UNIX market would have to choose between the AT&T or OSF approach, or support them both. Also, IBM had gained a firm foothold in the UNIX market.

5

UNIX International

On January 31, 1989, UNIX International, an organization created by AT&T and other suppliers that had a strong reliance on AT&T's System V UNIX technology, responded to the creation of the OSF. With much less marketing flair than the OSF, the new organization announced details of its charter, organization structure, and working relationship with AT&T. Because this announcement helped shape the open software environment, I present it in its entirety.

At the 1989 UniForum Conference, I interviewed Peter Cunningham, president of UNIX International. The text of that interview follows the UNIX International material. At the end of this chapter I have listed UNIX International's current membership. Figure 5.1 shows its roster of 240 members.

5.1 UNIX INTERNATIONAL—AT&T STATEMENT OF JOINT OPERATIONS

UNIX International, with strong support and commitment of AT&T UNIX Software Operation ("AT&T"), has created a working body with the charter to ensure the integrity of the industry standard, UNIX System V(R), and to guide its future growth as a standard. In order to capture the spirit of the cooperation of UNIX International and AT&T, the following is a statement of planned cooperation between them.

UNIX International and AT&T are committed to the success of their mutual relationship. The two organizations will work together to assure that UNIX System V continues to be a standard in the future. They

will protect its integrity by evolving UNIX System V to include new technology while maintaining continuity with the more than one million current users of UNIX System-based products. In order to best accomplish
this, it is the present intention of the two organizations that UNIX International will define the future features and functionality for UNIX System V
through an open process, and AT&T would accept that direction. The processes for defining the features and functionality and the interactions
between the two organizations would be set forth in a living document,
known as "Structures, Processes, and Products." Both organizations intend
to abide by the escalation procedures prescribed in such document, which
contemplates the use of the offices of UNIX International to resolve all
differences, except those which are inimical to AT&T's interests. Additionally, it is contemplated that AT&T will have a management incentive
plan, which will have as one of its elements AT&T's performance in meeting milestones mutually agreed upon with UNIX International.

Users and suppliers of UNIX System-based products have made significant and long-term commitments to UNIX System V. They have done
so on the basis of the current and expected capability of UNIX System V
and the expectation of continued availability of that technology. In recognition of this expectation, AT&T is committed to maintain the current
UNIX System V perpetual license through future releases. UNIX International is committed to provide timely and considered guidance on licensing policy, other than pricing, and AT&T is committed to incorporate
such recommendations to the extent consistent with applicable laws and
with good business practice.

It is with great optimism that UNIX International and AT&T proceed with their joint effort to continue to provide a truly participative,
open industry standard based on UNIX System V. We are convinced that
this arrangement will stimulate new creativity in the market and extraordi-
nary user benefits.

5.2   INTRODUCTION

This two-part document is an overview of the UNIX International
organization. The first section describes the structure of UNIX International: committees, staff roles, and associated outside organizations. The
second section describes the process through which UNIX International,
working with AT&T, X/Open, and other organizations, defines requirements for future UNIX System products.

Further detail on these subjects is available from UNIX International. Companies or persons interested in joining UNIX International should contact the organization for additional information.

5.3   COMMITTEES, STAFF, AND ASSOCIATED ORGANIZATIONS

5.3.1 Committees

UNIX International includes several permanent boards and committees, plus a varying number of specialized work and special interest groups:

- **Board of Directors**—an assembly of delegates from among all UNIX International members which sets overall organization direction
- **Executive Committee**—elected by the Board of Directors to be responsible for the operation of the UNIX International organization
- **Steering Committee**—elected by the Board of Directors to set product direction and guidance
- **Work Groups**—established as needed by the Steering Committee to study and report on specific business or technical issues
- **Special-Interest Groups**—formed for technical exchange between members on specific feature areas
- **Technical Advisory Group**—formed to solicit input and guidance from academic and research communities

The **Board of Directors** is an assembly of delegates from each UNIX International member which:

- Ratifies technical and business directions of the corporation
- Determines overall priorities for technical and business activities
- Makes changes to bylaws, dues, and the UNIX International Charter

The Chairperson of the Board is elected from among the Board membership. Voting weights on the Board of Directors are proportional to dues paid, but members voting on other committees each have one vote. The Board is expected to meet twice a year.

The **Executive Committee** reviews and approves or rejects, as the executive management committee, the following operational items:

- Annual budget and revenue plan
- Major new program initiatives
- Personnel actions
- UNIX International operations

The Executive Committee is responsible to the Board of Directors to ensure that UNIX International operations adhere to charter and expenditure policies. The Chairperson of the committee is elected annually from among its members.

Each Principal Member has one delegate on the Executive Committee, while General Members and Associate Members are together represented by five elected delegates. Executive Committee delegates are expected to be vice presidents of their respective organizations, but not necessarily the same person as their Board of Directors delegate. The chief executive officer of UNIX International is a voting member of the Committee, and a representative of AT&T USO is a nonvoting ex-officio member. The Executive Committee is expected initially to meet every 2 months.

The **Steering Committee** is responsible for providing attention and guidance to AT&T USO. This committee

- Establishes priority of work
- Develops technical plans and proposals subject to Executive Committee review
- Establishes Work Groups and defines Work Group charters (including deliverables and schedules)
- Oversees and directs the Work Groups as appropriate
- Evaluates Work Group reports and recommendations, and decides continuance or dissolution
- Establishes Special-Interest Groups and other subcommittees as required

The Steering Committee is not purely a technical body; it will take business and market factors into account when considering the future direction of the UNIX System.

Each Principal Member has a delegate on the Steering Committee, and there are five delegates elected from among the General and Associate Members. Delegates are expected to be senior product planners in their member corporations. There are three nonvoting delegates: an AT&T USO representative, the UNIX International Technical Director, and one other UNIX International director. The Chairperson of the Steering Committee is elected annually from among its members and represents the Steering Committee at Executive Committee meetings. Steering Committee bimonthly meetings are open to member observers.

Work Groups are established by the Board of Directors for a specified period on a particular technical, organizational, or business issue. For example, a Work Group may be formed with the responsibility for generating and monitoring a specific feature in an AT&T release. There will, however, be a small number of permanent Work Groups, such as the Licensing Work Group.

There is a practical limit on the number of Work Groups that UNIX International members and AT&T USO can support adequately. There will generally not be more than five at any one time.

Work Groups are composed of a variable number of members, including a UNIX International Project Manager, participants from member companies, and a chairperson who is appointed by the Steering Committee. Those who regularly attend the meetings of a particular Work Group have the right to vote in that group, but each member organization has a maximum of one vote per group.

Each Work Group will meet as often as necessary. Nonmembers may attend by invitation of the chairperson.

Special-Interest Groups provide a forum for technical exchange between members on topics where there is not yet an immediate, specific need. SIGs are self-forming: interested members join together, decide their own work program and procedures, and register their topic and membership with the Technical Director. Members are encouraged to avoid duplicating efforts within other industry and academic organizations. SIGs will be provided with administrative support for meetings, an operating manual, and production and distribution services for minutes and other publications.

The **Technical Advisory Board** serves as a technical review and consulting body for the Steering Committee, Work Groups, and staff. The Technical Advisory Board is made up of academic leaders in Computer Science and industry experts on the UNIX System. The Technical Advisory Board ensures academic involvement in the UNIX International technical process providing advice and information on current and upcoming technology.

5.3.2 UNIX International Staff and Responsibilities

There will be 15 to 20 UNIX International full-time staff plus secretarial and clerical support. UNIX International management will include the following key positions.

Chief Executive Officer. This officer oversees all UNIX International activities, provides general direction, and supervises all UNIX International directors and other staff. The CEO's specific duties include acting as the primary spokesperson for UNIX International, ensuring effective communication with AT&T USO, managing day-to-day company operations, creating major plans, and supervising major reports.

Director of Marketing and Promotions. This officer is responsible for communicating the message and mission of UNIX International to the press, standards bodies and other outside organizations, and the AT&T USO marketing staff. This director also oversees membership activities, and disseminates information to the membership at large.

Director of Business Operations and Planning. This officer administers the financial affairs of the organization including the budgeting process, establishment and management of financial controls, and related internal duties. This director is also the focal point for business relationships between UNIX International and AT&T USO, as well as with other outside organizations and individuals.

Director of Technology. This officer drives the UNIX International technical process defined in the next section, is a member of the Steering Committee, and may serve as vice chairperson of that committee. The director works with the Steering Committee and is responsible for achieving the technical objectives of the organization.

Project Managers. These staff members provide support for Work Groups including scheduling of meetings, distribution of minutes and other documentation, and monitoring the progress of action items. Each PM serves as a interface to AT&T USO to monitor progress of development activities, and to manage formal information transfer between organizations. They also serve as the liaison to other Work Groups for resolution of conflicts. All PMs report directly to the Technical Director, and report Work Group status to the Steering Committee.

5.3.3 Associated Organizations

UNIX International will have an especially close relationship to two other organizations: X/Open will be a major source of market requirements, and the AT&T UNIX Software Operation will be the source of UNIX System products.

X/Open is an international standards organization with a strong reputation for the creation of vendor-dependent procurement specifications.

In the past, X/Open has focused on selecting and creating standards around existing software products and specifications (e.g., POSIX). X/Open is now emphasizing its role as a primary specifier of industry needs, and focusing more on defining market requirements for new software. UNIX International has selected X/Open as a primary specifier of market requirements for a Common Applications Environment. To accomplish this goal, X/Open and UNIX International have defined complementary processes, as described later in this document.

Although UNIX International will have a close relationship with X/Open, UNIX International will consult with other sources of industry requirements (UNIX International members themselves, industry standards bodies, trade associations, endusers, independent software vendors, and others).

UNIX Software Operation (USO), newly created by AT&T, is a separate business unit that develops and markets UNIX System software. UNIX International and AT&T USO will interact on technical, business, and, to a limited extent, promotional matters. In particular, they will work jointly in the definition of the content of UNIX System releases.

With UNIX International input, USO will continue to be responsible for the creation of licenses, and for rules regarding the use of the UNIX trademark. UNIX International will provide no input on establishing prices for UNIX System releases and the trademark.

As in the past, USO will subcontract development to third parties where specific technical expertise is desired. The results of such work will be subject to the processes defined in the next section.

5.4   THE UNIX INTERNATIONAL TECHNICAL PROCESS

This section describes the process through which UNIX International collects market requirements from members and standards organizations, further refines them, and communicates with AT&T USO.

Most of this process occurs in step with the creation of a set of documents described below. These formal documents are expected to be made available to all UNIX International members. However, their specific use and further distribution still remain to be decided in order to protect intellectual property rights.

5.4.1 Documents

Product Roadmap—This multiyear plan for the evolution of UNIX System V is based on market requirements brought to UNIX International by X/Open and other sources.

- Specifies functionality (in the form of feature lists), strategy, and release dates

- Maintained by the Steering Committee

Release Feature List—This document includes an overview, a prioritized list of features for a specific release, and performance goals.

- Published 2 to 3 years prior to product release

- Contained in less than five pages

Requirement Specifications—This two-part document contains a summary and detailed definition of the features in a release.

- **Overview** section summarizes the major release features without technical details

- **Detailed Specification** section defines functional capabilities, non-functional characteristics (e.g., performance, reliability, compatibility), external interfaces, and design constraints of each major feature

- Specifies conformance to applicable industry standards and is detailed enough to be used by development, test, marketing, and documentation personnel

- Published 1-1/2 to 2 years before product release

Design Specification—This document describes a release feature and is composed of a detailed design section and a syntax section.

- **Detailed Design** section includes definition of modules, module interfaces, data structures, algorithms, and detail interfaces. It provides enough detail to ensure that there is no bias toward a particular hardware architecture

- **Syntax** section consists of draft manual pages

- Published 9 to 12 months before product release

5.4.2 Procedures

Step 1

- From the Product Roadmap and other inputs, the UNIX International staff and USO, with the concurrence of the Steering Committee, produce a Release Feature List.

- The release feature list document is submitted to the Board of Directors for ratification, and to X/Open for information.

- If ratified by the Board, the document is placed under change control. The process is continued with Step 2.

- If the Board rejects the document, it makes specific recommendations for changes. The UNIX International staff, USO contributors, and the Steering Committee revise the document, which is then submitted for ratification.

- If the document is not ratified in a timely fashion, an Escalation Procedure, described below, is initiated.

Step 2

Requirements Specifications for each major area are produced by AT&T USO, with input from Work Groups formed to address specific feature areas.

- Completed, Reviewed Requirements Specifications Overview sections are widely distributed to provide guidance for software developers.

- Detailed Requirements Specifications are announced in the UNIX International Newsletter and made available to UNIX International members.

Step 3

Design Specifications are produced by AT&T USO for each feature area in response to Requirements Specifications Documents.

- Work groups will promptly review the Design Specification for their areas.

- AT&T USO receives feedback from UNIX International.

- Interface definitions specified in the Design Specifications are repackaged into SVID format and distributed to all member companies, to X/Open for further review, and for possible inclusion in future standards.

- Design Specifications, in either draft of final form, are protected by marking them with a date of free release and having UNIX International members sign agreements to observe the dates appropriately.

Step 4

Copies of these specifications will be made available to UNIX International members as they are completed and updated. Notification of new or updated documents will be published in the monthly UNIX International Newsletter.

Change Control Procedure. Upon completion, the documents are entered into a change control system, after which change requests may be entered against them. Once a document has been entered, further substantial changes require formal review (usually by the originating committee) before inclusion. Changes will be clearly marked to distinguish them from the previous version.

Escalation Procedure. On matters where UNIX International and AT&T USO cannot reach agreement, the CEO of UNIX International and the president of USO are responsible for mediation of differences. Each takes steps to see if agreement can be reached before the formal procedure is begun.

AT&T is not expected to undertake activities that threaten the loss of intellectual property or the UNIX trademark, nor to undertake activities that would adversely affect its financial position or business operations.

If agreement is still not reached after the efforts of the CEO and the president of USO, both sides formally present their positions to the Executive Committee. A vote is then taken by the committee to determine if the UNIX International position will be endorsed (three-quarters majority required). If the Committee endorses the UNIX International position, the president of AT&T USO is required to formally respond with a rationale for any divergence from the UNIX International position. The response is sent to the Executive Committee and to AT&T Data Systems Group senior management.

5.4.3 Early Product Release

Software and Documentation. In order to help UNIX International members prepare their products for release as quickly as possible, USO will make incremental product additions available to UNIX International members as they are integrated into the USO development system. These "load points" are the earliest times at which added functionality is usable.

The load tapes will include a binary C compiler, the operating system, and associated commands and utilities. Hard-copy load notes will accompany each tape.

As with software, USO will distribute load tapes of machine-readable documentation.

Early-release recipients may not release products based on this technology until final release. At this point, early-release recipients may release products based on the technology. AT&T licenses will continue to be required.

Beta Sites. A small number of customers, who may or may not be UNIX International members, will be selected by USO as beta sites. UNIX International will review the lists of beta customers. As in the past, beta site testing is covered by a Beta Release License Agreement executed by the individual beta customer and USO.

Final Release. When system test is complete (i.e., when the final load meets the USO system test exit criteria), the product will be declared formally released and will be distributed to holders of the appropriate AT&T license.

5.5   UNIX INTERNATIONAL EXECUTIVE APPOINTMENTS— JANUARY 1989

Beside Don Herman, organizing chairman, and Peter Cunningham, chief executive officer, other UNIX International executives are listed below.

- Van Aggelakos—Office of the Chairman

Mr. Aggelakos is an assistant vice president, General-Purpose Systems Division, NCR Corporation. He joined NCR in 1967 and has held several sales and product management positions; most recently, he was director of product management for NCR's UNIX (R) systems.

- Tom Mace—Director of Marketing and Promotions

Mr. Mace, UNIX strategy manager at Unisys, has extensive product management experience at Digital Equipment Corporation, Raytheon Data Systems, and Convergent, most recently as Group Product Manager for Convergent's S/Series UNIX-based systems.

- Alan G. Nemeth—Director of Technology

Dr. Nemeth, corporate consultant at Prime Computer, is responsible for overall technical strategy. He previously held positions at the MIT Lincoln Laboratory and Bolt, Beranek and Newman, and has been involved with UNIX operating system technology since 1975. Dr. Nemeth is also

president of the USENIX Association, the professional technical association in the UNIX community.

- David I. Sandel—Director of Business Operations and Planning

Mr. Sandel is division manager responsible for UNIX System V
marketing at AT&T. He has 20 years of experience with AT&T and has
been involved in the evolution of UNIX systems in various technical support, product management, and marketing positions. Mr. Sandel also represents AT&T as an X/Open board member.

- Shuitsu Yoshida—Office of the Chairman

Mr. Yoshida is manager of UNIX development for advanced workstations at Fujitsu America. He joined Fujitsu in 1977, and his experience
includes research and planning of computer systems with special emphasis
on mainframe operating systems.

5.6   MEMBERSHIP CLASSES AND BENEFITS

The five classes of UNIX International membership or affiliation
are as follows:

Principal Member:

- Direct representation of the Board of Directors
- Membership on the Executive Committee and the Steering Com-
  mittee
- Participation in Work Groups
- Access to early documentation and source code with distribution
  fee waived (AT&T license required)
- May sponsor five Associate Memberships at no additional cost
- May use the UNIX International membership logo on promo-
  tional material
- Entitled to benefits of all membership categories
- Annual dues: $500,000

General Member:

- Direct representation on the Board of Directors
- Representation on the Executive Committee and The Steering
  Committee (Each committee includes a total of five representa-
  tives elected from the General and Associate Members.)
- Participation in the Work Groups

- Access to early documentation and source code for a minimum distribution fee (AT&T license required)
- May sponsor one Associate membership at no additional cost
- May use the UNIX International membership logo on promotional material
- Annual dues: $100,000

Associate Member:

- Direct representation on the Board of Directors
- Representation on the Executive Committee and the Steering Committee (Each committee includes a total of five representatives elected from the General and Associate Members.)
- Participation in the Work Groups
- Access to early documentation, including design specifications, for a minimum distribution fee (AT&T license required)
- May use the UNIX International membership logo on promotional material
- Annual dues: $10,000

Individual Affiliate:

- Receives the newsletter
- Eligible for discounts on selected documentation
- Annual dues: $50

Student Affiliate:

- Receives the newsletter
- Eligible to participate in annual software design competitions
- Eligible for UNIX International Scholarship Fund
- Annual dues: $25

5.7   INTERVIEW WITH PETER CUNNINGHAM, PRESIDENT OF UNIX INTERNATIONAL

Killen: It is delightful to meet you. You're ... you were just appointed recently as president of UNIX International.

Cunningham: That's correct.

Killen: Maybe you can tell us why 40 something computer companies around the world decided they needed to create another organization?

Cunningham: Well, Michael, as you've probably been aware, over the last few years the shape of computing has been changing significantly. And we have seen the dawn of a new age—the age of the power of the user. And I think it is true to say that a number of computer companies have required their product strategies to change to accommodate more flexibility, more performance, and more scalability in computing, and above all to consolidate on a standard operating system to provide that. Now, we at UNIX International have brought together some of the major companies in the industry from the USA and North America, from Europe, and the Far East to concentrate our energy on enhancing and taking forward the major open systems operating system in the industry today—UNIX System V.

Killen: All right. Let me stop you. So UNIX System V is AT&T's operating system. And that is the operating system that your group has banded together to promote and to try to make a super success in the world. Is that correct?

Cunningham: That is absolutely right. And let me just pick up on a point that you made there—UNIX System V is AT&T's operating system. I want to tell you that one of the reasons why we had the major companies of the world come together to band around UNIX System V is that, although the operating system was developed and invented in AT&T's Bell Labs, we now have a situation in the world where every major computer company ships a derivation of UNIX System V as part of its operating system for its computer product line. And so we have a position where AT&T would like us, the computer companies, who have dedicated their product lines around UNIX System V, to help them develop the operating system in line with the requirements of the users.

Killen: Now you said you're driven by the users. I think, of course, that's one aspect of why your organization was created. But wasn't your organization also created because

another group of computer vendors, specifically, the group
called the Open Software Foundation, decided to band
together and build their own operating system in direct
competition to AT&T UNIX System V?

Cunningham: Well, you know, Michael, there has been much press spec-
ulation, and many rumors and intrigues, as there always
are in our industry, about how the positioning of UNIX
International relates to the Open Software Foundation.
And I would like to use this opportunity to clarify for you
a little how our respective organizations relate. UNIX
International is not a development organization. UNIX
International exists to take the requirements of the many
computer companies around the world in terms of serving
their users and translate those into detailed specifications
which will improve and enhance UNIX System V as it
progresses throughout the nineties. In other words, what
we're doing is taking, if you like, the customers of AT&T,
who in the past have dedicated their computer lines
around UNIX System V, and we're forming an association
that will, if you like, do the product planning to take
UNIX System V forward and enable it to become even
more successful than it already is today.

Killen: So this is a bit of a shift from AT&T having total responsibility for product development to another organization
made up of your 40 or so members having some responsibility for product development.

Cunningham: That's correct. Let me finish the point in terms of the positioning of the respective organizations. The OSF have an
arrangement where they internally develop, through a process that they call their open process, software which will
be incorporated around an overall environment specification for operating systems. And we at UNIX International
basically are set to provide further requirements that we
take from our users and that we also derive from our input
from standards bodies and from associations such as
X/Open, and we then take these and crystallize these into
specifications that we would like AT&T's UNIX software
operations to implement. And AT&T's UNIX software

operation expressed a strong commitment to work in response to these requirements and to develop the operating system in exactly the way we, the major computer companies of the world, would like to see it evolve.

Killen: All right. Let me just change the tack for a moment. May I ask, What's your definition of open systems?

Cunningham: Well, you know, there is a lot of talk in the industry at this minute about quite what the word "open" means. And I think it's very important that when we talk about "open," we relate what "open" means back to the users. And to me that means the ability for the users to have their voice heard in the evolution of an operating system so that it develops in response to their requirements. And also that we ensure that we don't disrupt the users' development applications plans and systems plans by ensuring that we deliver compatibility and continuity. And that is one of the prime founding principles of the UNIX International organization. We feel that on behalf of our organization's members, that the prime reason why we came into being is to ensure that our customer's investment in UNIX System V based applications worldwide was not disrupted and was able to continue to evolve in an "open" manner.

Killen: By the way, if I look at an IBM dictionary of terms, loosely quoting them . . . "openness" means that the interfaces are well documented and made available to anyone. And they never address the issue of who controls the operating system. And that is sort of in line with the definition you have just presented. You're not pinning down that "openness" must be "not controlled," an operating system not controlled by a single vendor. You're not addressing that issue in your definition.

Cunningham: Well, Michael, I would like to respond to you on that point because I think that this is one of the areas that we have to clarify and explain. This is a very complex area. We believe that the best way to ensure that the operating system really is "open" is to work with our users through organizations like X/Open, through organizations like the standards bodies, to ensure that we take their input and crystallize that into specifications which can be used to evolve the future of UNIX System V. And when I talk about evolving the future of System V, I just don't mean technically, I mean also commercially, in terms of the changes that need to be made in the mechanics of the distribution of the operating system, that need to be incorporated to ensure that the operating system is freely available to anybody in the user community over the next few years.

Killen: All right, so your organization has formed this relationship with AT&T where your organization will advise AT&T on product development and will probably play some role in promoting that operating system. Let me ask, what happens, this arrangement you have, how long of a period will it last? Five years? Ten years? Is it possible that five, ten years from now AT&T will say: I don't want to listen to you anymore. I want to develop the operating system so I can optimize it for my own hardware offering. What guarantee do you have?

Cunningham: Well, I'm glad you asked me that question. The computer industry is a pretty fast changing place, but one of the significant changes that has occurred over the recent years has been the growth of open systems-based procurements, not only here in the USA, but significantly in Europe, and, of course, in Japan and the Far Eastern markets. And as I started out at the beginning of the interview, one of the points that I would make to you is that no longer are users and major governments prepared to put up with being locked into proprietary operating systems. What our organization seeks to do is to agree on specifications requirements, with AT&T, which they will respond to and they will commit to over time. Now you asked me why or how do we know that AT&T will honor that commitment? And to you I would say that the biggest possible reason why AT&T will move forward and will honor our commitments is we are their customers. I do not know of any organization that willingly ignores its customers and still survives over a period of time.

Killen: Well, I could argue that HP, IBM, Digital, and Apollo were all AT&T's customers, and those four companies felt that AT&T was not meeting the needs of its customers, and that's what provoked that group to actively put together the Open Software Foundation.

Cunningham: Well, you know, I think there that it is true that situation has evolved from the days when we had AT&T distributing UNIX System V, distributing the system among all the industry vendors to a situation where we now have another organization who have declared that their aim is to produce an operating system under something they call an "open" process. And it is equally true that that organization has a number of members. But I think I would make a point to you that our organization is basically comprised of those companies who have delivered and shipped a considerable percentage of the UNIX System V market over the last few years. It is comprised of the organizations who have had "open" architectures and who have basically delivered those systems to the extent that they represent about 75 to 80 percent of the UNIX systems marketplace. And that is why for us in UNIX International, one of the critical concerns when we established the organization was to ensure that the customers' investment and, indeed, our investment in serving our customers with our product lines, could evolve forward in a compatible manner.

Killen: So, for that reason, and the reason that AT&T has probably learned its lesson with respect to dealing with its customers and probably is going to be much more sympathetic with your needs, you expect to have a good long-term relationship with AT&T.

Cunningham: I cannot see any reason why AT&T would choose to ignore the requirements of its customers. To do so would be the utmost business folly. I don't believe you'll find, with the management in AT&T being as aware of the "open" requirements worldwide, that they would ever commit such an act.

Killen: All right. Let me ask, What's about to happen with respect to UNIX V Release 4? When will all of your members be able to offer that upgraded operating system to the software developers and the ultimate customers?

Cunningham: Well, one of the major announcements that we are making here at the show is that as a result of significant work done within UNIX International on behalf of all of our members over the last few months, we are pleased to be able to announce an early access program for our members.

Killen: What does an early access program mean?

Cunningham: Let me explain that for you. Every organization that is a systems integrator or a systems software provider requires to have access to the development code as an operating system builds up. And what we at UNIX International have done is to tailor a program in conjunction with AT&T's UNIX software operation, in order to provide them with that access so that they are able to develop their products as the operating system progresses and builds up and to be able to ship their products to market. And let me stress one point to you there—every organization will have equal access. There will be no favored access.

Killen: All right. So, I'm Amdahl. When would I get early access code?

Cunningham: Well, Amdahl, who are, to use them as an example, who are a member of UNIX International, would have, under this early-release scheme, access to the code starting in March.

Killen: All other members would have access to that.

Cunningham: All the members of UNIX International who are principal and general members would have access to that source code.

Killen: Are all members getting equal access? Yesterday, Scott McNealy called me. We had a discussion. I asked him about the development of System V Release 4 and his own OS. And I asked him, When is he going to bring out the equivalent to a System V Release 4? He said (to paraphrase) "We've been bringing it out all along, piece by piece. We've been a subcontractor of AT&T. So as we've been developing it for AT&T, we've been able to incorporate some of those developments." So, that seems to me

	that he has an extra early access, unless I'm paraphrasing him incorrectly.
Cunningham:	Well, you know, the position with Sun and AT&T has caused a lot of comment in the industry over the last year or so. I'm glad to take a chance to put the situation straight. Under this arrangement with UNIX International, we will evaluate technologies for incorporation into future releases of UNIX System V, together with AT&T's UNIX Software Operation. And what that means is that no organization, I repeat, no organization, will have a favored subcontractor relationship with AT&T's development organization. It will be UNIX International's responsibility in response to those requirements that are being fed through from our users, and from the standards bodies, and from bodies like X/Open to examine technologies for incorporation into UNIX System V. There will be no favored relationship in the development of the operating system release in response to those requirements. So, Sun, just like any other systems integrator, is part of UNIX International and receives no special access to the development of the releases of the operating system.
Killen:	All right. The creation of your organization, in a way, levels the playing field.
Cunningham:	That's correct.
Killen:	What are some of the new rules that computer companies must adhere to to be successful, now that all of your members will get releases at the same time. Are there new dynamics for being successful in the . . . you're from ICL if I remember correctly. . . .
Cunningham:	That is correct. There certainly are, and, you know, one of the reasons that we took a while before we announced our organization is to develop a process that accords equal participation, and equal access to over 50 companies worldwide is not an easy task. And it takes a lot of time to work out the detailed mechanics and the detailed logistics of how each of those companies can be included in setting down the requirements for future versions of UNIX. And we have developed, as I say, this process which allows

each company to participate at a number of levels. We
have an executive committee, which is comprised of members who basically look after the business and the commercial charter for our organization, and we have a product
planning committee, which we call our steering committee, who in response to the requirements that are coming
down from the various sources that I outlined earlier, set
up various working groups to examine particularly exciting areas of technology to be included. And let me give
you an example there. One of the areas that we are currently concentrating quite a bit of effort on is to look at
multiprocessing, which we believe will be a major requirement for systems architectures in the nineties. And, in a
truly "open" fashion . . . .

Killen: Multiprocessing. For the masses out there, what is multi-
                   processing?

Cunningham: Multiprocessing allows, basically, the ability of a com-
                   puter to use a number of processes to tackle jobs of work
                   at the same time. And it has been for a long time an area
                   where the computer industry has required to gain advan-
                   tage, in terms of utilizing systems architectures a little bit
                   more effectively, in other words, to harness the ability of
                   several processors to concentrate on a particular job or
                   task at a single time. We believe that the true way to
                   develop this openly is to consult with the industry, consult
                   with academic institutions, and then to work through our
                   "open" process to arrive at the technology to be incorpo-
                   rated into UNIX System V future releases.

Killen: I got that. If you were at ICL today, an ICL strategist,
                   what advice would you give ICL for playing in this new
                   so-called level playing field environment?

Cunningham: Well, you know, the advice I would give them is the same
                   advice I would give any major systems company who
                   were concerned with the requirement to develop their sys-
                   tems in an "open" manner and to provide total solutions.

Killen: In a competitive world.

Cunningham: In a competitive world. You said it. And that is to basi-
                   cally concentrate their efforts on participating in a process

which will allow them to have a say in the way that the operating system is developed. And what that means is working in our work groups, which cover areas from licensing and conformance for the operating system to multiprocessing, as I've just talked about, to other areas such as looking at their demands for commercial transaction processing.

Killen: So people should get involved.

Cunningham: People should get involved. This is their chance to have a say in the way the operating system moves forward.

Killen: You also mentioned different types of computing requirements, like commercial, and I would like to ask – you and I know, right now, that UNIX is very limited to the technical communities. Five years from now, where will UNIX be, your System V?

Cunningham: Well, you know, firstly, I'd like to take issue on what you say about UNIX being limited to the technical community. Because I believe that's one of those old myths that seems to be perpetuated from year to year and is an easy question to bring a response to.

Killen: Let me ask, do you know any companies running their business on UNIX?

Cunningham: I can tell you that in Europe and here in the U.S. . . . .

Killen: ICL? AT&T?

Cunningham: ICL runs various parts of its business on UNIX-based systems. And I can tell you, furthermore, we're not talking about computer systems companies. In the U.S. government, in governments all around the world, various administrative processing tasks and office automation are being done on UNIX-based systems. Furthermore, mainstream transaction processing is now occurring in several areas in the U.S. and in various parts of Europe, for example, hotel reservations and hotel tracking systems are all based around UNIX-based systems.

Killen: (Out of time.) You've been a great guest.

See Figure 5.1 for UNIX International membership company list.

88 Open Consortium Ltd.
Aoor/Altos Corporation
Addamax
Advanced SW Technology Research Institute of Kyoto
Aggregate Computing, Inc.
AIR Company Limited
AIS
Alenia (Aeritalia & Selenia)
Alliant Computer Systems Corporation
Altos India Limited
Amdahl Corporation
Andersen Consulting
Aoyama Gakuin University
Apple Computer
Arix Corporation
ASCII Corporation
ASHISUTO
AT&T
Auburn University
AVCOM Systems, Inc.
Bank of America
The Boeing Company
C. ITOH Techno–Science Co., Ltd.
Cadence Design Systems, Inc.
Cambridge Technology Group
Canon Inc.
CBIS
CCL/ITRI
Centre National d'Etudes des Telecomms.
CETIA
Chinese University of Hong Kong
Chorus Systemes
Citibank
Com Food Software GmbH
Commodore International Limited
Computation Center, Osaka University
Computer Associates International, Inc.
Computer Center, Tohoku University
Concurrent Computer Corporation
Control Data Corporation
Convex Computer Corporation
Cornell University
Cray Computer Corporation
Cray Research, Inc.
CREO
CSK Corporation
Czech Technical University

Dansk Data Elektronik
Data General Corporation
Datapoint Corporation
Dell Computer Corporation
Diab Data AB
Digi International
Dist–Universita' di Genova
DMR Group, Inc.
Dolphin Server Technology A.S.
Dublin City University
DuPont Fibers
Edinburgh Portable Compilers Ltd.
Edinburgh University
EG&G Idaho, Inc.
Elea
Electronic Engineering Laboratory, Daikin
EMSCA
Emulex Corporation
Encore Computer Corporation
Epoch Systems, Inc.
Ericsson
ESIX Systems, Inc.
ETRI
Exxon Production Research Company
Facom Center Association
Facom Software Association
Faculty of Engineering, Hokkaido University
Far East Computers Pte Ltd.
Fellesdata A/S
FIAT AUTO S.p.A. Sistemi E Informatica
FPS Computing
Fuji Xerox Co., Ltd.
Fujifacom Corporation
Fujitsu Limited
G.C. McKeown Co. Ltd.
German UNIX Users Group
GIPSI S.A.
Gradient Technologies, Inc.
HaL Computer Systems
HCL America Inc.
Hyatt Hotels Corporation
ICL
Imperial Software Technology Ltd.
Indian Institute of Technology, Bombay
Information Service Industry Association of R.O.C.
Informix Software
Ingres Corporation

Figure 5.1 – UNIX International Membership (8-7-91), page 1 of 3

Institute for Information Industry	Oki Electric Industry Co., Ltd.
Integrated Computer Solutions	Olivetti
Intel	Omron Corporation
INTERACTIVE Systems Corporation	Open Technology Ltd.
IO Power	Oracle Corporation
IXI Limited	OSA
J.C.Penney, Inc.	OTSUKA SHOKAI
JSB Computer Systems Ltd.	Pacific Dunlop Limited
Justsystem	Patriot Partners
KAIST	Petroleos de Venezuela, S.A.
Keio University	PFU Limited
Kmart Corporation	Phoenix Technologies
Kubota Pacific Computer, Inc.	Pick Systems
KYOCERA Corp. OA Systems Group	Polnet Technologies
Lawrence Livermore National Laboratory	POSIX Software Group
Lionel Singer Corporation, Inc.	Prime Computer
Locus Computing Corporation	Project Manager Base ADP
MANA Systems Limited	Pyramid Technology
Mannesmann Informationstechnik	Rechenzentrum Universitat Stuttgart
Marriott Corporation	Retix
Marshfield Clinic	RIACT
Matsushita Electric Industrial Co., Ltd.	Ricoh
Mead Data Central	Samsung Electronics (SEC)
MEITEC Intelligent Technology Corp.	Santa Cruz Operation, The
Mentec International Limited	SANYO
Michigan State University Computer	Sanyo/Icon
Laboratory	Scientific Software, Inc.
Micro Focus	Sector 7 Software
MIPS Computer Systems, Inc.	Seiko Epson Corporation
Mississippi State University	Seikosha Co. Ltd.
MITRE Corporation, The	Sequent Computer Systems, Inc.
Mizar/Integrated Solutions	Sequoia Systems
MODCOMP	Sharp Corporation
Motorola Computer Group	Sigma Systems, Inc.
National Centre for Software Technology	Silicon Graphics, Inc.
National Computer Board, Singapore	Simula–Servizi Di Informatica
NBI, Inc.	SISA ACCOUNTING Software
NCR Corporation	SMT–GOUPIL
nCUBE	Software Japan International
NEC Corporation	Software Research Associates, Inc. (SRA)
NEC-NET Group	SOFTWAY Pty Ltd.
Ngee Ann Polytechnic, Singapore	Solbourne Computer, Inc.
Nihon Unisys Limited	Solucions Informatiques S.A.
Nippon Steel Corporation	Sony Corporation
Norsk Data	Southwestern States Bankcard Association
NTA Japan Technociates	SPARC International
NTT Data Communications Systems Corp.	SPEKTR
NUC	SRI

Figure 5.1 – UNIX International Membership (8-7-91), page 2 of 3

Stardent Computers, Inc.
State Institute of Applied Chemistry (GIP)
STATSKONTORET
Stollmann GmbH
Stratus Computers
Sumitomo Electric Industries Ltd.
Sumitomo Metals
Sun Microsystems
Swedish Defense Force
Swedish Telecom
Swiss Federal Institute of Tech. (EPFL)
Sybase
Systems Strategies, a NYNEX company
Tadpole Technology plc.
Tandem Computers, Inc.
Tata Consultancy
Tata Unisys Limited
Tatung Co.
Technical University of Budapest (BME)
Teradata Corporation
Tetra Ltd.
Texas A&M University, Computing Services
Texas Instruments Inc.
The Netherlands Central Bureau of
    Statistics
Tietotehdas–Group/Open Systems
TIS Limited
TIVOLI Systems, Inc.
Tokyo Electric Co., Ltd.
Tokyo University, Computer Center
Tokyo University, Dept. Information Science
Toshiba Corporation
U.H. Corporation
UniRel srl
UniSoft Group
UNISOL Corporation
Unisys Corporation
United States Air Force
United States Military Academy
Universita' Degli Studi Di Milano
University of Bergen
University of British Columbia
University of Erlangen, Dept. Computer
    Science
University of Helsinki
VERITAS Software, Inc.
Wal–Mart Stores, Inc.

Wang Laboratories, Inc.
Wipro Infotech Limited
Wollongong Group, Inc. (The)
Wyse Technology
Xerox Corporation
Yokogawa Electric Corporation

Figure 5.1 – UNIX International Membership (8-1-91), page 3 of 3

6

OSF Revisited

Sometime after the OSF was announced, I invited David Tory, its first president, to be a guest on my television show, "High Technology with Killen & Class." I asked Tory a number of questions about the OSF, UNIX International, and open software systems. His answers provide additional insight into the role the OSF plays in the open software industry.

In this chapter I am including a portion of that interview. At the end of the chapter, Figure 6.1 lists the OSF membership as of August 1991.

6.1 INTERVIEW WITH DAVID TORY, PRESIDENT OF OSF

Killen: David, why was the OSF created?

Tory: It was created for a variety of reasons. One of the important aspects of the industry and UNIX environment was that an organization (AT&T) ran the development of UNIX on a vendor independent basis. What resulted was all of the companies that wanted to have a UNIX-based facility, a scientific engineering workstation area, were dependent on that one UNIX kernel.

The problem was that it was a fairly limited kernel, and all the companies that needed it had to then develop their own proprietary additions to that kernel so that they could actually use it with their hardware and offer solutions.

Killen: The kernel is like the bottom, the base, of it.

Tory: That's right, that's right. As long as all the vendors had that
           problem, then there was a stability, if you like, among the com-
           petitive stability. And what happened was that AT&T, which is
           the company that owns UNIX and developed UNIX, established
           a relationship with one of the vendors which was Sun Microsys-
           tems, which resulted in an imbalance of power, if you like, a
           change of stability.

           Because of the result of that, it was felt that Sun and AT&T
           together would drive the development of UNIX in the direction
           that Sun wanted, and therefore it would become vendor-specific.
           And the other companies, the companies that were in competi-
           tion with Sun, recognizing what a strong marketing organization
           Sun was and how entrepreneurial they were, felt that that would
           be a very unfair advantage, and as a result, over a period of
           some time and through various manifestations, the Open Soft-
           ware Foundation was created to establish a vendor-neutral devel-
           opment organization to establish an alternative UNIX base.

Killen: So all these companies were using AT&T's UNIX kernel, and
           all of a sudden AT&T formed an alliance with Sun that sort of
           tilted the playing field, and your organization was created to tilt
           it back so there might be a level playing field.

Tory: Well, in fact, they changed the rules a little bit further. Not only
           did they want to establish some sort of equilibrium, what they
           also wanted to do was to remove the constriction of having an
           organization develop what was going to be an open software ker-
           nel, without due regard to the needs of the organizations that
           were licensing that kernel. And what they wanted to do was cre-
           ate a truly open environment, hence, Open Software Foundation,
           where the process of development was based on market need
           and the needs of the licensees, in terms of the type of kernel
           they wanted.

Killen: They (the OSF founders) wanted to create a new environment.

Tory: It was really the sponsors, or the forefathers, if you like, the
           founding fathers of the Open Software Foundation, which was
           eight of the industry players that said that we can't, there's no
           way that any one company will be so altruistic as to continue to
           develop an operation to the benefit of all competitors. So what's
           necessary is to set up an organization which is independent of

any vendor; neutral entirely, to create an "open" platform, which is independent and, therefore, entirely neutral. And it was the charter that was created by the founding fathers, which is what we work with now as the Open Software Foundation.

Killen: The OSF is committed to "openness."

Tory: Yes. It all revolves around the definition of the word "open." "Open" software, in terms of the software that needs to be developed or needs to be brought to market to be offered by the Open Software Foundation, and the way that is developed—to be entirely "open." And what is meant by the "open" process, which is the way the software actually gets selected and agreed upon, if you like, by a market constituency, which is our member base.

Killen: What are "open" systems? What's your definition?

Tory: That's a good question because it's becoming a rather redundant phrase. "Open" is becoming part of the buzz phrase of the industry.

What we mean by "open" is something which is independent or neutral of any vendor. It's a software product which will work across multiple platforms. In other words, it is truly portable. It doesn't depend on the architecture, either software or hardware architecture of any particular hardware environment, and, therefore, does not gain any, does not provide any vendor with any significant benefit over any other vendor. It is entirely independent to that extent. Therefore, the portability question is very important.

Another aspect of "open" software is the interoperability. That means that it can work on a number of different platforms, and if the same operating system is sitting on two or three different platforms, no matter who the vendor is, it will work as though it's one large operating system, and, therefore, the different boxes, different nodes, if you like, in the network are largely transparent to the user. And the third area is scalabilty. Scalability is very important because you need an operating system that can work with a small box, a small node, up to the very largest box, such as a microcomputer right up to the largest computer, like a Cray or something like that. That's the basis of an "open" environment.

Killen: So a fundamental tenet of your definition is that no one vendor controls the operating system.

Tory: That's right.

Killen: There is an alternative organization to yours—UNIX International. They promote the development of a standard for the UNIX environment. Is that an "open" environment?

Tory: UNIX International, in fact, is attempting to do a job that has to be done. The difference is that UNIX International consists of a group of companies that are attempting to, force is too strong a word, to *require* AT&T to be open about what they are doing in the development of their operating system. AT&T has retained control over the final specification definition and the development process that goes into their operating system, UNIX V.4, which is being developed at the moment. And the UNIX International consortium are a group of companies that are attempting to provide direction to AT&T, so that AT&T gets some market sense or some sense of the market need for their product. The problem with UNIX International and the problems they face is that ultimately AT&T controls its own destiny. And it's an advisory capacity as much as anything else.

Now I think it is absolutely vital that UNIX International continue to do the job they are doing and be given every opportunity to continue to force AT&T and maintain AT&T's honesty in a sort of quasi-"open" process. But that's what they are, primarily—very different organization from the Open Software Foundation.

Killen: You describe UNIX International as an advisory group to AT&T. You describe your own organization as a Foundation that develops software technology like independent software companies such as Microsoft. Maybe you could put into perspective the difference between your organization and someone like a Microsoft.

Tory: Well, the first thing is that the Open Software Foundation is a foundation, a nonprofit organization that's been set up by a large number of companies, well, a number of very large companies in the industry, and is supported by an increasingly large membership of software companies, hardware companies, government organizations, end users. It's increasing all the time. That organization, the Open Software Foundation, has been given responsibility for bringing to market a licensable product which satisfies the charter that's been laid down for the Open Software Foundation—that is, that software should be entirely "open" based on my previous definition.

Killen: And a Microsoft is developing software for its own . . .

Tory: For commercial, for commercial benefit. It is a profit-making organization. That's right.

Killen: And it's one entity, but you're multiple entities together.

Tory: That's right. One of the differences is that we don't take responsibility for bringing to market, an offering, a public offering. We have the capability, through the "open" process, to bring into our organization technologies from throughout the industry that satisfy a specification that's been defined by our membership. It's evaluated; if the technology that comes in meets the specification, then we will adopt that technology. Now, normally when we go out on what's called an RFT process, request for technology process, which is the "open" process we talk about, we get multiple companies offering their technology, and then the process of evaluation must take place to determine which is the best technology from that which has been received.

Now the membership, to start with, our membership, and that's why it's very, very important that we're recognized to be driven by our membership, determine, initially, the short list of technology which does satisfy that specification. The members themselves have defined the specification to start with, so it's very much a member-driven process. Only at the final stages does the OSF then take responsibility for making the final choice. And that's done on a vendor-neutral basis through the principles that we've identified before.

Killen: Now one of the technologies that your organization selected was developed by IBM to a great extent.

Tory: Yes—AIX/UNIX operating system.

Killen: What are you doing with what IBM has sold you?

Tory: IBM has licensed to us a product which is, in fact, AIX Release 3, which is in the process of being provided to us. What we do with that particular example, and there are other examples of software we're dealing with, is, first of all, ensuring that it conforms to the portability standards that we require, that it conforms to the industry standards that we have already committed to, such as POSIX, and XPG3 from X/Open, and so on.

Tory: Next, we provide validation tweaks to ensure that anyone else who wants to license that source code has a mechanism to validate that it does satisfy requirement, or if he wants to make, or that organization wants to make changes, that the changes are within that validation process.

Thirdly, we provide documentation which describes very carefully and very clearly not only the code itself and what it does, but the mechanism wherein it can be ported. And that's what we provide when we license it back out again. Now having done that, of course, we then obviously add technology to that so we're building a larger and larger operating system facility which will become OSF/1, which is what we expect to release.

Killen: Now there's always been controversy about Sun working too closely with AT&T. Right now, I believe Sun claims they are a subcontractor on Release 4 of System V. And as a subcontractor, they develop some technology, and therefore they have access to that technology ahead of possibly all of the UNIX International members. What about the case of IBM? Are they working on developing AIX for you and does that give IBM a competitive advantage in terms of time?

Tory: What they are doing is licensing to us technology that they already have. They have made a commitment to AIX across their whole range of products—hardware, from mainframe, midrange, OS/2, the OS/400, and even the RT. To them AIX is part of a twin strategy, which, in fact, Terry Lautenbach talked about today in his keynote speech.[1]

So what we have done, and what OSF did when it was formed, when it looked for an alternative to AT&T's product kernel, which is our nucleus, the evaluation of the technology that was available determined that the AIX Release 3 was the best technology to license. So we licensed that technology. We're not subcontracting to IBM to develop something for us. We're licensing

1. Terry Lautenbach (of IBM), keynote speaker at the 1989 UniForum Conference, San Francisco, CA.

technology that exists, and then we're using that as a platform to build our own operating system standard, again based on the "open" system, the "open" standard that we talked about earlier.

Killen: All right, I just heard that IBM has delayed introducing AIX to the marketplace. Are they delaying turning over code to you?

Tory: No. They have a number of different AIX development processes. What they are delaying, in fact, is certain aspects of AIX Release 2 that relates to the 370, relates possibly to OS/2, although that version is being released, I hear, next month, I hear—anyway, and certain components in that. The AIX Release 3 version that we're receiving is the AIX Release 3 that is being developed in Austin for the RT workstation, and there's no delay on that workstation version of AIX at all.

Killen: All right. Your operating system that you are developing is called the OSF/1. When will software developers have access to it?

Tory: Part, again, of the open process is that anyone who is a member not only is able to help in the specification definition process, but also the evaluation of the technology against that specification.

And what they are able to do is have early access to the source code as it becomes available. We call that "code snapshots." And any member, on signing a nondisclosure agreement, can receive, and has already received, and a large number of them have already received, from us since December of 1988, "snapshots" of the source code. So they look at the code; they add value to it.

Killen: Now the UNIX International group spearheaded by AT&T is claiming that at the end of the summer their System V Release 4 will be out. That's approximately 6 months ahead of your organization. And I believe your organization has no basic operating system technology out there. Do you find this a competitive disadvantage?

Tory: No. See, we're not trying to develop a product that competes with UNIX V.4. We're trying to develop an "open" system, "open" software system for the future.

Our version of OSF/1 would be the first release of something that's going to go on for years, expanding, getting bigger, being more comprehensive in terms of what it does.

Tory: UNIX V.4 is one further release in the history of UNIX, which is now 20 years old. UNIX V.4 comes after V.3. AIX Release 3 is a rearchitected V.2. So, it's a staged approach. But what we're looking for is providing something that our sponsor companies felt was needed in the marketplace to open up, to act certainly as a catalyst in the industry, to bring together all these varying 200 types of UNIX implementations into a UNIX or UNIX-derivative "open" system facility, which obeys the rules of the "open" software definition.

          We need to go a little bit further than that, because the Open Software Foundation is doing two things. It's not only developing OSF/1, the "open" software platform. It's also developing components through, again, the RFT process. We released, for example, in fact, we announced, we didn't release, we announced the decision on the RFT process that produced the user interface. What we call the user environment component, which has been named OSF/MOTIF, and if you go around the UniForum (Conference), you will find a large number of companies already showing early versions of OSF/MOTIF.

          Now OSF/MOTIF will form part of OSF/1. It's being developed so it will work with OSF/1. However, OSF/1 will not be available until the time I said, but OSF/MOTIF itself will be available in the summer.

Killen: People can start writing software right now using OSF/MOTIF?

Tory: Yes. And OSF/MOTIF is running on a number of different hardware and operating system platforms. It's been developed to be truly portable. That means it's not only going to be portable as far as the hardware platform is concerned, but also the particular version of the operating system. We sell source code to vendors. We sell the portability of source code to vendors.

          OSF/MOTIF will be sold in source form with a number of what we call reference ports, where it's already been ported to a number of different platforms. The individual software vendor (ISV), whoever that might be, then has the capability to port that anywhere else that he wants. The early users of OSF/MOTIF will probably be people who use V.4 or V.3, or whatever, because OSF/1 will not be available until it comes out at the end of the year.

Killen: So somebody who is developing applications on V.3 could uti-
lize OSF/MOTIF to develop their next generation of an application, and then when your OSF/1 comes out, they can use that as
a platform in place of . . .

Tory: Yes, they could. It's their choice based on what they believe the
market needs, which is, again, part of the "open" process. We're
not forcing down the throat of our sponsors or our members
what we license. What we license is based on the "open" process, which we believe provides us with an understanding of
what the market needs. If we made the wrong choice, people
will not license our software.

Killen: So it seems to me that you're not developing just a replacement
for AT&T System V Release 4; what you're developing is a
totally different operating system environment. Are you going to
call it "UNIX"?

Tory: Well, we'll call it "UNIX-derivative" as long as we license any
part of the technology which is based on UNIX. We've got to
reference that fact, because it's a trademark which is owned by
AT&T. We're calling it "OSF/1," but it's derived from UNIX,
and we must recognize that fact.

Killen: This seems to be a major rewrite, a major restructuring. Why is
IBM planning to pay AT&T a royalty?

Tory: Well, because what AIX Release 3 is is a restructured development, if you like, of V.2. And the V.2, it's a UNIX V.2 that
comes from AT&T, and the license is required from AT&T to
use V.2 so it can be redeveloped and extended, and we're adopting that so AT&T technology is contained within the product
that we've got.

There is a very significant similarity between what we're doing
and what AT&T is doing. There are also certain different structural architectural differences. But what is happening, what is
changing the whole process, which is making it difficult, why
there's argument and controversy in the marketplace is because
people forget that all the statements made by AT&T, by UNIX
International, by X/Open, by OSF, by all the other organizations
that they're all adopting and following the standards that are
being set in the industry means that they largely are working
according to common standards and, therefore, as far as the end

user is concerned, the people using it, those standards are going to make those products look more and more alike.

So there's much greater similarity in terms of the future of these operating systems than dissimilarity. The changes will affect the performance, they'll affect the ability to add further value to the product, and so on. But the standards themselves as defined by and accepted, in a very public way, by all organizations, and exactly the same standards, to a large extent, means that those products will look alike. And the major benefit to the end user will be the competitive position of two companies developing to satisfy a common market need.

Killen: May I ask you, right now, where is UNIX technology with respect to serving the needs of the customer?

Tory: In some cases it's in a very good position, because it was developed, it started 20 years ago, to satisfy the needs of a niche market, which was the scientific, engineering marketplace . . .

Killen: Is it still there?

Tory: It's still there, but it's rapidly increasing. OSF/MOTIF is a very clear indication that UNIX is going to break out of this somewhat more limited niche market to become a much more commercially viable offering.

Killen: When do you see UNIX offerings clearly fulfilling commercial applications—the kind you would run your business on?

Tory: I think if you talked to certain software companies like SCO, Santa Cruz Operation, and so on, that they would say that it's already arrived. But it's still a very tiny percentage of the total marketplace. The reason for that as much as anything is that you need the system integrators, the ISVs, the independent software vendors, and the hardware companies to really start providing a wide range of application solutions which will use these. That's what's driven all the other proprietary operating systems success in the marketplace. And they'll do that when they see that the UNIX environment is coalescing, and the catalytic action that the OSF is providing is to coalesce the UNIX marketplace.

6.2   OSF UPDATE

The new OSF/1 operating system has been announced and has received support from some of the world's largest and most significant computer companies, most of whom plan to offer OSF/1 releases.

Digital Equipment Corporation announced that it would make the new OSF/1 operating system the basis for the company's next major release of its ULTRIX operating system and would ship a merged ULTRIX/OSF/1 product. The company also said it has created an OSF/1 developers' kit that would be available for use on the DECstation 3100 systems.

In late 1990 the OSF also achieved several new milestones with its OSF/MOTIF graphical user interface.

Approximately 1000 source code licenses have been issued and MOTIF is now available from 60+ different companies for use on more than 120 different hardware platforms and 40 operating systems. MOTIF can be used on virtually every major desktop system, including personal computers and workstations from IBM, Digital Equipment Corporation, Hewlett-Packard, Groupe Bull, Hitachi, Siemens Nixdorf Information Systems, Philips, Intel, MIPS, Dell, Sony, NEC, and Sun Microsystems.

6.3   MEMBERSHIP OF THE OSF

In August 1991, I received an updated list of the OSF's membership. According to the OSF, it now has more than 300 members, however, Figure 6.1, which follows on the next two pages, shows only 173 members—those that have been formally announced.

88 Open Consortium Ltd.
Academia Sinica
Acer, Inc.
Adobe Systems
Advanced Computing Support Center, Inc.
Andersen Consulting
Apple Computer
ASCII Corporation
Asea Brown Boveri
Atlantic Richfield Company
Barclay's Bank PLC
The Boeing Company
Bolt, Beranek & Newman
BP Exploration, Inc.
Brown University
Cadence Design Systems, Inc.
Cano,n Inc.
Carnegie Mellon University
Centre for Development of Advanced
    Computing
Centre Universitaire d'Informatique
CETIA
Chalmers University
Chung-Ang University
Chorus Systems
Columbia University
Computer Associates International, Inc.
Computer Institute of Japan Ltd.
Concurrent Computer Corporation
Convex Computer Corporation
Cornell University
Cranfield Institute
Cray Research, Inc.
CSK Corporation
Data General Corporation
DECUS
Digital Equipment Corporation
EG&G Idaho, Inc.
Ecole Nationale Superieure d'Ingenieurs
    Electriciens de Grenoble
E.I. du Pont de Nemours & Co., Inc.
Electronics and Telecommunications
    Research Institute
Encore Computer Corporation
Exxon Production Research Company
Fallmann and Bauemfeind GmbH
Frame Technology Corp.

Fraunhofer Institute for Information & Data
    Processing
GKSS Forschungszentrum Geesthacht
    GmbH
Goddard Space Flight Center
Gradient Technologies, Inc.
Groupe Bull
HP/Apollo
Hitachi Ltd.
Hughes Aircraft Company
IBM
IMAG
INEGI
Information Presentation Technology, Inc.
Institut fur Wirtschaftsinformatik
Institute for Information Industry
Institute of Systems Science at the
    National University of Singapore
Integrated Computer Solutions
Intel
Interactive Systems Corporation
Intergraph Corporation
Intergraph Graphics Users Group
IXI Limited
iXOS Software GmbH
J.C.Penney, Inc.
Keio University
Kontron Elektronik GmbH
Landmark Graphics Corporation
Lawrence Livermore National Laboratories
Leibniz Rechenzentrum
Locus Computing Corporation
Mamram Computer Center
Mannesmann AG
Martin Marietta Corporation
Massachusetts Institute of Technology
    Information Systems
Matsushita Electric Industrial Co., Ltd.
Mead Data Central
Mentor Graphics Corporation
Michigan State University
Micro Focus
Microsoft Corporation
Mitre Corporation
MIPS Computer Systems, Inc.
Motorola
Mt. Xinu

Figure 6.1 – OSF Membership (8-1-91), page 1 of 2

NASA Software Support Environment
   Project
National Computer Board
The National Institutes of Health
The National Instituto for Higher Education
   (Ireland)
National Semiconductor Corporation
Naval Underwater Systems Center
NCR
NKK Corporation
New Jersey Institute of Technology
New York University
Non Standard Logics
North Carolina State University
Northeast Parallel Architectures Center
Objectivity, Inc.
Omron Corporation
Oracle Corporation
Petrotechnical Open Software Corporation
   (POSC)
Philips
Princeton University
Project Athena, Massachusetts Institute of
   Technology
Quantum GmbH
Quest Systems Corporation
Raytheon Company
Retix
Ricoh Company, Ltd.
Research Institute for Advanced Computer
   Science (RIACS)
Royal College Maria Cristina of El Escorial
Royal Institute of Technology
Royal Signals and Radar Establishment
Samsung Group
The Santa Cruz Operation
Schlumberger
Sematech
Sequent Computer Systems, Inc.
Sharp Corporation
Shell Development Company
S.I.A.
Siemens Nixdorf Information Systems
Sierra Geophysics
Silicon Graphics, Inc.
Simpact Associates, Inc.
Software AG

Software Research Associates
Sony Corporation
Stanford University
Sumitomo Electric Industries Ltd.
Superconducting Super Collider Laboratory
Tandem Computers Incorporated
Tatung Institute of Technology
Tecsiel S.p.A.
Tektronix, Inc.
Texas Instruments, Inc.
The Royal Dutch/Shell Group of Companies
The Swedish Telecom Group
Tivoli Systems, Inc.
Transarc Corporation
Trusted Information Systems, Inc.
Unilever PLC/NV
University of Alaska Fairbanks
University of Calgary
University of California, Berkeley
University of Cambridge
University of Guelph
University of Illinois at Urbana–Champaign
University of Iowa
University of Lowell
University of Maryland
University of Massachusetts
University of Michigan
University of Milan
University of Southern California
University of Texas
University of Tokyo
University of Tromso
University of Utah
University of Vermont – EMBA Computer
   Facility
University of Virgnia
University of Washington
University of Waterloo
Uppsala University Computing Center
Verband Deutscher Maschinenund Anla-
   genbau e.V. (VDMA)
Visix Software, Inc.
Wang Laboratories
Xerox Corporation
Yokogawa Electric Corp.
Zentrum fur Graphische Datenverarbeitung

Figure 6.1 – OSF Membership (8-1-91), page 2 of 2

7

The Level Playing Field

In an industry that uses the fuzziest definitions and terminology that have ever existed, the concept of a "level playing field" is an imaginary concept in competitive time and space. Those who talk about it would have us believe that true competition in the computer industry will develop through "standards" and "open systems," which, in turn, will result in the best technology at the lowest prices for users. At the present time, no one in the open systems game really knows what the impact of open systems will be on their own businesses, much less on the users of such systems.

Perhaps now the definition of "open" should be modified to read "controlled by a group of consenting competitors operating outside the privacy of their parent organizations." Regardless of semantics, the purpose of "open systems" is to attract enough users to eventually become at least de facto standards for the benefit of those who had the foresight and "generosity" to give freely of their time, effort, and treasure to develop and promote them.

7.1   A LOOK AT THE PAST

To better understand the strategies, tactics, and politics of standards development it is important to take a look at the past.

Lewis Carroll, a mathematician and logician, wrote *The Hunting of the Snark, An Agony in Eight Fits* in 1876. Claude Shannon, the father of information theory, wrote *H/logN* in 1948. In 1963, the American Standard Code for Information Interchange (ASCII) was introduced employing a 7-bit code with no parity recommendation. Essentially, a level playing field was established for information interchange with a code set (alphabet) of 128 characters (N in Shannon's equation). The fact that practically all computers would eventually have an 8-bit compare character (byte) meant that source coding at the most fundamental level would be "half-standardized."

ASCII provided for the Roman alphabet (in upper- and lowercase form), for decimal digits, and selected symbols and control characters that could be freely interchanged between computers and terminals. As we shall see, practically all other standards are snarks, but for 7 bits, ASCII is real. However, the eighth bit provides another 128 characters that hardware "architects" and software "designers" can use to express their creativity and individuality. It permits the snark of compatibility and portability to remain elusive.

The irritation of terminal settings, the blandness of ASCII text stripped of its incompatible formatting characters, and the agony of connectivity can all be traced to the bumpy, competitive half of the level playing field which resulted from failure to heed the warning of $H/logN$. Excess bits (and freedom of expression) increase information entropy, and it is necessary to expend energy in order to avoid the natural tendency toward chaos. That energy today is manifested by

- Enormous systems integration projects, which are necessary if incompatible code sources (computers) are to communicate with each other
- Frantic efforts of vendors to develop "standards" or to "open" their proprietary systems so that they may become de facto standards

All these efforts perpetuate the myth of the level playing field when, in fact, they were designed to either secure or attack the high ground already established by the competition. The competitors have played an expensive and costly game, and the users, who must ultimately foot the bill, will eventually run out of both patience and resources. Let's rerun some former games.

7.1.1 The ASCII Fiasco

When ASCII was introduced in 1963, IBM was well along with the design of its System/360 line of computers which would become a de facto standard for commercial data processing. The original System/360 and its long line of successors represent information internally in extended binary coded decimal interchange code (EBCDIC), a standard from the punch-card days.

IBM, a representative on the committee that developed ASCII, maintained that EBCDIC was already a standard for information interchange, card image processing was then standard for commercial computer systems, and why change now? However, if a change were to be made, there were code sets that were technically superior to ASCII.

When ASCII came up for a vote, IBM's "reasoning" went something like this: (1) all computer companies had the same vested interest in EBCDIC as a standard, (2) IBM did not want to appear to be throwing its weight around, and (3) it was "obvious" that ASCII was not a good enough code set to warrant change. With this brilliant reasoning, the IBM representative on the committee was instructed to abstain from voting.

Other committee members' reactions were quite simple: (1) IBM had the most invested in EBCDIC since it dominated punchcards; (2) if IBM didn't care enough to vote on ASCII, why should they vote against it; and (3) adoption of ASCII might cause IBM some problems with its new computer product line.

Since the committee was weary of hunting the standard code-set snark that would satisfy everyone and was having fits agonizing over 8-bit vs. 7-bit codes (the technical merits of which few members had detailed understanding), it took the easier, softer way and approved ASCII. There you have it, folks, just a little example of the tactics and politics associated with standards development at the most fundamental level. Little strategy was involved, and no consideration was given to any potential problems that might be caused for users.

When IBM was in the early stages of software development for the System/360 line, an estimate showed that it would cost $1 million to support the ASCII bit in the PSW (program status word). How much ASCII has cost IBM over the years is problematic, but one thing is certain—IBM has never employed similar tactics in any standards effort since that time; major IBM products, such as the System/3X, did not even support ASCII terminals.

7.1.2 Language Stories

Language stories are important because they bring into play the world's largest computer user—the federal government. It was the federal government that first specified there be a level playing field, the motivation for which varies from the blatant politics associated with the geographic location of vendors to legitimate concerns about alternate sources of supply and antitrust. However, for better or for worse, procurement policies of the federal government have dictated that it install a variety of computer hardware, and communications between these diverse systems has been an obvious problem from the start. One of the first "solutions" was COBOL (COmmon Business-Oriented

Language), which came from the United States Department of Defense. Once again, history is instructive.

IBM invented FORTRAN (FORmula TRANslator) in the 1950s, and it rapidly became a standard for engineering and scientific programming. By the time the Conference on Data Systems Languages (CODASYL) was convened at the Pentagon in 1959, IBM was in the process of developing a "commercial translator" (COMTRAN) intended for use by its commercial customers. This language was offered as a commercial language standard. However, while CODASYL was theoretically composed of "computing personnel from the computer industry, user organizations, software houses, and other related groups," the meeting was dominated by the major computer vendors and the Department of Defense.

The result was the rejection of COMTRAN, and CODASYL proceeded with the development of COBOL—all players started on a level playing field. RCA announced the first operational COBOL compiler at an ACM (Association for Computing Machinery) meeting in 1960, and COBOL has become a de facto standard for commercial data processing. At the present time, existing lines of COBOL source code are reported to be approaching the one trillion mark, and this is, in large measure, the sacred "programming investment" of which everyone is so wary.

Several pertinent comments, all of which are important as the OSF, UNIX International, and others work on their software standards, should be made about COBOL:

- It was supposed to solve the "portability problem"; it didn't.

- Many false claims were made for it, one of the most ludicrous being that management would be able to read COBOL programs and understand what those crazy programmers were doing.

- Some of what were considered to be the most powerful features of the language (for example, permitting data definition to specify editing that will take place as a side effect of output) were originally incorporated because complex instructions were available on IBM's commercial "data-processing machines." Other vendors, such as RCA, incorporated such complex instructions as an afterthought in their computer systems to facilitate compiler development.

- While the lure of English-language programming seemed so intuitively attractive, the language has not been highly regarded by either professional programmers or casual users. It is too "clerical" for the highly skilled; too complex for casual users. This has led to a proliferation of other languages and tools.

* Indeed, the process of standardization practically assured that CO-BOL would not be able to keep up with the times. New versions have been slow to win approval through an inevitably laborious process; it is much easier to come out with an entirely new language than it is to change a standard. COBOL has essentially been frozen in the 1960s.

Since IBM is a significant factor in this analysis, it is important to review its strategy and tactics in language standardization.

When the gift of COMTRAN was rejected by CODASYL, IBM had no alternative but to support COBOL if it wanted to do business with the federal government. Therefore, COBOL was announced as a supported language for the System/360.

However, since IBM knew its customers had minimal investments in COBOL (less than 5 percent of program libraries were in COBOL at the time System/360 was announced), the company decided to bring out a new and better language as a standard for the new system. IBM was willing to sacrifice its own child, FORTRAN, and its users' investments in that language (FORTRAN accounted for 75 percent of the program libraries among its engineering and scientific customers), to standardize on a new language—PL/1 (Programming Language/1).

IBM persisted in establishing PL/1 as a standard despite the pleading and advice of its customers and the internal bickering in the Programming Systems Department itself.

A letter from one major customer directed to the then IBM vice president of development stated, "Please, for our benefit, and the benefit of our children, and our children's children, don't announce a new language with the new product line." The plea was obviously rejected.

After the announcement of PL/1, a prominent member of SHARE (the IBM user group) asked point blank whether IBM intended to stop support of other languages in favor of PL/1. Upon being assured that this was not the case (although it was, in fact, IBM's strategy), the SHARE member stated he was glad because "FORTRAN users aren't going to switch to PL/1, and the federal government is going to make you support COBOL"—he was right!

IBM, pitted against the world of competitive vendors, its customers, and the federal government, could not sell (or force) the acceptance of PL/1. However, it tried; and with even minimal support from any quarter, it would probably have prevailed. It did not prevail because

- Competitive vendors did not want another language to develop and support, especially one that would give IBM a competitive edge.

- Programmers have a natural built-in reluctance to change languages, so customers did not adopt it. (This reluctance probably extends to operating systems also.)

- The federal government had no intention of abandoning its efforts to standardize languages, and IBM did not expect it to do so. (IBM has always viewed the federal government as a separate market, and its strategy has always been to keep its commercial customer base from becoming a level playing field.)

The point is that it is only when the rest of the world joins together that IBM becomes thwarted in its efforts to establish standards for the commercial data processing market. And seldom does the rest of the world join together because IBM usually has its loyal customer base squarely on its side. The case of PL/1 is the exception that proves the rule—the playing field is seldom level when IBM is on the field.

In 1978 the Computer Science and Engineering Research Study (COS-ERS) concluded a 3-year project for the National Science Foundation with a weighty document that contained the following statement: "In considering software methodology research, one problem is how to put new methodology into practice. The pressures of local economies often force people and organizations to use obsolete techniques even though newer ones are clearly better. Nowhere is this better illustrated than the current pervasive use of FORTRAN and COBOL. If software practices continue to drift, in 20 years the U.S. will have a national inventory of unstructured, hard to maintain, impossible to replace, programs written in FORTRAN and COBOL as the basis of its industrial and government activities. Conversely the Soviets may very well have a set of well-structured, easily maintained and modifiable programs in more modern languages, because, in fact, they plan to leapfrog FORTRAN and CO-BOL. In this case the competitive process of selecting efficient industrial processes among feasible alternatives will be impaired in the United States, but facilitated in the Soviet Union. We could then face a software gap more serious than the missile gap of some years ago."

This is a disturbing statement from many points of view, not the least of which is the federal government's involvement in the standards process. Bear this statement in mind as we analyze the tactics, strategies, and politics of the standards process because it becomes even more pertinent in today's environment. For while there is hope that "programs" can be translated to another language or replaced, complex data base systems and computer networks can literally become "hard to maintain" and "impossible to replace."

7.1.3 Hardware Hieroglyphics

Prior to the advent of IBM's System/360, competitive mainframe architectures flourished; there was no standard (de facto or otherwise) for hardware. At that point in time computer architects still believed that if you built a better mousetrap, the world would beat a path to your door. However, the success of IBM's compatible line of hardware soon made it clear that 70 to 80 percent of the commercial mainframe market was firmly committed to IBM. For all practical purposes, the other competitors were confronted with playing the game deep in their own territory.

The fact that the System/360-370 hardware architecture became, and has remained, the major commercial data-processing standard had little to do with technical excellence. The architecture wasn't all that exciting in the early 1960s, and it hasn't improved much since. For example:

- The RCA 601 was available before IBM's System/360 was announced and many considered it to have superior hardware architecture. It had register sets associated with each programming space, tagged memory, multiple levels of address modification and indirect addressing, an excellent interrupt system, etc. (In fact, the Bell System, which tended to operate like a "minigovernment" in seeking alternatives to IBM computers, had a substantial number of RCA 601s on order for commercial applications such as billing.)

- The Burroughs B5000 had been announced with "reverse Polish notation" (the operands preceded the operators) and virtual memory. (With RISC architectures, compilers are becoming critically important once again. Who knows, maybe some of the world will go stacks- and "parentheses-free.")

- A shift in attitude on the part of the mainframe computer industry was a major contributing factor in the establishment of the IBM System/360 hardware "standard." It acknowledged that building better hardware mousetraps was not the name of the game being played.

This acknowledgment led some to adopt an "if you can't lick'em, join'em" strategy. General Sarnoff of RCA addressed a joint computer conference in the late 1960s, at which his subject was standards. He had provided the leadership necessary to have the television industry adopt a standard of compatible black-white and color television. The good General was promoting not only standard computer languages such as COBOL, but also potential hardware "standards."

Shortly after this RCA announced the Spectra/70, a "nearly compatible" System/360 look-alike. Someone had convinced General Sarnoff that 99 percent compatibility was enough; to go 100 percent would risk lawsuits from IBM. When RCA started an extensive recruitment campaign for programmers in Poughkeepsie (NY), IBM had some conversations with RCA that reinforced this conclusion. RCA destroyed itself writing systems software for a 99 percent-compatible hardware system and trying to sell 99 percent compatibility to IBM customers.

From IBM's perspective the need for standardization had been clear. It had been confronted with maintaining four distinct architectures (14XX, 7080, 707X, 709X), and it was entirely too expensive to develop systems software for such architecturally different systems. However, the System/360-370 architectural standard was not the result of divine inspiration. As one old-timer stated at the time IBM announced MVS/XA, "XA really stands for 'extended accommodation,' not extended architecture." The System/370 architecture became a standard for mainframe data processing as a result of the loyal IBM customer base and Gene Amdahl.

Amdahl pioneered software-compatible mainframes and proved that if you are going to adopt a de facto hardware standard, it had better be 100 percent compatible in terms of instruction set and general architecture. In this environment, it also became apparent that it was absolutely essential to run systems software as produced by the primary vendor and that the performance of that systems software was influenced by the actual implementation of the instruction set. (For example, Amdahl found that its initial, sloppy implementation of the Execute instruction resulted in measurable degradation of total systems performance, because that rather obscure instruction was used extensively in IBM's implementation of its operating system.)

True hardware-software compatibility provided some means for customers to measure directly the price-performance of competing mainframes. After Amdahl became a viable contender in the IBM mainframe market, it became increasingly difficult for the loyal IBM customer to justify substantial differences in price-performance based on the color of the hardware boxes. It also benefited all customers because competition did, in fact, improve mainframe price-performance more rapidly than the traditional IBM price-performance curve.

The ancient hieroglyphics carved into stone on the cave walls clearly tell us that 99 percent compatibility with a de facto hardware standard may be worse than no compatibility at all; the key to success is systems software compatibility and hardware-software synergy. PC-cloners only verified this fact.

7.1.4 Data Model Tales

GE announced the development of Integrated Data Store (IDS) before IBM announced System/360. IDS was a data base management system (DBMS) that defined the network model, and GE proposed that data base management facilities be included in COBOL. When IBM was questioned about whether such facilities were to be included for the new product line (System/360), the corporate level answered: "We don't need that, we have ISAM (Indexed Sequential Access Method)."

Since GE was one of the largest IBM computer systems users, Charlie Bachman (the father of IDS) had access to the IBM user organizations (Guide and SHARE), and he lobbied for IDS's acceptance as a standard. Despite the formation of "data base task groups" in both organizations, IBM resisted adopting IDS. This ended in the development of the hierarchical data model and IMS. Bachman had more success with CODASYL and the network model became the "CODASYL model."

There was more to IBM's resistance of the CODASYL model than the usual "not invented here" attitude. IBM certainly knew about the problems associated with file transfer among various systems requiring the same data (or even a datum) and also recognized the need for data management of direct access storage devices. However, internal "experts" disagreed about the solution to the still ill-defined problems. IBM let many flowers grow:

- Access methods such as ISAM were put forth by some, such as the corporate "expert."

- Inverted file structures were incorporated into many internal "management information systems" to facilitate information retrieval. Some thought this solved the data management problem.

- IMS and the hierarchical model became official products for customers.

- IBM's internal order entry system was developed using BDAM (basic direct access method); to the best of my knowledge, flat addressing remains at the heart of this IBM system 20 years after development (despite IBM's best efforts to bring its internal systems into conformance with what it recommends for its customers).

Then, before the 1960s were over, Dr. Edgar F. Codd was busy working on the relational model.

Standardization on a single DBMS or data model during the 1960s was premature and doomed to failure. In fact, many data models and DBMSs will survive, inevitably, into the foreseeable future. However, with the increased complexity of computer-communication networks and an expanded definition of "data" to include images, graphics, text, voice, and video, as well as traditional encoded data, the problems of information entropy identified by Shannon so long ago become paramount. The effective management of data in a distributed environment becomes the energy necessary to avoid chaos. Without improved standards for data interchange, these costs will become prohibitive for both users and vendors. (More on this later.)

7.1.5 The Operating Systems Saga

The initial efforts to achieve portability of applications through CO-BOL were attempted before there were such things as operating systems, a term that came into being with IBM's System/360. Previously, "operating systems" incorporated a varied set of functions and services classified as monitors, executives, supervisors, input/output control systems, loaders, etc.

IBM originally planned to have a single System/360 operating system (OS/360) and the initial design specifications for that monster called for it to run on systems from the 16-kilobyte Model 30 up to the top-of-the-line 1-Mbyte Model 65. Without belaboring the long history, IBM needed to "decommit" OS for the smaller machines and to develop simple disk and tape operating systems (DOS and TOS). The major operating systems families evolved slowly over the years along two separate lines—the "mainstream" [OS to OS/MVT to VS2 to MVS to MVS/XA (Multiple Virtual Storage/Extended Architecture) to MVS/ESA (Multiple Virtual Storage/Enterprise System Architecture)] and the little orphan DOS [DOS through various stages to DOS/VSE (Virtual Storage Extended)]. Despite IBM's best efforts to upgrade its customers, the dichotomy between full-function and relatively simple operating systems has persisted for 25 years. Today, 50 percent of 9370 customers continue to use DOS/VSE. So much for one operating system for all users.

That is not all. IBM poured millions of dollars into the development of a timesharing system (TSS) before it announced its virtual storage hardware-software systems. The multiple and diverse operating systems environments led to the need for a special operating system for the development environment—VM (virtual machine)—which struggled for years to achieve full support from IBM as a commercial product. And the complexity of the "regular" operating systems were too much for the small business environment that grew up around the IBM System/3X, minicomputers such as the venerable Series/1, and controllers such as the 3790 and 8100. A whole list of alphabet soup sprouted around these—CPF (Control Program Facility), SSP (System Support Programs), EDX (Event Driven Executive), DPCX (Distributed Processing Control Executive), DPPX (Distributed Processing Programming Executive), etc.—all of which can be classified as operating systems. It is a safe assumption that IBM didn't get itself and its customers into this mess by design. There are different operating environments out there, and they require different operating systems.

IBM should have learned a number of lessons about operating systems during this long and trying experience:

- It is difficult to standardize on operating systems across market segments—customers don't like to change.

- It is expensive for customers to shift operating systems or even to convert to new versions within the same general system.

- It is expensive for vendors to develop, maintain, and support multiple operating systems.

However, it is all worthwhile if the operating system is viewed as the primary means of account control. An operating system can be the bond that binds customers to the hardware, and the whip that forces them to move along the vendor's prescribed technological path, and the burden that requires ever-larger processors.

The "success" of the compatible line of IBM mainframes has been a systems software rather than a hardware success. The systems software design objective was to move all processing and data bases to ever-larger IBM mainframes. Generally speaking, this has been a remarkably successful strategy.

The major resistance to IBM's "stepping-stone" strategy of selling ever-larger hardware-software systems has come from interactive computing on minicomputers. Call it distributed processing, networking, departmental processing, personal computing, or whatever suits your fancy—anything that starts to off-load IBM mainframes is viewed with alarm in Armonk.

7.1.6 Networking—An X-Rated Epic

By 1970, it was apparent that a processor hierarchy was inevitable; minicomputers were already in existence, and even IBM engineers were talking about "computers on a chip." Off-loading functions from mainframes over a hierarchical network was the obvious cost-effective technical solution, even if it didn't appeal to IBM on a business basis.

Timesharing had come out of the academic environment into the commercial marketplace. As long as there was only isolated use in the corporate world, through either individually installed minicomputers or purchase of outside services, a bizarre synergy developed between the central data-processing facility and these pockets of resistance. The expenditures for timesharing were used as justification for upgrading mainframes to absorb this non-IBM workload. When it was found that it was more expensive to do the same work under TSO (IBM's mainframe timesharing option), the user departments would "downsize" again. Then another corporate audit would reveal the "outside expenditures" and the MIS department would justify another mainframe upgrade by absorbing the work again.

This cycle was all to IBM's benefit, regardless of cost to the customer, and the isolated pockets of resistance were tolerated. However, by the early 1970s, even IBM had to recognize that distributed processing networks promised more cost-effective solutions for on-line transaction processing, and this posed a threat to IBM mainframes.

As an alternative to distributed processing (IBM has never liked that term), IBM decided to announce a mainframe-oriented networking strategy called SNA (Systems Network Architecture). Its evolution has been painfully slow, frequently misguided, and always directed toward the primary objective of keeping as much processing as possible on IBM mainframes. However, SNA has become the standard on much of the commercial playing field. It has slowed the development of true distributed processing; it has been enormously successful from IBM's point of view; and it will be around for years to come—make no mistake about that.

- SNA permitted IBM to consolidate 35 major communications software products and 15 different data link controls into a cohesive communications system. For IBM, SNA would be deemed successful if it became nothing more than an internal development standard.

- However, we must also recognize that SNA did, in fact, establish a conceptual framework where there was none. It was inevitable that it would attract the attention of other vendors.

- SNA is an outstanding example of a proprietary architecture becoming a de facto standard, thereby initiating alternative standards activity.

SNA, announced in 1973, threatened to tilt the playing field in IBM's favor by establishing an architecture of layered protocols that would be necessary as networks grew in complexity. Despite its shaky start, by 1977, SNA installations approached 1000 and were expanding rapidly. At this point, ISO (International Standards Organization) formed a subcommittee to develop standards for a model of Open Systems Interconnection (OSI) and for the exchange of information between distributed systems. By 1980, SNA had 2500 installations, and ISO/OSI was still enmeshed in the standards process. In 1986, IBM announced its intention to support OSI for the purpose of "connectivity" to SNA—an SNA now expanded to 20,000 installations.

For those customers who suffered the expense and frustration of building (or attempting to build) distributed processing networks using 37X5 communications front-ends and 3790 and 8100 cluster controllers, I can only sympathize—they were all part of the plan to keep processing on the mainframe. It is also possible to view these boxes (along with mainframe channels) as reduced instruction set computers. The only difference is that they were specifically designed, packaged, and supported to restrict their function and use. They served their purpose well against minicomputers, but the advent of the PC changed all that—the controlled evolution of distributed processing gave way to revolution once stand-alone PCs started linking up to mainframes.

Thus, the mainframe remains the master of all it surveys in the SNA-oriented networking world; and while IBM first started to preach "connectivity" and "openness" only from necessity, it is proceeding from a position of great strength.

7.1.7 Performance Measurement Fables

The concept of an open, level playing field implies that there will be some way to measure performance. To invent a better mousetrap, you have to define "better." Standards assist in performance measurement by at least clarifying what we are trying to measure. For example, a better mousetrap isn't worth much if you are trapping elephants. On the other hand, a trap for elephants will seldom catch very many mice.

In performance measurement, two general categories must be considered—hardware and software. Taken individually, there is no question that hardware performance is easier to measure than software performance. However, on today's playing field, the perceived hardware-software "effectiveness" in improving "productivity" is frequently the category used to determine the competitive "winners." The difference between measuring perceived "effectiveness" and measuring hardware is similar to that of judging gymnastics floor exercises and clocking the 100-m dash.

However, measuring the performance of computer hardware is far from being as simple as clocking the 100-m dash. It is more equal to a race where runners, at various times, run on an Olympic-quality track, through a swamp, and scramble up the side of a mountain, and some runners wear track shoes, some a sturdy set of brogues, and others hip boots. Over the years, we have all come to realize that there is no one appropriate way to measure hardware performance across either computer architectures or application sets.

Cycle times and MIPS (million instructions per second) all suffer because they do not consider bandwidth, and if bandwidth is considered, the larger word size may not process any faster because smaller integers are being processed. Then, the actual implementation of the instruction set itself can vary considerably, and averages are of little use since certain instructions will be more frequently used. (Remember the Amdahl case.)

Various instruction mixes have also been used, but these suffer from the obvious fact that these mixes are applications-dependent. When crossing architectures, other features such as addressing and indexing become significant in performance. [IBM, in its MACHAN performance measurement system, which was designed for both internal and competitive "machine analysis," employed the Gibson Mix (a suite of programs for testing hardware developed by old-timer and IBMer, Jack Gibson) for scientific and commercial data processing, but then saw fit to add "brownie points" for architectural features.]

All this led to the development of various kernels, benchmarks, and synthetic jobs. Kernels are code fragments—the inner loop that is so critical in most scientific processing; benchmarks add I/O activity, and thus provide a better measure of systems performance, including peripherals; synthetic jobs are artificial programs designed to exercise all of the components of the systems based on "job mix." Their purpose is to provide a "shell" for constructing benchmark-like jobs.

One thing learned from the advent of System/360 was that hardware performance measurement becomes a relatively meaningless exercise—the systems software is what must be measured. Gene Amdahl, in particular, was fiercely protective of his hardware implementation. He constantly complained about the impact of systems software, especially virtual storage systems. (Seymour Cray had a similar aversion to virtual storage, believing the overhead of complex memory management would destroy high-performance systems.)

There is no question that operating systems determine the performance of computing systems, at least from the users' perspective. This became more than obvious when early virtual storage systems started to "thrash" and users could clearly see that no productive work was being accomplished. Therefore, hardware-software systems performance is normally measured in "throughput" and/or response time, both of which clearly demonstrate that something is being accomplished. Thus, transaction rates and the number of terminals that can be supported (with some specified response time) have become measures. Two simple questions can be raised about these measures:

- What kind of transaction is it? (A simple update of a flat file, or an update of a distributed data base?)

- Response time for doing what? (Calculating $A=B+C$, or querying a large data base?)

Thus, the lessons from the past tell us that performance measurement of computer systems is far from an exact science. However, there is an even more alarming concern—How do we measure the value of the information being produced by computers? The fundamental law of information theory tells us that "more is not better" and that "faster" is becoming highly suspect. What now?

7.2   A LOOK AT THE PRESENT

Our long look at the past was prompted by the déjà vu I feel when looking at the present. Before proceeding with a detailed analysis of the trend toward standards and open systems, we need to look at what is currently going on.

7.2.1 Code Sets

Code sets work in Europe would adopt an 8-bit code for native language. Japan, which does not have the benefit of a simple alphabet, is continuing work on developing systems software with a 16-bit compare character so that Kanji can be represented. [The cost of development and the impact of a 16-bit compare character on performance could be substantial, but vendors who want to compete on the Pacific Rim are going to be forced to look beyond ASCII (American Standard Code for Information Interchange).]

7.2.2 Languages

Languages continue to proliferate, and efforts at standardization may not help at all. In fact, a good way to ruin a language is to make it a "standard" and then try extend to it to satisfy everyone. The Tower of Babel wouldn't be so bad, but there are signs of a trend toward "multilingual capability" by having one language invoke another. Here the problem becomes one of data structures (call them objects, if you will)—the various languages don't treat them in the same manner at all. In addition, for the neophyte who cannot speak even the simplest computer language, we want to point and use icons, the "look and feel" of which are subject to litigation. It is rather like saying that teams playing football cannot use the same formations.

7.2.3 Hardware

The sudden attention being given to "standards" and "open systems" is prompted by the brash attempt of Johnny-come-lately Sun Microsystems, which, having gained a competitive advantage with RISC technology, wants to declare the game over by standardizing on the SPARC chip. Since Sun is making noises about wiping out everything from the desktop up to supercomputers, with special attention being given to minicomputers, its generous offer has not been well received by its RISC competitors, especially since it teamed up with AT&T in an attempt to seize control of UNIX as the standard operating system. Then, of course, there are the questions about patents associated with RISCs.

7.2.4 Data Models

It would seem that the data model question has been settled. The relational model is mathematically defined and is the obvious choice for distributed data bases and systems integration. But, wait just a minute. There have been questions and problems with the implementation of relational systems from the beginning. Dr. Codd is very protective of his child and very specific about what it takes for a data base system to be "fully relational." He has suggested that terms such as "tabular" and "semirelational" be used for systems that do not meet his criteria. A recent article by Dr. Codd was titled "Fatal Flaws in SQL" and if that isn't enough to give those standardizing on SQL (Structured Query Language) pause, consider the fact that IBM's rights to the relational model are substantially more clear than Apple's rights to the MAC (Macintosh) interface. Then, of course, other data models will not (and should not) disappear, especially with an ever-expanding definition of "data" as that which incorporates "everything stored in a computer."

7.2.5 Operating Systems

I have already discussed IBM's failure to standardize on operating systems. About 4 years ago in a public meeting of its large-scale systems users, IBM made the statement that UNIX was "just about where VM was 10 years ago in IBM's thinking." Since then, IBM announced SAA in formal acknowledgment that its internal attempts to standardize on operating systems failed, and it has joined the Open Software Foundation and provided AIX as the UNIX kernel.

While I will discuss UNIX in chapter 10 of this book, I should point out here, that now, UNIX is technically 4 or 5 years behind the state of the art for commercial processing, and SAA provides for the tight integration of communications, operating systems functions, and data base management functions. The "Operating Systems Saga" continues, and UNIX is merely the latest episode.

7.2.6 Networking

Strange murky worlds sometimes get summed up under the general classification of "networks." By networks I mean all "code sources," including human beings. The question then is how to make the networks "open" to everyone, when we can be reasonably certain, barring unforeseen progress in genetic engineering comparable to that envisioned by Huxley in *Brave New World*, that the humans are not going to be standardized. Standards to connect hardware-software products have been slow to evolve, and the current emphasis on connectivity is about 15 years too late. However, the "human connection" is an important consideration for vendors. Consider the following:

- The government is beginning to emphasize equal access to information for all systems users. While vendors have been somewhat concerned about the ramifications for the physically handicapped (for example, the blind), equal access might also apply to the wide range of human potential as well. Do we standardize human interfaces and access to information at the kindergarten level?
- Some time ago, two major universities installed advanced networks on campus, including wonderful new phone systems that have caused no end of problems. As one information systems (IS) director

asked: "Have you ever been confronted with (the problem of) telling university professors that you are going to run a training program on how to use the telephone?" Tradeoffs between function and ease-of-use are as old as the computer industry, but the problem hasn't even been solved for the simplest terminal!

- In a study of usability conducted for a major computer vendor, one customer stated quite simply and succinctly: "Tell them to standardize on the keyboard—that would help more than anything else."

- Nontrivial problems associated with networking and the "information age" are beginning to surface; most of them have to do with communications between human and machine code sources. To say that computer and communications architects and engineers do not understand these problems is obvious; to say the same about those selling and installing such networks is both an understatement and frightening. (Remember the great stock market "adjustment.")

7.2.7 Performance Measurement

For the last three years, *Computerworld* has published a special supplement called "The Premier 100." These companies are reportedly "The Most Effective Users of Information Systems"—it says so right on the cover. The methodology, which was developed with the assistance of some leading IS consulting firms, is based on the following six criteria and weighting factors: (1) IS budget (the more spent, the better), 30; (2) 5-year profit average, 15; (3) current market value of major processors (the higher the better), 15; (4) percentage of budget spent on staff (the less spent on staff, the better), 10; (5) percentage of budget spent on training (the more spent, the better), 15; and (6) the ratio of personal computers and terminals to total employment, 15.

Even a cursory analysis of this formula reveals that it is based on the following assumptions, which we present along with our comments:

- The higher the IS budget (as a percent of revenue), the more effectively companies are employing information technology.

(This criterion is deemed so important that it is weighted twice as heavily as any other factor. This seems to be based on the confused notion that the value of output, or desired results, is directly related to the amount invested to achieve those results. In light of the fact that a high percentage of information systems projects are never completed, or never used, this criterion distorts the meaning of "effectiveness" and rewards big spenders.)

- The higher the profit growth for a 5-year period, the more effectively companies are employing information technology.

(Since we assume that "profit" or quality service at low cost is a goal of most organizations, we have to agree with this criterion. However, to arbitrarily attribute profit growth to the effective use of information technology is quite another matter. It would be more appropriate to correlate investment in information technology with profits, and that is precisely what we will attempt to do.)

- Newer processors (mainframes and minicomputers, as specified in the criterion definition) are assumed to be more "effective" than older, fully depreciated processors that obtain the same results.

(The assumption that those on the leading edge of technology more effectively use information technology may be encouraged by vendors and some IS personnel, but technology for technology's sake is not very popular with prudent business executives.)

- By rewarding companies that have the lowest staff/budget ratio, this criterion contains the premise that it is always better to invest in hardware, packaged software, and outside services rather than internal IS personnel.

(Perhaps this is a reaction to the current tendency to blame the central IS function for all the failures of information technology to meet vendors' claims and users' expectations. However, there is absolutely no evidence to show that increased investment in hardware and outside information services results in more effective use of information technology by an organization. In fact, we only need look at the federal government's use of systems integrators to produce evidence to the contrary. And, on the outside chance that the developers of this model depend on end users to replace IS personnel in effectively using information technology—the record is at least as bad.)

- The higher the proportion of the IS budget spent on training, the more effective the use of information technology.

(Superficially, this seems to make sense. However, combined with the reward for a low personnel budget, this criterion can be paraphrased as follows: It is better to hire cheap, inexperienced people and train them than it is to hire good experienced people in the first place. Or, a concomitant conclusion would be that it is "good" to lose people once they are trained and their salaries rise, because this would lower the salary budget and increase the training budget.)

- The more terminals and PCs you have per employee, the more effectively you use information technology.

(There is no proof that companies with more terminals or PCs per employee use their information technology more effectively or that individuals use the specific technology more effectively. In fact, as we have seen, the installation of tens of millions of PCs in the 1980s failed to achieve the originally stated objective of improving office productivity.)

When the original Premier 100 listing was published in 1988, we spotted several companies on the list that had experienced major systems problems. For example, a major bank was close to bankruptcy because information on loan portfolios was 90 days after the fact and the implementation of a new trust accounting system resulted in a catastrophic failure, which led to the bank's sale of its trust business. And, a highly touted airline reservation system had a bug and underbooked flights on the parent airline during the vacation season, which required the CEO to explain poor corporate earnings to the financial community. Nevertheless, such companies, by spending heavily on information technology, managed to make the Premier 100 list of "most effective users of information systems."

We performed some statistical analysis on the Premier 100 companies and determined that the correlation coefficient between the "effectiveness ratings" and profits was only 16. When you consider that profits are included in the rating with a weighting factor of 15 out of 100, that is as close as you get to no correlation. We also looked by industry, and while the range varied from +.29 for the petroleum industry down to -.48 for financial services, it was obvious that there was no significant positive correlation between the effectiveness ratings and profitability, even within industry.

We really thought the Premier 100 would be laughed out of existence after the first year, but that didn't happen. The ratings still do not correlate with profitability. In 1988 the correlation coefficient was 11, and it remained the same in 1989. However, this hasn't stopped the Premier 100. In fact, *Computerworld* is now having an Annual Awards Dinner for the big spenders at which speakers, such as Peter Keen, assure them that information technology "infrastructures" cannot be cost-justified. That must be reassuring.

Mr. Keen presents much the same argument that James Martin made about building the "big bang" corporate data bases of the 1970s. Such major undertakings cannot be cost-justified because you don't know the specific applications that will "benefit." Therefore, you should capitalize the effort required to build these data bases, even if you do not know what their value will be. This requires an act of faith and trust that we feel is beyond what most CEOs and chief financial officers (CFOs) have in information technology, regardless of whether their heads are built on the "Taylor model."

One financial analyst has promoted RISCs based on charts comparing dollars per MIPS for mainframes, minicomputers, and RISCs. Even the popular trade press has a better feel for performance measurement than that. *Computerworld Focus* (10/5/88) defined MIPS as follows: "The MIPS measurement calculates the execution of a command off a microprocessor (some don't know the difference between commands and instructions; that's progress). MIPS are used to compare very similar architectures." At least that definition indicates you shouldn't compare apples, oranges, and zucchini; however, the confused technical performance measurement is not the real problem here.

In "The Premier 100—The Companies Investing Most Effectively in Information Systems," published in September, 1988, I found the following:

- A correlation coefficient of less than 2 between the ratings assigned and the 1987 profits of these "premier" companies. That is more than a little scary, especially when profit is one of the factors considered in the methodology.

- While the introduction to the report stresses the necessity for a commercial organization to "leverage its MIS strategy to gain a competitive edge" and warns that "we will soon enter an era when the ability to do this will become absolutely essential to survive and prosper," I found the following:

  - The four highest-rated insurance companies were among the lowest in relative profitability (profit was less than 30 percent of the leading company), whereas the ninth-rated company was the most profitable.

  - Five of the ten top-rated banks had losses in 1987.

  - The fourth-rated retailing establishment had the highest IS budget as a percentage of revenue and lost money in 1987.

  - Among the top-rated utilities, the company with the highest IS budget as a percent of revenue had the lowest profit ratio, and the

10th ranked company had the lowest IS budget and the highest profits.

When using this methodology, if an information systems budget decreased by 10 percent and profits increased by 10 percent, the effectiveness rating would go down!

A somewhat embarrassing incident occurred the week following the publication of "The Premier 100." In the September 19, 1988 issue of *Computerworld*, two articles appeared on American Airlines, which always has a leading reputation for using computers for competitive advantage. Let's take a look:

- American Airlines was ranked eighteenth in effectiveness among the top 100 companies and second in the "Transportation and Other Services Category." (Actually, it was first among transportation companies since McGraw-Hill was lumped under this category and came in first.)

- American Airlines also had the second highest ratio of IS budget to revenue within the category (McGraw-Hill being highest here also), but had the second lowest profit ratio among the eight companies in the category (one of the "premier" companies having had a loss).

- The first article reported that the United States General Accounting Office concluded that the Sabre system is making excessive profits and needs more stringent regulation by the federal government to prevent "anticompetitive abuses." (Remember the level playing field.)

- The second article reported that "flawed software" in the Sabre system cost American Airlines $50 million in revenue during the 1988 peak travel season. (A spokesperson for American stated: "We gave away $50 million in revenue that we should have carried for American.")

- It was concluded that more rigorous testing of software changes is required; this 25 years after the Sabre system was developed.

- I doubt that the CEO of American will gain much solace from the fact that his company is making the "most effective" use of information systems technology of any transportation company.

- I also doubt that the federal government will be able to readily reconcile "competitive abuses" with "effectiveness."

One gets the impression that we do not yet have a standard for performance measurement in terms of the effective application of information systems technology. As we approach the wonderful world of IS standards and "connectivity," some feel that computer processing power will become a commodity. If this is true, some customers are going to start wondering what you really do with a train load of pork bellies. I doubt that getting a "great deal" will sufficiently justify buying either pork bellies or MIPS.

In commercial data processing (as opposed to scientific computing), it all comes down to the concept borne of the "information age," that information has value—a concept yet to be clearly articulated, a concept of value without metrics. In a truly open environment where processing becomes a commodity, we need an invention to demonstrate the value of information to those human nodes on the network (or at least to those footing the bill for the technology). The nature of such an invention was clearly defined by von Neumann and Morgenstern nearly 50 years ago in *Theory of Games* and *Economic Behavior* when they stated that to make progress in the social sciences, it was "to be expected—or feared—that mathematical discoveries of a nature comparable to that of calculus are necessary to make progress in the field." This hasn't happened.

Computerworld introduced its "Premier 100" report as follows:

Imagine spending $160 billion and not being able to account for it in any hard and fast manner.

That is the dilemma facing U.S. companies, which will spend that much in 1988 on information technology.

More MIPS per dollar, standards, and open systems aren't going to solve the users' dilemma. The old game ain't going to play in Gualala, much less in Peoria and points east. A new type of game will be required on the level playing field of open systems.

7.3   A NEW TYPE OF GAME?

Do any of us really believe that all the recent talk about standards and open systems means that the fundamentals of the game have changed? Do any vendors really want a level playing field? Do users want vendors to play on a level playing field? Don't both users and vendors want the home team to have an advantage? These questions are not really very difficult to answer.

Certainly the strange sight of IBM, DEC, HP, and some of the founding partners of X/Open "volunteering" to clean up some rough spots on the playing field was curious, indeed. Those inclined to believe in the Easter Bunny and the Tooth Fairy read great significance into the new wave of "openness" this portended. In the early stages of the open systems "movement" rumors abounded that AT&T would join the OSF any day, and all would be sweetness and light. What really happened is that AT&T was picking its team. I won't comment on the lineups except to say that the remnants of IBM's earliest competitor, Unisys, is on the "other" side (IBM and Remington Rand used to argue about whether round or rectangular holes should be the standard for punch cards) along with Amdahl, an early UNIX believer because AT&T is one of its big customers.

At the first meeting of the two teams, a problem immediately surfaced—whose ball would be used? OSF's position was that "best of breed" should be the criteria for selecting the base technology. USV thought it should be "what is best for the greatest number of UNIX licensees" and pointed out that for most UNIX users, UNIX System V would give the shortest and easiest migration path to future advancements in UNIX technology. Since the two teams could not agree on whose ball would be used or the rules of the game, which was highly predictable from the start, the USV team moved to its own end of the field to play its own game.

Let's face it, the standards wars haven't changed at all. They are all about competitive advantage and disadvantage. Most of them come about when the game is over and the winner receives the de facto standard cup. As soon as that happens, the losers immediately declare that the real championship game will be played when the de facto standard is opened to everyone and a real standard is established.

The game hasn't changed, and the game isn't new. It looks terribly familiar, except for two important differences:

1. IBM, having apparently become a recent convert to "openness" and standards, has actually agreed to join a team rather than compete alone against the rest of the world.

2. The conduct of the spectators (users) has changed considerably —from the polite atmosphere of Wimbledon in the 1920s, where spectators wouldn't even cough for fear of distracting the players, to the insatiable demands for new thrills of the original Colosseum, where the players didn't receive very much consideration (much less a level playing field).

It is important to analyze both of these phenomena to conclude how the game may change in the future.

8

The Mountain in the Middle

IBM's SAA stands like a mountain in the middle of the playing field, making all talk of an overall level playing field meaningless. There may be "mini-playing fields" around the base of the mountain, but the mountain dominates the environment. The mountain may be clouded in mist at any given point in time, but this does not mean it is "vaporware"—it is real. The fact that IBM has deigned to come down from the mountain does not mean the mountain has moved or that IBM intends to open the mountain to mere mortals—the IBM mountain is proprietary. There is no question where IBM lives, where its heart is, or where its future lies. The fact that it is playing the open systems game with UNIX is similar to the company president who plays softball at the annual picnic; his motives and objectives are entirely different from those of the other players.

Why IBM is playing this game, and what the likely outcome will be are analyzed later in this book. But first, a few words of general advice.

I have cautioned IBM customers many times that IBM, regardless of any stated commitment to its customer base, is not a philanthropic organization, and they should not expect it to be. I now caution IBM's OSF teammates that IBM is not an egalitarian team player—at least not in terms of its long-range objectives. To paraphrase F. Scott Fitzgerald concerning the very rich: "IBM is different from the rest of us." Don't ever forget it! I also caution UNIX International's members who, now that they have banded together, may think they can ignore the IBM SAA mountain, that a bandwagon behind UNIX System V only prepares one to climb the foothills!

8.1 SAA—A MONUMENT TO FAILED "STANDARDS"

As mentioned previously, SAA may be viewed as a monument to the failed standards that IBM has attempted to establish internally, among its customer base, and within the computer industry. In the previous chapter, I reviewed some historic standards efforts in the industry. I would now like to make two every important points:

1. Standards that have been established within in a particular market segment or within a particular user segment fail when extended beyond their normal bounds.

2. Such standards fail for two reasons: ease of use and price-performance.

To understand why IBM needed to build the SAA mountain, let's look at what IBM knew, what IBM did, and what happened.

8.1.1 What IBM Knew

Before IBM announced System/360, a major customer study was conducted to determine the most important attributes of systems software. All major customers in the United States were surveyed, and the response rate for completed questionnaires was 83 percent. The response rate was so high because this was really IBM's first attempt to obtain user input into the software development process. One portion of the study asked users to rank attributes of systems software in order of their importance (with 1 being most important, 2 next, etc.). The message could not have been clearer.

Figure 8.1 plots the relative importance of the attributes of programming languages. Unlike ratings, rankings do provide meaningful measures of relative importance. Those on the chart were computed based on the following formula: (highest possible sum — individual sum)/(highest possible sum — lowest sum) × 100. Obviously, the attribute having the lowest sum has been assigned a value of 100. This makes it the most important attribute, since customers ranked the attributes based on 1 being most important and were asked to continue with their rankings as long as the attributes were at all appropriate. (I provide this detail because many market researchers do not seem to understand the difference between ratings and rankings, and weird conclusions are frequently reached.) The chart shows the following:

- Ease of use—programming (EOP) was the most important feature of all languages; hardly surprising.

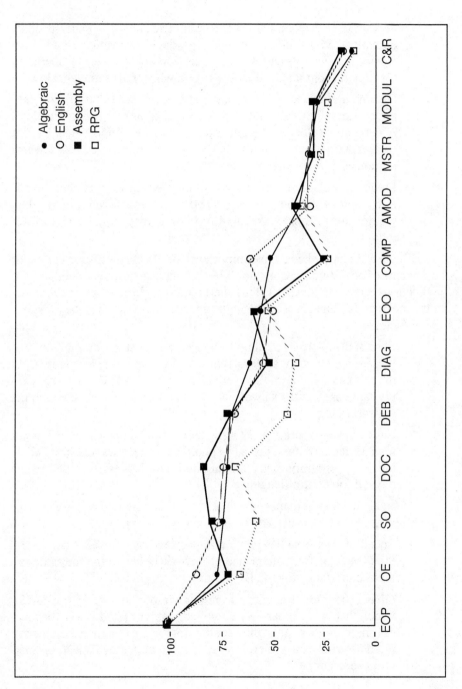

Figure 8.1 – Relative Importance: Languages (*Source: IBM*)

- Performance factors. Object program efficiency (OE) and speed of operation (SO) follow with relative importance ratings tending to cluster between 70 and 85, the exception being ¬peed of operation for Report Program Generators (RPGs), which falls somewhat lower.

- Documentation (DOC), which is an "ease of use" or "usability" factor, clusters tightly around 75 percent. (There is something practically eerie about documentation and its consistent importance. Recent studies on systems usability have revealed unchanged relative importance 25 years later.)

- I won't comment on the other attributes except to say that compatibility across machine lines (COMP) received lower ratings than would have been expected (this finding may still be significant today).

Figure 8.2 charts the relative importance of the attributes for the major components of operating systems (don't let the quaint terminology bother you; the functions remain to this day). This chart requires a little more explanation, but the message is clear. Ease of use in the generic sense remains the most important factor.

- Ease of use—programming (EOP) was the most important factor for IOCSs, which, in those days, required "programming" separate from the primary languages that were then in use (FORTRAN and assembly language; COBOL was not prominent in 1963); so the result is not surprising.

- Ease of use—operating (EOO) was the most important attribute of loaders and monitors, just as it should be. [The relatively low importance of "programming" for monitors and loaders was before the days of job control language (JCL).]

Once again, "performance attributes" tend to assume the same relative importance to the "ease-of-use attributes."

- Speed of operation has relative importance ranging between 73 and 90. (The 90 is for loaders, and probably would assume the same relative importance for PC-DOS today.)

- Object program efficiency has relative importance of 75 for IOCSs, which then were separately compiled, but was rated lower for loaders and monitors, since the user did not think of them as being compiled. (Performance, therefore, is covered under the "speed of operation" category.)

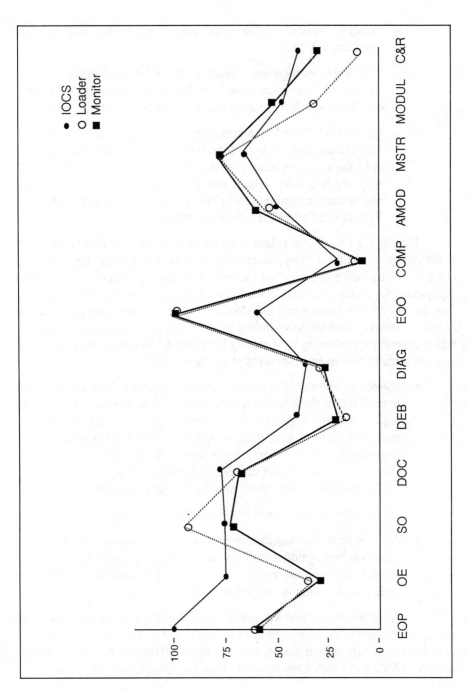

Figure 8.2 – Relative Importance: Operating Systems (*Source: IBM*)

- "Documentation" assumes its usual importance and is clustered around 75.

- "Minimize storage requirements" has relative importance comparable to "documentation" for "operating systems" (and little did they know how much storage would eventually be required).

- Once again, the relative importance of "compatibility across machine lines" is shockingly low. It is obvious that the users considered the major operating systems components to be "bundled" with the hardware, which was then "different" for commercial and scientific applications. (This result will be analyzed later in light of OSF and UNIX International.)

Figure 8.3 charts the relative importance of the attributes for sorts which, at the time of the study, accounted for approximately 22 percent of all computer time being used by both commercial and scientific users of IBM equipment. Of course, this was in the tape-oriented, batch-processing days before the use of disk storage and DBMSs. Direct-access storage, on-line transaction processing, and DBMSs should all diminish the importance of sorting, right? (I shall pursue the topic of sorting later with some surprising results.) At any rate, this is how users responded many years ago:

- "Speed of operation" and "ease-of-use operating" had identical ratings of 100 as the most important factors. This is something of a statistical surprise since 170 respondents to the survey ranked speed of operation as most important as opposed to only 35 for ease-of-use operating (even documentation was ranked first by 44 respondents). However, it does reflect the overall balance of importance between the "ease-of-use" and "performance" categories of attributes.

- Documentation falls right in behind those two categories as usual.

- As you start to consider developments in computer architectures, data base management systems, and performance, why sorting is important will become readily apparent, even beyond the fundamental code set and collating sequence considerations.

In summary, what IBM knew was that ease of use and performance of systems software were very important to users, and compatibility was not. In addition to the information presented in the charts, IBM also knew that its customers had a clearly stated resistance to changing programming languages.

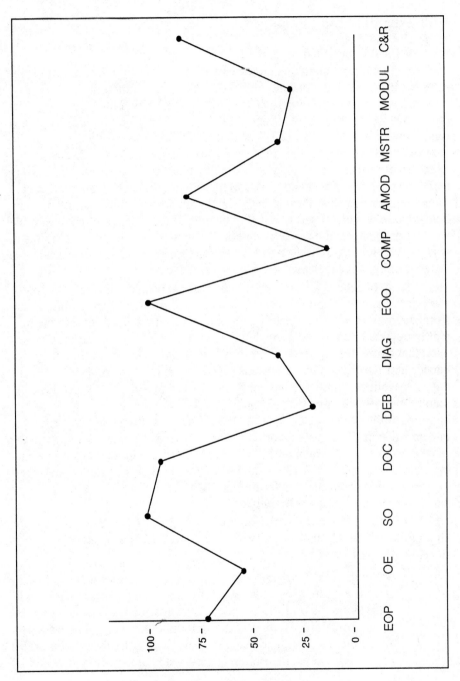

Figure 8.3 – Relative Importance: Sort (*Source: IBM*)

8.1.2 What IBM Did

With this information in hand, IBM proceeded to develop the most complex operating system that has ever existed, even though it formally established ease of use as the primary design object. Added function was confused with ease of use, contributing to the resulting complexity. Future IBM customer surveys were directed toward determining customer preferences for added functionality in the mistaken belief that more function would contribute to ease of use. By directing the surveys toward functions that the Programming Systems department thought were important or represented an "interesting technical challenge," it was possible to manage the "wish list" and obtain customer support for what Poughkeepsie's systems programmers wanted to do. And what they wanted was to develop one big kludge that would solve all the world's problems and provide compatibility across machine lines. One result was the creation of a JCL that was more prone to programming errors than the programming languages themselves.

Then, of course, since "ease of use" was the primary design point, problems of "object program efficiency," "speed of operation," and "minimizing storage requirements" were sacrificed (or at least rationalized) during the normal trade-offs that always occur in systems development. An attitude developed that computers existed primarily to run the systems software being produced, and user "problem programs" were considered secondarily. To this day, the feeling among systems programmers is that if you "keep the CPU (central processing unit) busy," you are achieving good performance. While hunting for the performance "snark," IBM systems software led its customers into an Alice in Wonderland world of always having to run faster to stay in the same place. Later "virtual storage" would translate into more real storage, and big chunks of systems software would have to run in V=R (virtual equals real) to achieve even minimal performance. IBM created a strange topsy-turvy world with its performance looking glass.

I mentioned IBM's abortive attempt to establish a standard language for all programming with PL/1; there is an interesting and significant aside to that story.

- At the first IBM Programming Symposium (a gathering of IBM programmers from around the world) in the 1960s, a presentation was made on the use of PL/1 to write systems software. When queried about the details of what was being done, the programmers determined that the language being used was "a PL/1 subset, with extensions." As one recalcitrant maverick stated at the time: "I would be

hard put to see the difference between that and a new language."
Nevertheless, an internal "standard" was established that systems
software would be written in the so-called PL/1.

• At the second IBM Programming Symposium held a year later, a
presentation was made on the use of FORTRAN to write a FOR-
TRAN compiler. This piece of wizardry was accomplished in response to the PL/1 edict through the simple expedient of permitting
assembly language subroutines to be used. The motivation of this
particular group was to "prove" that anything written in PL/1 could
be written in FORTRAN; and despite the PL/1 edict, this compiler
was released as an IBM program product. The same recalcitrant
maverick stated at the time: "I think things are out of control in Programming Systems."

While not directly related to the internal programming language wars
but pertaining more to the whole "programming mess," a short time later three
levels of IBM management were thrown out of the game. And even though
IBM called it being put in the "penalty box," they never returned to positions
of responsibility. They were a corporate vice president and group executive, a
division president, and the director of Programming Systems. IBM had "bet
the company" on System/360, and Programming Systems had nearly lost the
game. IBM's System/360 experience is important because it profoundly af-
fected both IBM's willingness to gamble and its view of systems software.
While analyzing IBM's SAA, one of my associates called an IBM "old-timer"
and asked whether the System/360 experience had faded in the memory of
current IBM management. He replied that it has become even stronger, because it is now firmly entrenched in corporate folklore.

8.1.3 What Happened

The grand concept of one hardware-software architecture for all computing environments, based on ease of use and performance, started to come
apart at the seams before it was ever sewn together. Differentiation of hardware, languages, operating systems, and data base management systems has
proceeded ever since the IBM big bang of "compatibility" was launched nearly 25 years ago. By the time SAA was announced on March 17, 1987, IBM
had developed many "partial differential solutions" to the fact that users need,
want, and demand different levels of performance and ease of use from their
hardware-software systems.

Figure 8.4 presents a rough diagram of the systems software mess that has proved confusing to IBM salespersons and customers and intolerable to IBM management. Just a few words on some of these systems, proceeding from top to bottom on the figure.

TSS and ACP appeared practically as soon as IBM realized that one operating system (OS/360) wasn't going to do the job.

- TSS was in direct response to GE selling its "timesharing system" (which later became MULTICS) to both MIT and Bell Labs—two high-visibility accounts. Tom Watson, Jr. wasn't very happy with these developments. IBM was forced to concede that there was more to timesharing than the OS/360's QTAM (queued terminal access method) and the System/360 architecture could support. IBM invented virtual storage in the form of the "Blau Box" (which did address translation) overnight and embarked on a costly software effort that never came anywhere near paying for itself.

- ACP (Airline Control Program) came about because it was immediately apparent that OS/360 could never support the high on-line transaction rates required of airline reservations systems. The original version, Programmed Airline Reservation System (PARS), was started in the 1960s as "program product" under the Data Processing Division (the sales organization). ACP, not restricted to airlines, has been employed in other high performance on-line transaction processing environments, such as banks.

Despite the confusion about ISAM and data base management systems, which I briefly discussed previously, IBM separated DBMSs as subsystems, where they began to acquire a life of their own.

While Information Management System (IMS) was part of the standards wars over data models, it managed to push the hardware and customer resources to the limit —some major customers literally could not find enough days of processing time to reorganize their data bases. As one customer stated: "IMS has managed to use up more CPU cycles than even IBM could ever have imagined in its wildest dreams." Another, when asked how much it cost to convert to IMS, commented: "We don't know, and I don't think we want to know."

IBM found it difficult to use IMS in its major in-house systems. Its order entry system (AAS — Advanced Administrative System) was originally developed using BDAM (Basic Direct Access Method) files and proved impervious to conversion for decades. IMS was also too rigid to permit major or-

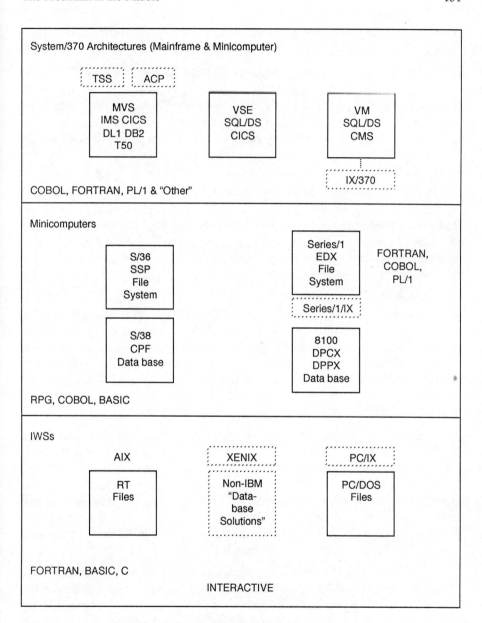

Figure 8.4 – Partial-Differential Solutions

ganizational changes, and therefore proved to be inappropriate for internal planning systems also. (Imagine IBM being unable to reorganize.)

Meanwhile, the relational model (System R) was sitting in IBM's San Jose Laboratory. Its performance was so bad that not even IBM would announce it. As IBM continued to develop "optimized" versions, one IBMer was quoted as saying: "Being better than awful can still be pretty bad." Now that DB2 (Database Two) is officially out the door, it is expected to drive the demand for MIPS through the next large mainframe generation.

The VSE story has already been told. Because of hardware requirements for both speed and memory, IBM mainline operating systems strategy never really got off the ground. DOS to VSE systems have resisted all attempts to kill them off not only because of hardware-software performance but also because of ease of use. Top-of-the-line IBM systems software requires nursemaiding by systems programmers, and applications programmers find it all but impossible to comprehend. It is complexity piled upon complexity.

VM/CMS was developed for systems programmers (so that they could run different operating systems on the same machine), was later promoted as a conversion tool, and eventually acquired full recognition when IBM recognized that the whole "operating system mess" was not going to go away and would probably get worse. IBM formally committed "equal resources" to MVS and VM development only within the last 6 years. When IBM announced its mainframe version of UNIX (IX/370), it was only natural that it run under VM.

The language wars have already been described, except to state that in addition to procedural languages the terminology merchants have started to classify languages by "generations." I am inclined to agree with Ted Codd, the father of the relational model, that "there has never been a definition of a 4GL worth its salt." I prefer the term FGL which can stand for first, fourth, fifth, . . ., future. It merely recognizes that languages evolve and are a matter of personal preference, and that no one language should be forced beyond its capability. What is easy for one person is not easy for another.

This brings us to the System/36, which traces its genealogy back to the System/3, which was designed for the first-time computer user and even featured funny little punch cards. (This was the last gasp of the unit record types within IBM.) The System/36 was designed for small businesses in terms of both performance and ease of use. Small businesses did not require fast arithmetic, and management of small businesses didn't want anything to do with "programmers." This resulted in the following:

- A computer that literally replaced unit record equipment—sorters, collators, and tabulators—but attempted to keep punch cards around in its initial version.

- The System/36's programming language was always intended to be an RPG. RPG was originally developed for those who were familiar with "wiring a board" to generate reports on a tabulator. The view of data was that of a deck of sorted punch cards.

- The System/36 evolved over time into a general-purpose office system with workstations attached. The workstations gradually replaced IBM word-processing equipment (magnetic tape and magnetic card Selectric Typewriters and Displaywriters). IBM coined the term "word processing" before personal computers were invented.

- The System/36 line of equipment has been extremely successful for IBM as a small business system; its installed base peaked around 300,000 systems. It attracted an enormous base of applications software and established a standard of ease of use for "real business applications" which has not been seriously threatened by either personal computers or departmental processors. Its customer base is extremely loyal.

- However, the System/36 was far from a success as a departmental processor in large organizations:

  - Because it was oriented toward batch processing of sequential files, it did not have a data base management system.

  - Personal computers could provide an attractive alternative, in cost and functionality, for many office functions; specifically, for word processing.

  - IBM did not know how to support it or sell it as a departmental processor. In fact, to those who were System/370 architecture-oriented, it was a real "odd duck," a throwback to a bygone era, and one without a clearly defined growth path. (Popular sentiment within IBM was to kill the beast before it did more damage. That this didn't happen is important.)

- There is one other less-than-casual observation about the ease-of-use characteristics of the System/36. The ease of use of the relational model is based on the simple, intuitive view of data arranged in unsorted tabular form, and the relational algebra operates on these tables without the need for "navigation." A deck of punch cards provides a similar tabular representation, albeit sorted, and when you "wired a board," your navigation was complete.

The System/38, originally called FS (Future System), was IBM's only serious effort to replace the System/370 architecture. It developed out of the frustration with developing systems software, and the thought was to engineer as much systems software as possible right into the hardware. The FS effort resulted in the following:

- According to one ex-IBMer, "The engineers found out that they make mistakes too and hardware is more expensive to debug."

- An enormous write-off. A then-prominent IBM corporate executive reportedly said: "I can understand throwing away $100 million here and there, but a half-billion dollars is enough to make anybody nervous."

The official reason given for the failure to replace the System/360-370 architecture was that IBM did not want to impose the conversion effort on its customer base (remember the IBM customer reaction to the conversion to IMS). From the time IBM pulled the string on FS, it has waged a highly successful campaign (and perhaps for good reason) emphasizing the importance of "protecting the customers' investment in software."

The System/38 is the only product that came out of the abortive FS development effort. Its hardware-software architecture was substantially more advanced than that of System/370 in terms of addressing capability, data base management, and general ease-of-use characteristics. Bringing up applications on the System/38 is substantially easier than on the System/370 architecture machines, and those familiar with both become enthusiastic System/38 supporters. It has been the best kept secret in the IBM product line, especially in the United States.

The Series/1, proudly announced as a minicomputer in the early 1970s, was targeted to what IBM felt was the proper role of a minicomputer—process control. That required an operating system with a good interrupt system for handling "real-time" applications, and it was limited enough to pose no threat to conventional data-processing applications. It turns out that it has been a "series of 1"—it has been around for about 15 years and keeps popping up in strange places.

IBM customers discovered the Series/1 was superior to the 3705 as a front-end communications controller. (What wasn't?) But IBM discouraged this because the 37XX series has been extremely profitable and really doesn't do very much. When IBM announced UNIX (IX/370) for System/370, the Series/1 showed up as a controller for remote terminals. The irony in this seems to have been lost on practically everyone. Sometimes it is difficult to know whether IBM has a sense of humor.

At any rate the Series/1 is still around, and it must be one of the most profitable products IBM ever developed. It is a reduced instruction set computer which remains rather firmly in its market niche—running elevators, monitoring power and laboratory equipment, etc.

IBM attempted to address the "minicomputer problem," that is to say, distributed processing, with System/370 architecture machines (43xx and 9370) and failed.

Another IBM "solution" to the distributed processing problem was a series of cluster controllers (3790, 8100, etc.). They turned out to be a classic case of sloppy terminology.

- The 3790 was announced along with SNA, and one IBM salesperson proclaimed that IBM had embraced distributed processing. One afternoon was enough to convince any knowledgeable person that the 3790 was nothing more than a cluster controller, obviously designed to keep virtually all processing on the System/370 host.

- When the 8100 was announced, it was hailed by the trade press as IBM's "plunge into distributed processing," because two operating systems proudly used the term in their title — DPCX (Distributed Processing Control Executive) and DPPX (Distributed Processing Programming Executive). Even superficial analysis of the 8100 hardware-software architecture was enough to reveal that it was not a solution for true distributed processing. However, there were those determined to "make it work" (or IBM would make it work), and many IBM customers really got burned on the product.

- For the benefit of those customers, DPPX remains around after the 8100 has died, but it never became a "major IBM computing environment." Under SNA, all significant processing has remained on large host mainframes. One of the main factors for the failure of the 3790 and 8100 (other than poor performance) was ease of use. As my company and I warned at the time the 8100 was announced, "Beware of an operating system that has the word 'programming' in its title."

We are all familiar with the story that, when IBM needed an operating system for the PC, they tried to track down Gary Kildall [the developer of CP/M (Control Program for Microcomputers)], only to have him miss an appointment because it was a nice day to go flying over the Monterey peninsula. Thus, Bill Gates got the opportunity to develop PC-DOS. However, there are several important points about this whole episode:

- It cost IBM more money to reach the make-buy decision on the PC operating system than it did for Gary Kildall to develop CP/M.

- It cost IBM more to monitor the Microsoft contract than it did for Microsoft to "buy" PC-DOS and package it for IBM.

- IBM has individuals scattered all over the world who could have developed an operating system at least as good as PC-DOS, and IBM should be aware that really good software products have traditionally been originated by small groups operating outside the "normal" IBM development process.

- This raises many questions about the strategy, tactics, and politics of software development within IBM. I will not attempt to answer all of these questions except to state:

  - IBM is fully aware of what is required to develop and maintain an "industrial-strength" systems software product.

  - By IBM standards, neither PC- nor MS-DOS nor UNIX are industrial-strength products at this time. (What comes out of OSF probably will be industrial-strength.)

  - With the exception of UNIX, IBM's industrial-strength products will be proprietary. (Even IBM's version of UNIX will probably remain proprietary in many of its more important functions.)

  - IBM's investment in these products will be protected by license fees, lawsuits, and its continuing refusal to release source code.

During the 1980s the "partial differential solutions" presented in Figure 8.4 became intolerable to both IBM's customer base and, perhaps, even more importantly, to IBM management. The permutations of hardware systems, networking "solutions," operating systems, and data base management "solutions" were practically infinite, and more seemed to be arriving all the time. (UNIX and relational DBMSs are good examples.) IBM had so many teams, with their own game plans, running around on the field that neither IBM management nor customers knew what the game was or against whom it was being played. IBM has been very successful with management by contention, and chaos on the playing field would traditionally benefit the IBM team(s); but in the 1980s, it all threatened to stop working.

New levels of ease of use and price-performance were being established by microprocessor technology, and end users within the corporate environment were able to buy some of the technology they needed within departmental budgets and without the benefit of the "experts" in the Information Systems department. When processing power became distributed throughout the organization, the demand for "corporate data" was inevitable. Call it off-loading, downsizing, distributed processing, distributed data bases, or anything you like—IBM's strategy for maintaining account control through the centralized data on large mainframes was threatened as never before.

The economics of hierarchical computer-communications networks destroyed traditional economy of scale in the early 1970s. IBM fought the good fight for nearly two decades against minicomputers. During that time it managed to equip the mainframe "glass house" with bulletproof windows. However, its first real venture into open systems (the IBM PC) had unanticipated success and results—the genie was out of the bottle once and for all. The days of dumb terminals tied into enormous mainframes as a "networking solution" was over. IBM customers wanted – no, demanded – the ability to tie together diverse computing systems, which are now being called "enterprise systems."

I have harangued the industry and IBM about a "proper" hierarchical network of mainframes, minicomputers, and intelligent workstations since the early 1970s (yes, there were microprocessor-based terminals prior to personal computers). In early 1987, Dr. A. L. Scherr published a paper titled "Structures for Networks of Systems" in the *IBM Systems Journal* (vol. 26, no. 1, 1987). In that article Dr. Scherr concludes:

> In this paper, we have looked at a full spectrum of possibilities. It is difficult to escape the conclusion that each type of system has a significant role to play, and it is difficult to imagine technology changes that would eliminate any one of the types (mainframe, minicomputer or microprocessor). Each type of system represents unique advantages that argue strongly for its usage. Thus, we conclude that multiple-tier systems will be in general use, particularly in large corporations, for many years to come.

On March 17, 1987, IBM announced its SAA. Many people agree that it is developing slowly. Regardless, the entire industry is going to be playing in the shadow of that SAA mountain for a long time. It would be the utmost folly to ignore it in any serious analysis of any important issue in the information systems industry.

9

The SAA Mountain

My company, Killen & Associates, Inc., has devoted a substantial amount of resources to the detailed analysis of SAA. Three reports provided a comprehensive view of the key elements of IBM's SAA strategy:

- *IBM's SAA Strategy: Impact and Opportunities* (July 1987)
- *IBM's Distributed Data Base Strategy: Impact and Opportunities* (March 1988)
- *IBM's AS/400 & SAA: Impacts and Opportunities* (September 1988).

I also wrote *IBM: The Making of the Common View* (Harcourt Brace Jovanovich, 1988), which provides some insight into how the SAA strategy was created.

I have focused all this attention on SAA because I firmly believe that IBM is literally betting the company on it, even though there may be some in IBM who are unaware of the full significance of what they are undertaking. Ken Olsen's "snake oil" story on UNIX has been widely quoted, but if UNIX is "snake oil," then SAA is a bitter pill that must be swallowed before we can get well and prosper. I shall review why I think this medication is necessary for all of us, not just IBM.

9.1 A WALK AROUND THE GLASS HOUSE

IBM has made the mainframe "glass house" secure with bulletproof glass through the use of its proprietary systems software—an impenetrable mass of complexity, which, while it has caused the fragmentation depicted in

Figure 8.4, nevertheless stands alone as the bastion of "corporate data" on which the promise of the "information age" is based. As a systems programmer commented in the early days of OS/360, "when you consider what it does, it is a miracle it works at all." Today, MVS/ESA is combined with a dual-database strategy incorporating IMS and DB2. For those who have built this type of glass house, not only are vendors unable to shoot their way in, but the owners can't break out even if they want to—they might as well be prisoners.

SAA is a blueprint for extending the bulletproof glass walls to include much that is now outside and to provide open gateways for guests who might like to enter and have a look around. Figure 9.1 presents the plan for the expanded glass house. Let's quickly walk around before taking a guided tour.

9.1.1 Common User Access

The stated objectives of the Common User Access (CUA) are

- CUA will be designed for the user and optimized by the particular workstation. (Some IBM customers have stated that the most important thing IBM could do to improve ease of use would be to standardize its keyboards.)

- The CUA will define the basic elements of the end-user interface and how to use them. The elements to be specified include

  - Screen layout

  - Menu presentation and selection techniques

  - Keyboard layout and use

  - Display options

- The primary goal is "to achieve (through consistency of user interface) transfer of learning, ease of learning, and ease of use across the range of IBM Systems Application Architecture applications and environments."

- The SAA announcement stated that IBM-developed software would adhere to the definition of the CUA "over time," and that the definition would be published so that both customers and software vendors can develop programs that follow the definition.

From an ease-of-use point of view, it can be stated that any non-SAA "computing environment" connected to the SAA architecture will either have to adopt the CUA standard or not be easily usable by those in either environment.

9.1.2 Common Programming Interface

The Common Programming Interface (CPI) consists of a variety of languages and services. The languages include "common" higher-level languages, an applications generator, a procedures language, and 5GL (fifth-generation language). The services consist of data base interface, query interface, presentation and dialog interface, and distributed services.

Objectives for the Common Programming Interface were stated as follows:

- The languages and services of the CPI will permit the development of applications that: "can be integrated with other applications and ported to run in multiple IBM Systems Application Architecture environments." It is specifically stated that the CPI is the applications programming interface to the SAA systems (my emphasis).

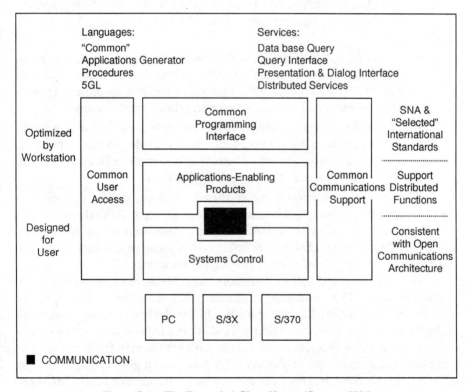

Figure 9.1 – The Expanded Glass House (*Source: IBM*)

The initial elements that were announced are as follows:

- Common higher level languages supported are
  - COBOL based on ANS Programming Language COBOL, X3.23–1985 Intermediate Level
  - FORTRAN based on ANS Programming Language FORTRAN, 77 level
  - C based on the draft proposed ANS Standard (X3J11)
- The Applications Generator will be based on "elements of the interfaces" found in the existing Cross-System Product (CSP).
- The Procedures Language will be based on the existing REXX language.
- The Database Interface will be based on the ANS Database Language SQL, X3.135–1986, and IBM's SQL.
- The Query Interface will be based on an "extension of the interfaces" found in the existing Query Management Facility (QMF) product.
- The Presentation Interface will be based on "extensions to the interface found in key elements" of today's Graphical Data Display Manager (GDDM) product which provides services to present textual and graphic information on displays, printers, and plotters.
- The Dialog Interface will be based on "extensions to the interface" found in today's EZ-VU product which provides for the definition, display, and management of textual information and menus, and for the control of screen flow within applications.

The announcement states that additional elements will be defined and the elements named above will be extended. (For example, RPG II was named as a common language when the AS/400 was announced in the summer of 1988). The "long-range goal is to define a comprehensive and productive set of IBM programming development languages and services."

For both users and software vendors, the message is clear—if you want portability across SAA computing environments, you should develop applications using CPI. This is a hard offer for vendors to decline because it automatically expands their potential markets as changing technology constantly redefines how applications should be distributed over the mainframe, minicomputer, and personal computer hierarchy. [A good, and highly visible, example of the effect that SAA had on software vendors is the case of MSA (Management Sciences of America), which announced in 1987 that it would develop applications for DEC's VAX. After SAA was announced, the decision was reversed and MSA returned to the IBM fold where it is developing applications for the SAA environment. Just the announcement got a major player back on the IBM team right away.]

9.1.3 Common Communications Support

IBM stated that the Common Communications Support (CCS) would consist of extensions to existing communications architectures. It would be based on SNA (hardly a surprise) and "selected" international standards. It would support distributed functions, and would be consistent with open communications architecture.

The SAA announcement stated that CCS will be used to interconnect SAA applications, SAA systems, communications networks, and devices. Interconnection will be achieved through consistent implementation of designated communications architectures in each of the SAA environments. The announced communications architectures will be "building blocks for distributed function to be detailed in future announcements of Common Programming Interfaces and IBM Systems Application Architecture applications."

Unlike the other elements of SAA, IBM had been selling "connectivity" for some time and the SAA announcement was merely a "reaffirmation" of IBM's Open Communications Architectures announcement of September 16, 1986. The primary architectures announced for SAA support were listed as follows:

- Data Streams
  - 3270 Data Stream
  - Document Content Architecture (DCA)
  - Intelligent Printer Data Stream (IPDS)
- Applications Services
  - SNA Distributed Services (SNADS)
  - Document Interchange Architecture (DIA)
  - SNA Network Management Architecture
- Session Services
  - LU Type 6.2 (Logical Unit Type 6.2)
- Network
  - Low-Entry Networking (LEN) Node
  - X.25

- Data Link Controls
  - Synchronous Data Link Control (SDLC)
  - IBM Token Ring Network

Since it made this general commitment to "openness," IBM has proceeded to demonstrate it by joining the OSF and X/Open and by releasing a series of product announcements. In September 1988, IBM gave the OSI model its official blessing under the greater SAA umbrella. It will now be possible to interconnect with third-party products for electronic mail under X.400 and for file transfer under OSI/File Services. In addition, NetView was substantially enhanced as a multivendor network management system.

As IBM Vice President William O. Grabe stated at the time of these announcements: "We are committed to doing whatever is necessary to give customers what they require to communicate enterprise-wide. We will do whatever it takes." This indeed seems to be an open door to the SAA glass house. It appears that competitive vendors are free to enter and solicit business inside the glass house and that IBM customers are free to select competitive products and systems. Mr. Grabe doesn't think many IBM customers will be foolish enough to listen to the door-to-door salespeople who might call, for reasons he explained when the AS/400 was announced (and which will be presented in the next chapter of this book). However, just in case some do, the SAA glass house has a blockhouse that contains some pretty heavy shackles designed to keep most IBM customers from exiting through the open door.

9.1.4 Common Applications

The promise of all this is that software developers (both users and vendors) who conform to the supported standards of CUA, CPI, and CCS can develop applications that may eventually be easily portable across the major IBM computing environments. But there is a big difference between systems and applications software. IBM is not attempting to help vendors develop systems software and will defend its proprietary systems software (just ask Fujitsu how much it costs to look at IBM's operating system source code).

The definition of applications software was never intended to include DBMSs, regardless of the current propensity to classify them as "applications," and SAA is going to present systems software vendors with some problems. A good case in point is Cullinet, which presented all kinds of market research studies showing IBM losing market shares to IDMS, even after DB2 was announced. Unfortunately, market research studies didn't stop Cullinet from suffering terribly in the marketplace when it discovered that you can't make a product relational by simply changing the label. Cullinet then tried to slowly recover by developing products for Digital's VAX, but has since been acquired by Computer Associates. (Now, market research studies are showing enormous gains for UNIX in the "commercial market.")

SAA is a real challenge for systems software vendors and a real opportunity for applications software developers.

9.1.5 Uncommon "Computing Environments"

Figure 8.4 depicted the fragmentation that occurred after IBM's noble attempt to establish one hardware architecture (System/360-370), one operating system (OS/360 to MVS), and one programming language (PL/1) in the 1960s. When IBM announced SAA, three "major IBM computing environments" were identified: the PC, S/3X follow-on (AS/400), and S/370 architectures. However, IBM later reportedly said that despite SAA, there would probably have to be "at least five operating systems supported in the foreseeable future."

My associates and I speculated at announcement time that the five had to be MVS (ESA), VM, VSE, the S/3X follow-on operating system (OS/400), and OS/2 Extended Edition. It could clearly be seen through the walls of the "extended glass house" that these operating systems would have to become more tightly integrated into a single "network operating system." Our analysis led us to conclude that (1) the management of distributed data bases was the only means of achieving this integration and (2) the System/3X follow-on product (AS/400) was the key to distributed data base management.

The little black box at the center of the "expanded glass house" (Figure 9.1) holds the key to IBM's new open-door policy. It is a blockhouse designed to restrain those customers who might think of straying away, and it has ample "holding power" for any guests who accept the hospitality of connectivity that SAA offers.

9.2 A PEEK INSIDE THE BLOCKHOUSE

As pointed out earlier in this book, IBM had two serious weaknesses in its early operating systems development: networking (timesharing) and data base management (DBMSs). These caused fragmentation in the operating systems functions and ignored the fact that a single large mainframe can be viewed as a communications network, and a communications network (either local area or wide area) can be viewed as a single "computing system." Therefore, not only did all of the various operating systems depicted in Figure 8.4 evolve along their own paths, but SNA and DBMSs were split out where they developed "lives of their own." SAA's ultimate objective is to tightly integrate communications, operating systems, and data base management systems across the major IBM computing environments described above. We are just beginning to get a taste of this tight integration in several developments.

The AS/400 has relational data base management facilities and communications capability built into the hardware. Its architecture features one-level addressing (currently 48-bit, but easily expandable to 64-bit) which goes beyond that of even the "Extended Architecture" (XA) versions of System/370 machines. It treats both data and programs as tables or arrays, and treats main storage and disk storage as a single area. In a true distributed data base environment, applications development for networked AS/400s would not consider where disk storage is located on the network.

The PS/2 with OS/2 EE and the MCA also quite clearly integrate communications and data base management facilities. The disclosure of "bus mastering capabilities" that permits other intelligent devices to control the Micro-Channel becomes especially important when you consider that an "intelligent device" could be an AS/400 on either a LAN (local area network) or WAN (wide area network). It is precisely the capability needed to provide true distributed data base management.

I use the term "true distributed data base management" because few people seem to understand what a distributed data base is, and most experts don't like to talk about them very much in public. The most important reason for this is that there are still unsolved technical problems with distributed data base management; no one as yet has an "industrial strength" distributed data base management system on the market (although some vendors have forged ahead with commercial implementations of IBM's R* research effort). I think that IBM has a reasonable and workable plan for "true distributed data base management"—that is the primary secret of the blockhouse.

9.2.1 What Does This Mean?

Simply put, this means that the user and systems development staff need not concern themselves with the age-old question that has been around the industry for a couple of decades—where data or programs reside.

In this environment, distributed data base management and network management become synonymous. Together, these two provide account control as it has never been exercised before. (Those who enter the glass house's open door may find themselves in the blockhouse where the door swings only one way.)

This also means that IBM may have the key to the effective integration of the complex systems of the 1990s, provided that applications developers adhere to the SAA recommended standards. SNA, operating systems, and distributed data base management systems will be tightly integrated and layered at all levels of the processing hierarchy.

9.2.2 Who Needs It?

Practically everyone in a commercial environment needs it. The PC "revolution" has distributed processing power to end users on an uncontrolled basis. Data are distributed over a variety of mini- and personal computers today. It is no longer a question of whether data will be distributed; they already are, in a variety of uncontrolled and unmanageable text, spreadsheet, and data base files.

The question is whether these distributed data bases can be managed with data integrity, synchronization, privacy, and security. More specifically, can the data support the information that is being produced in such great volume? Pretty reports, graphics, and presentations are all fine and good, but they are only as reliable as the supporting data. We currently live in a high-entropy information environment. Information overload is real, and there is every indication that quality is decreasing while volume is increasing.

The old mainframe glass house had one big advantage—it did address the issue of quality of data. It is a paradox that IBM's highly centralized, mainframe-oriented strategy now appears to have been the right thing for most companies. For years, my associates and I encouraged, first, the centralization and establishment of data-processing standards, then the "orderly distribution of processing" back to end users. SNA was an interminably long process with which I lost patience. The PC revolution was not, and is not, an orderly process; and it will take a lot of energy to restore order if chaos is to be avoided. IBM's highly centralized strategy may indeed have been a wise choice for most customers.

It will not be too difficult for IBM to convince most of its customers that data base integrity, synchronization, privacy, and security are important. If SAA will truly provide for distributed data base management, IBM will be able to expand the glass house and be very open about it. It is holding all the high ground before the game begins. However, I would add that IBM will be very slow at doing this.

9.2.3 What About the Level Playing Field?

Assuming that the mountain isn't going to go away and that the expanded glass house perched at the summit will become ever more prominent as its architecture is constructed (and both of these assumptions are more certain than any forecasts currently being published), vendors can play any of three distinct games:

- Accept the mountain and play a variety of games on what remains of the level playing field
- Storm the mountain and attack the fragile-looking glass house directly
- Ignore the mountain and pretend that it isn't there

The first game deals with industry standards and "openness." IBM has provided a chart that depicts its view of how this game will be played (Figure 9.2). While this chart will be analyzed in more detail later, I need to make several comments now.

- The rules of the game according to IBM are that all of the "servers" listed on the proprietary side are SAA (and therefore IBM) hardware-software systems. These servers will be tightly integrated through OS/400 and OS/2 EE as described above. While System/370s may be considered servers, they don't work very well that way—they are too accustomed to being hosts in the glass house.
- Since IBM released this chart, the company has become actively involved in OSF, whose purpose is to simplify the interfaces between the proprietary and the open side of the architecture. We can now be reasonably comfortable that UNIX will be the supported operating systems link with the "OEM" (original equipment manufacturer) world.
- Since IBM is in the process of extending NetView to the open side of the architecture, there should not be any question about how the big guy who lives on the hill feels about which "peer" will be more equal when the game begins.

The second game, trying to invade the glass house, implies that you must also crack the blockhouse of distributed data base management, as it will evolve under SAA. IBM has also released the outline of a "distributed data reference model" (Figure 9.3) that depicts quite graphically the shackles that bind SAA.

Logical conversations occur between (and among) requestor and server processes at the various levels of the new, tightly integrated, network operat-

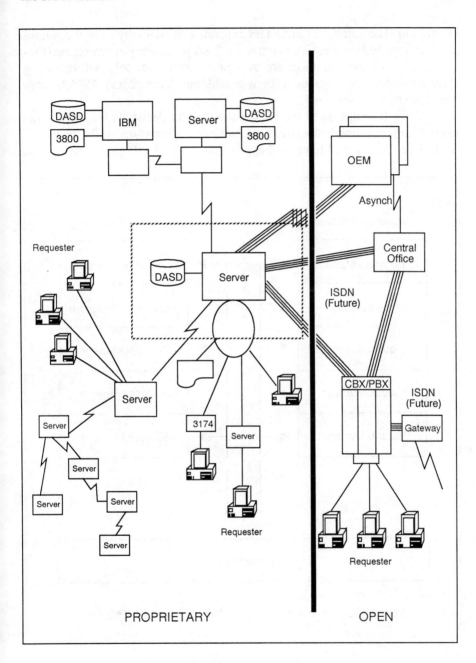

Figure 9.2 – Proprietary and Open Architecture (*Source: IBM*)

ing system. The number of interfaces expands exponentially from those link-ing the supported open environment to the SAA proprietary environment (Fig-ure 9.2). And these interfaces are truly proprietary. Not only will operating system source code continue to be withheld, but the PS/2 and AS/400 hard-ware also become involved.

Some time ago, IBM and Fujitsu accepted the decision of the arbitrators in their long-standing battle over mainframe operating systems. By the time it is all over, Fujitsu will have paid approximately $0.5 billion for the right to

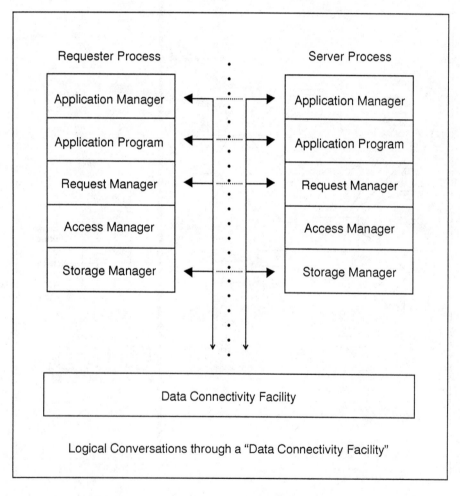

Figure 9.3 – A Distributed Data Reference Model (*Source: IBM*)

pore over the source code of MVS, and most of this falls straight to IBM's bottom line. (AT&T probably won't net nearly that much from its Air Force contract.) That should be a humbling experience for the whole industry. And what Fujitsu is paying for is not even the most important part of IBM's SAA grand strategy! In fact, one might suspect that the classic System/370 hardware-software architecture is obsolete.

While both of the above games present some pretty tough realities about the nature of the level playing field, they are not nearly as dangerous as ignoring (or not understanding) the nature of the mountain in the center of the playing field, and IBM's ambitious plan for expanding the glass house. That can lead to delusions of grandeur in which a rock emerging from the turf on the playing field is confused with the beginning of a mountain—it just isn't going to happen in our lifetime.

That brings us to UNIX.

10

UNIX—A Survivor on the Field

By now, the UNIX story has been told many times in many places. From *The Bell System Technical Journal* (now *AT&T Bell Laboratories Technical Journal*) to special supplements in *Computerworld*, the story has been documented with both remarkable clarity and the hype that Ken Olsen of Digital referred to as "snake oil." My purpose is to put UNIX, as it is envisioned in the commercial computing environment of the 1990s, into some reasonable perspective.

UNIX is certainly not in proper perspective at the present time. It is being torn apart by a phenomenon which, quite appropriately, was identified by Lady Lovelace (who has some claim to being the world's first programmer), when she observed that with computing developments, such as Babbage's analytical engine, there is a natural propensity to first "overrate" their value and then, when they do not meet our expectations, to "undervalue" them. This "Lovelace Cycle" has been clearly evident in practically all developments in the computer industry since that time.

Since my company and I started researching UNIX, a minor Lovelace Cycle has occurred in the trade press. First, AT&T got the Air Force contract for $1 billion of "UNIX systems," and then 6000 UNIX systems came crashing to earth because a hacker took advantage of a known security weakness in the system. The old Army Air Corps song used to go "we live in fame or go down in flame," and perhaps it still does. We haven't heard the end of this story, and I will get back to it later.

Earlier in this book, I stated that UNIX was at least 4 or 5 years behind the more advanced operating systems for commercial data-processing environments. This is not meant to deprecate UNIX or its developers; UNIX has been an extremely valuable tool when used within the environments for which it was intended, and its limitations have been clearly defined in the *AT&T Bell Laboratories Technical Journal.* The problem is that it is now being "overrated," viewed as the solution to all the world's problems (a common characteristic in our industry), and this could trigger the classic Lovelace-Cycle reaction of "undervaluing" it, even in environments for which it is well-suited.

10.1 FROM BELL LABS TO OSF AND BEYOND

UNIX was developed by Bell Laboratories in the late 1960s because the famous GE timesharing system (MULTICS) that ran on the GE 645 mainframe computer was "too expensive" for an application that was being developed. The applications developer decided that it would be cheaper to port the application to a Digital PDP-7 minicomputer even if it was necessary to write the systems software to support the application. In other words, a quick-and-dirty "operating system" could be justified because of the price-performance spread between the GE mainframe and the Digital minicomputer. This is significant for two reasons:

1. At precisely the same time, it was found within IBM that a "what if" forecasting application [complete with a IBM 2250 graphics CRT (cathode ray tube) and light pen] was "too expensive" to run on an IBM System/360 Model 165 mainframe, and it was possible to justify developing both the software and hardware interfaces to hang disk storage and the 2250 on the only thing IBM had that looked like a minicomputer—the IBM 1130.

2. Twenty years later, we are finding that classic minicomputer-based timesharing systems are "too expensive" to run certain applications, and we can cost justify putting a microprocessor-based intelligent workstation (IWS) on the individual's desk. The fact that UNIX appears to be the operating system of choice for the IWSs does not mean it is the key issue—if it didn't exist, we could justify the development of a new operating system to take advantage of the improved price-performance of the technology.

The hardware-software system developed for the IBM 1130 included a link to the IBM mainframe for file transfer and was actually more responsive to today's requirements than the early UNIX system. The reason the system never saw the light of day in a customer environment was that IBM has spent 20 years denying the relative economics of mainframes and minicomputers.

Bell Laboratories, on the other hand, had no vested interest in the computer industry at that time and freely and openly made UNIX available to other research organizations and the academic world. UNIX has survived and thrived.

UNIX turned out to be ideal for the academic world where computer science was just emerging as a discipline. It was simple enough for an individual to understand an entire operating system; it was constructed to facilitate change; and its developers encouraged improvements. A cult of UNIX followers developed at universities; and more importantly, generations of computer scientists were graduated who had been trained on it, and generations of engineers and scientists were graduated who had used it. When these graduates enter the business world, they still want UNIX.

However, being an "open system" in the truest sense of the word, UNIX really lost its identity over the years. There is currently no such thing as UNIX as an operating system; UNIX is a generic term for a type of operating system. AT&T cannot take credit for, and is not responsible for, all the hundreds of UNIX-based versions and look-alike systems that are out there.

Now that AT&T acquired NCR and has a new start in the computer business, it will try to capitalize on UNIX, and that is certainly its right and privilege. However, the current emphasis on making (or declaring) a UNIX standard while proclaiming its "openness" is unlikely to have positive results in either direction.

10.2 AS AN OPERATING SYSTEM

While this book cannot go into any detail about operating systems design, it is important to understand the functions and characteristics of operating systems. The implementation of operating systems functions have exhibited certain general characteristics (or design points) depending on processor level. The functions listed in Figure 10.1 are the five major abstractions that have characterized operating systems development over the years. Implementation has been added to the list so that implementation technologies can be characterized.

Several abstractions have developed concerning the actual use of processors (computers). Generally speaking, operating systems for the three levels of processors (mainframe, minicomputer, microprocessor) tend to be implemented with the following emphasis:

- Mainframe operating systems have traditionally emphasized a batch, multiprogramming environment with terminal access a secondary consideration.

- Minicomputer operating systems have been developed with emphasis on an interactive, timeshared resource.
- Microprocessor operating systems have been developed with emphasis on the direct interaction of a single operator with the processor.
- While these primary process abstractions have become somewhat blurred as they have been implemented across processor families, they remain necessary.

Operating System Functions	Processors		
	Mainframes (& 370 Servers)	Minicomputer "Servers"	PC/Intelligent Workstations
Process	Multiprogramming	Timesharing (Interactive)	Interactive
Memory Management	Real (Automated)	Virtual	Real (Manual)
Protection & Security	Centralized	Work Unit	Personal
Scheduling & Resource Management	Priority	Real Time	Manual
System Structure	Centralized	Distributed	Stand-alone or Connected
Implementation	Software Firmware	Hardware Software	Hardware Firmware Software

Figure 10.1 – Operating System Distribution

Memory management, in terms of bringing programs and data together for processing, is the inherent characteristic and challenge of the von Neumann architecture. It has become increasingly complex as the on-line memory hierarchy has become more complex.

- Operating systems in a mainframe "production" environment tend to automate the use of real memory—"jobs" are scheduled, programs are located and loaded, executing program(s) remains resident in memory, and data are processed through these programs. (Even if the operating systems provide for virtual storage, memory management tends to be real for production and systems programs.)

- Minicomputer timesharing operating systems started with the assumption that each user should experience the feeling of having exclusive use of the whole machine, including processor memory. The logical extension of this was to permit the user to have access to virtual memory that was larger than real memory.

- Current PC operating systems bring users face to face with the realities of memory limitations. Indeed, current PC operating systems bring users face to face with the realities of operating system limitations, when such operating systems even fail to automate (or permit) the use of real memory.

The protection and security of programs and data are acknowledged problems at all levels of computer systems. These problems become especially troublesome in complex computer-communications networks. It is an area in which precious little progress has been made, and the complexity of the problem seems to advance more rapidly than the ability to solve it. Only the crudest abstractions are currently available to address protection and security.

- At the mainframe operating system level, centralized protection and security through limited and controlled access have generally proved less than adequate to prevent hackers, much less computer professionals, from penetrating supposedly secure systems.

- At the minicomputer level, physical security of the work unit (and computer) has been the primary protection and security abstraction. Once connected to networks, minicomputer operating systems (such as UNIX) have generally failed to provide even the level of protection and security available through centralized mainframe systems.

- At the personal computer level, protection and security depend on the operator of the system. When connected to a network, the protection and security of data and information on the network become dependent to a large degree on individuals. (The experience with software pirating should give us pause when making individual integrity a significant component of protection and security.)

- There are no known technical solutions to the security problems inherent in the complex information flow that is implicit in complex networks.

Scheduling and resource management obviously become more complex in a network environment; there are more resources to schedule and more queues to manage. The mathematics of queuing networks is the relatively restricted province of a few specialized theorists (and some practitioners) in operations research. The application of queuing network theory to resource scheduling in operating systems has primarily evolved in connection with performance prediction and evaluation where the algorithms have been found to give surprisingly good results. Advanced networking architectures (such as SAA) will raise the complexity of network performance management to entirely new levels. At present, the following operating systems' emphasis can be observed:

- In the large mainframe environment, the primary scheduling abstraction has been one of priorities. While the priority scheduling process within the system itself may have been automated, the assignment of priorities frequently has not been. (A long-running job for the president of the company will be permitted to override the wisdom that priority should be given to short jobs if system performance is to be maximized.)

- Since the basis for timesharing is to give each individual user the feeling of having the full use of the system, resource management is supposed to provide at least the illusion of real-time response. Thus, subsecond response has become a primary objective (based on some rather questionable research on the impact of such response on individual productivity), and it is normally accomplished by throwing more hardware resource at the problem.

- At the personal computer level, the operator currently has control over the scheduling of the total resource and becomes sensitive (through experience) to relative impacts of various applications while operating in a stand-alone mode. As soon as the intelligent workstation is connected to a network, each individual operator competes with all others for resources, and sensitivity to resource use diminishes.

The fundamental system structures associated with operating systems at the three processor levels, while they may seem obvious, are important because they must all be integrated under the complex networks that will be commonplace in the 1990s.

- Mainframe operating systems are highly centralized and assume that the mainframe is the center of the processing universe.

- Minicomputer operating systems assume a distributed environment and are structured with a more egalitarian point of view, interacting with other systems on something approaching a peer-to-peer basis.

- Personal computer operating systems have been designed to be differentiated on the basis of individual preference in terms of accessories, tools, peripherals, etc. The fundamental choice of whether the system will be stand-alone or connected to a network has been left to the individual. Such freedom of choice is seriously restricted as operating systems functions and data bases become distributed over the network.

The implementation technologies of operating systems tend to follow patterns based on the anticipated use of the processors and their time of appearance. The mountain in the middle of the playing field (SAA) heralds a time when substantial shifts will occur across these technologies.

- Mainframe operating systems originated after the hardware was developed. Therefore, they have been implemented primarily in software with some performance assistance from firmware after the fact. (Relocation hardware for the implementation of virtual storage, and extended addressing for the implementation of MVS/XA, are the exceptions that prove the rule.)

- Numerous examples of minicomputer hardware and software systems being designed on a complementary basis can be pointed out. The Singer System Ten for point-of-sale applications dates back over 15 years; Tandem stressed such integrated hardware-software design from the beginning; and the IBM System/38 was the outgrowth of IBM's major effort to "engineer" software into the hardware.

- While personal computers were developed before operating systems were available for them, imaginative and flexible use of hardware and firmware to assist in systems software implementation and performance has been firmly established. For example, when purchasing add-on RAM (random-access memory) for Apple II computers, some vendors add a Z-80 coprocessor with the CP/M operating system to the memory board practically free of charge. It opens up a whole new applications set for those users.

UNIX stands alone as an operating system that was developed and has evolved in response to the needs of users of the system. This is a tremendous advantage, and it is the reason UNIX has such a loyal following among users. Developed originally as a timesharing system for a minicomputer platform, UNIX is now being promoted as the open standard operating system that spans all levels from desktop to mainframe and beyond to supercomputers.

UNIX is summarized most frequently by quoting from D. M. Ritchie and K. Thompson (its developers) in a joint paper written for ACM in 1974:

> It offers a number of features seldom found even in larger operating systems, including:
>
> (i) A hierarchical file system incorporating demountable volumes,
>
> (ii) Compatible file, device, and inter-process I/O,
>
> (iii) The ability to initiate asynchronous processes,
>
> (iv) System command language selectable on a per-user basis,
>
> (v) Over 100 subsystems including a dozen languages.

I would like to state from the beginning that a file system is not a data base management system. Data base management systems came about because very early on, files were found to be extremely difficult to manage across commercial applications, not because people could not pass them from one program to the next and keep track of them, but because the structure and content of the data elements had a way of changing. As early as 1960, the flow of data through pairwise connectivity across major commercial applications programs and systems was becoming unmanageable. That is the reason DBMSs were created. That is also the reason the IS function remains sensitive to problems of data base integrity, synchronization, privacy, and security in a distributed data base environment—MIS (management information system) professionals remembers how it was when flat files reigned supreme.

The Bell System Technical Journal (vol. 57, no. 6, part 2, July-August 1978), which was devoted to the "UNIX Time-Sharing System," provides ample documentation on the development of the system to that point in time (including an article on the file system by Ritchie and Thompson). It is not necessary to go into any technical detail. UNIX did not pretend to be anything more than it was—a minicomputer timesharing system. In *The AT&T Bell Laboratories Technical Journal* (vol. 63, no. 8, part 2, October 1984) UNIX is no longer identified as a timesharing system but is declared "The UNIX System." It has obviously spread its wings, preparing for flight.

Three articles are of particular interest in that issue:

- "A UNIX System Implementation for System/370"
- "The Evolution of UNIX Performance"
- "UNIX Operating System Security"

I will very briefly review those articles to make certain points about the applicability of UNIX.

10.2.1 UNIX on Mainframes

The initial porting of UNIX to mainframes occurred around 1980, when Bell Laboratories was developing the 5ESS switching system. The UNIX system had been selected for the project because of the availability of the Programmers Work Bench which can achieve substantial productivity improvement in a development environment. By late 1980, the project required nine PDP-11/70s to provide enough "programmer work benches" for all of the programmers associated with the project. These nine computers were linked over a high speed network with drivers written for UNIX.

It was then the trouble started. An extract from "A UNIX System Implementation for System/370" describes it:

> The fragmentation of the project over nine different computers caused significant additional work. The low-level compiled objects that were compiled on nine computers had to be networked onto one computer for the final linking before generating the final switching program output. The final products had to be distributed back to the eight computers so that final changes could be linked into the full system for private testing. Also, periodic auditing had to be done to ensure that all computers had the same common data and that the compilers and other tools remained the same on each system. The project was continuing to grow, and adding more minicomputers was not the best solution, because the auditing and networking overhead would increase on all the minicomputer systems.

Originally, a "direct port" of UNIX to a System/370 was going to be implemented, but this idea was rejected because

> The Input/Output (I/O) architecture of System/370 is rather complex; in a large configuration, the operating system must deal with a bewildering number of channels, controllers, and devices, many of which may be interconnected through multiple paths. Recovery from hardware errors (or software, we might add) is both complex and model-dependent. For hardware diagnosis and tracking, customer engineers expect the operating system to provide error logs in a specific format; software to support this logging lends itself to the use of paging for memory management; the UNIX system used swapping. Finally, several models of System/370 machines provide multiprocessing, with two (or more) processors operating with shared memory; the UNIX system did not support multiprocessing.

Therefore, the system as constructed consisted of three classes of programs operating at three levels: (1) user-level programs (user-written and those provided by the UNIX system), (2) a UNIX System Supervisor which provided the essential UNIX kernel, and (3) the Resident Supervisor which "(supports) the multiprogramming of UNIX system processes, provides low-level system calls, and manages the physical configuration"—in other words, all the complex work of a mainframe operating system.

For the Resident Supervisor, AT&T selected IBM's TSS (an IBM programming disaster from the 1960s), and IBM worked with AT&T to successfully port the UNIX System to mainframes. Each UNIX system process (user-level program and the UNIX System Supervisor) executed within its own 16-Mbyte virtual memory. The most complex part of the implementation was process synchronization of the UNIX System Supervisor with the Resident System Supervisor (TSS) which provided for paging and multiprocessing. (I might add that process synchronization should not be confused with data base synchronization in a distributed data base environment. The latter is much more complex!)

Both IBM (AIX) and Amdahl (UTS) implementations of UNIX depend on "resident supervisors" to provide the more complex essential functions of mainframe operating systems. While it is fair to call UNIX a System Supervisor, it cannot be termed a "mainframe operating system" under these circumstances. I contend that networks of both minicomputers and intelligent workstations need even more complex operating systems functions than mainframes do. Once these levels of complexity are reached, UNIX does not qualify as an operating system; in such an environment, it is more properly called a "subsystem supervisor."

10.2.2 Performance

This section is not intended to compare UNIX performance to the performance of its multitudinous versions or to other operating systems. I only want to point out that UNIX trails other operating systems in terms of suitability for the commercial environment. You can see the traces of UNIX's "quick-and-dirty" development in what has had to be done to improve performance in the 1980s. For example, a paper on UNIX performance ("The Evolution of UNIX Performance") points out the following:

- The original UNIX systems were implemented using linear table searches. In the 1980s when UNIX was implemented on mainframes (described above), "the key linear table searches have, one by one, been replaced by higher-performance ones" (hashing is mentioned most frequently). It was then reported, "the table search revisions have been a main factor in improved kernel performance." This is not surprising. What is surprising is that UNIX should have been around for over a decade using linear searches in the guts of the system.

- Around 1960, complete operating environments, written in a language that automatically generated binary searches for tables both within the compiler, which was written in its own language, and in the generated object code of applications systems were developed for the IBM 705 and 7074 computers. (The compiler also used direct hashing on the symbol tables on recompilation.) This was for machines with 40 and 50K of memory. (One of the reasons given for linear searches was small memory size of minicomputers.)

- In the early 1970s, it was found that IBM was doing linear searches of device tables in OS/MVT, and any self-respecting systems programmer knew that one of the most productive ways to improve performance was to replace the table searches. I know that IBM was belabored for using linear searches by at least one major customer.

- The point is that those who have implemented major commercial systems have known for years that table handling is among the most important determinants of performance, not only in the system, but in the generated applications. The developers of UNIX had little sensitivity to this, nor could they be expected to since UNIX was not developed for the commercial environment.

The paper also discusses the fundamental structure of the UNIX System, which features data transfers between processes through the famous "pipes." Essentially, this amounts to copying data from the sender process into kernel buffers and then from these into the address space of the receiver.

- Considering the fact that UNIX has gained much of its fame for increased productivity due to the reusability of discrete filters (relatively small carefully crafted programs and utility programs that are connected by pipes), pipes and filters are the key to process flow (performance) in UNIX applications.

- Even the simple description of how data-transfer pipes work should be enough to convince anyone familiar with major data-processing applications that there is an inherent performance problem (in the intermediate movement to system buffers and the management of these buffers) when the pipes-filters concept is applied to complex transaction processing. (It is akin to someone with high cholesterol going on an egg-and-steak diet, and the results are nearly as predictable.)

- The primary research being done at Bell Laboratories in the 1980s centered on the rates at which pipes can transfer data using different block sizes and on different hardware. Everything is relative, and with more powerful hardware and larger block sizes the rate can be increased. (However, remember that "being better than awful can still be pretty bad.") The problem that I am concerned with is the inherent limitation of the process structure—pipes and filters.

Here I will depart from the *Bell Systems Journal* to obtain an opinion on the performance characteristics of pipe-filter packaging. According to Brad J. Cox (*Object Oriented Programming—An Evolutionary Approach*, Addison-Wesley Publishing Company, 1986):

> This is one of the most potent reusability technologies known today. The small tools are neatly encapsulated, easily documented, and require no recompilation (e.g., their source code does not have to be available) to re-assemble them to solve problems that their builder never imagined. Nonetheless, this technology is not a panacea for packaging reusable code. For one thing, passing bytes along a

pipe is orders of magnitude more costly than passing arguments between two subroutines. More importantly, pipes
only carry streams of bytes, not the highly structured data
that abounds in system building. You cannot pass a pointer
or a linked list across a pipe without great difficulty.

The above should give practically any commercial applications developer some warning that a massive coronary may be imminent for data-processing applications. (An early implementation of COBOL on System/360
moved characters in a subroutine, the linkage of which took 40 times as many
instructions as the move would have taken if generated in-line. This is inserted
for all those who might be developing compilers for RISC machines.)

However, there is more than performance to worry about in Mr. Cox's
statement. Of particular concern is the whole concept of linking together reus-
able code for purposes the author "never intended" in any major commercial
system. Not only will performance suffer, but regardless of how good the documentation is, some of the filters are not going to work the way the "assembler" of the application may expect. Problems of debugging and maintenance
(which are not going to go away) could become horrendous, and the argument
that the system should not be misused doesn't help—the capabilities will be
misused.

The AT&T Bell Laboratories Technical Journal article on performance
improvement goes on to discuss many other areas of improvement that were
being addressed in the early 1980s—improvements that became commonplace in the operating systems for the commercial market during the 1970s.
That performance improvement in UNIX is still possible is beyond question.
For example, analysis of the "worm" that brought 6000 UNIX-based systems
to a whimpering halt revealed that the crypt routine (used to check passwords)
in the worm was "nine times faster" than the Berkeley UNIX version in common use. That brings up the question of security, which may make any concerns about performance relatively unimportant.

10.2.3 Security

Because of the reported and rumored weaknesses in the UNIX operating system, I had read "UNIX Operating System Security" before the famous
"worm" appeared. It is a highly professional assessment of some of the security problems the entire computer industry faces in the evolving network environment. It points out the tradeoffs that must arise between user-friendly
systems that encourage easy access and security. Before getting into the tech-

nical details of security, the paper points out that if UNIX is used the way its creators "intended it to be used," it could never be secure. Specifically, the paper stated:

> Such open systems cannot ever be made secure in any strong sense; that is, they are unfit for applications involving classified government information, corporate accounting, records relating to individual privacy, and the like.

While it would be possible to stop right there, some of the more detailed information in the paper becomes even more significant in light of the untimely security breach.

In discussing the set-user id (SUID) facility, the author commented: "Over the years it has provided truly horrid security flaws in various versions of the system. Some early versions of the mail command that ran superuser so as to be able to write in protected mailboxes could be coaxed to do things like appending lines to the password file." And, "A lax attitude about SUID programs, combined with a 'quick and dirty' programming style, can produce disasters." Then there is a statement that practically needs decrypting: "Escapes from SUID programs—child processes that are given a shell—are highly unrecommended." (Highly unrecommended?)

There follows a discussion of "Trojan horses" which are substantially more dangerous when the intruder assumes the identity of a UNIX "superuser" (systems administrator). Then the security problems associated with networking are raised, and the paper gets to the issues that matter most to this book.

Specifically, the uucp (the file transfer program between UNIX systems) and cu (the "call UNIX" program) are discussed in some detail. The following statement is attributed to Mr. R.T. Morris in an unpublished paper titled "Another Try at uccp" (reference no. 7 of the subject paper):

> The uucp program that is used by most UNIX machines was not written with security in mind. It can do just about anything, and it is up to the system administrator to restrict its capabilities. The restrictions needed are by no means obvious. The cure is to rewrite uucp so that it is able to deliver mail, copy files to and from spool directories, and to send out data only when it has initiated the connection. We have done this in our research environment some time ago. (Presumably at the National Security Agency.)

The subject paper then proceeds:

> The cu program can be a security disaster. Banning it from a machine or restricting access to devices will do no good at all, for the obvious reasons. The best that can be done is to educate users: 1) Do not use cu from a machine that is not trusted. 2) Do not use cu to a machine that is not trusted. 3) Do not browse on a remote machine.

Then parenthetically the statement is made:

> (This advice is remarkably similar to that which parents give their children: 'Do not go for a ride with a stranger.')

In retrospect, this little homily should have been accompanied by an additional bit of parental advice that children should not mug the little old lady who gives them a ride.

Under a section titled "Misguided Efforts," the paper then explores the problems associated with certain mechanisms which, while intended to collect evidence of "possible chicanery," can actually weaken systems security.

- When discussing the problem with logging the use of the su program (used to temporally change the user id) in sulog, the paper concludes that the practice presents a risk to the system administrator, but none for the knowledgeable intruder. Then, heaven help us, the paper makes the recommendation that rather than keep the log on the computer (which is obviously vulnerable), it should be taken off the machine where it cannot be accessed by even the superuser and, instead, should be printed out at the console! (The only possible justification I can see for this is that we wouldn't have UNIX to kick around anymore but could concentrate on physical security.)

- Password aging is discussed, and while it is conceptually sound, the paper notes that the "password" feature in UNIX has an algorithm that "from a security standpoint, is just awful."

- And it continues on to discuss recording unsuccessful login attempts, disabling accounts based on unsuccessful logins, and all of the "people problems" associated with maintaining security in the easy-going UNIX environment.

It would be difficult for any prudent person to disagree with the official warning that "such open systems . . . are unfit for applications involving classified government information, corporate accounting, records relating to individual privacy, and the like" after reading "UNIX Operating Systems Security." It was hardly necessary to have the celebrated "worm case" to convince me that UNIX may be "unfit" for a broad spectrum of commercial applications, but the incident certainly provides food for thought as it continues to unfold.

First of all, the paper appeared over 6 years ago, and the uucp and uc problems evidently continue to plague the system. Supposedly a systems programmer at UC Berkeley left a "trap door" in a mail program when it was distributed. He knew it was still there and did nothing about it. One source was quoted as saying that a thousand people knew there was a hole in the system but didn't take advantage of it. This has also been described as a relatively harmless prank that perhaps will serve a useful purpose. For some reason this type of logic isn't impressive.

First, the lax attitude about security that seems to pervade the UNIX environment is alive and well. The attitude in the academic environment seems to be "So what? That's UNIX."

Second, with a system as porous as UNIX seems to be, it is hardly reassuring that no classified files were destroyed during the worm incident; it only makes one wonder how many files have been illegally accessed by those more serious than the school boys playing games. ("UNIX Operating Systems Security" cites the propensity for systems administrators to cover up security problems and points out that this is just what the "bad guys" want them to do.)

The mere fact that UNIX is excellent for training computer scientists means that you have a whole cadre of smart guys (good and bad) who know the weaknesses of the system, and many have even worked on the system (early on, it was reported that R.T. Morris was a summer intern at Bell Labs and worked on UNIX security, but I haven't heard much about that recently). One wonders how many trap doors are hidden in the released products and how many illegal superuser Trojan horses are lurking around the networks.

It has also been reported that NSA (National Security Agency) tried to keep Purdue University from releasing information concerning its analysis of the "worm." A report from Purdue indicates most of the code was "awful," but the crypt module was highly sophisticated and looked as if it had either been written by someone else or "lifted." NSA once had an open order for AT&T UNIX systems that was never exercised to any major extent for unexplained reasons. Some strange games are being played around UNIX in the federal government, all of which should give us pause.

Then during the week of November 27, 1988, the Defense Communications Agency cut the connection between Milnet and the rest of the network because another "intruder" penetrated a VAX system of a defense contractor. Evidently the intruder gained entry through a loophole in an "anonymous File

Transfer Protocol (FTP)." Evidently a fix to close the loophole had been post-ed on Internet in late October. It is frightening to think that merely posting the fix could be an invitation to "test" the loophole, but now everyone is being careful not to identify the FTP in public. It appears that UNIX has become such an issue that we are all expected to ignore the fact that it is being paraded in public with no clothes on.

So all the major computer vendors in the world are tugging over the UNIX bone, and little consideration is being given to who out there really wants it. The market forecasts (sometimes made by those who wouldn't know an operating system from a word-processing package) all indicate that UNIX use is exploding. If this is true, it is unquestionably because the system is easy to use. And as "UNIX Operating System Security" concludes:

> At the beginning of this paper it was noted that UNIX sys-tems, when used for the purposes and in the environment for which they were designed cannot be made secure. The supporting arguments for that statement should now be clear.

They are. Let's quickly look at environments.

10.3 THE UNIX ENVIRONMENT

UNIX was designed and implemented for a research-and-development environment. Thompson and Ritchie were engaged in "programming re-search," not applications programming. Essentially, UNIX can be character-ized as a system that is "easy to use" by those with scientific and engineering backgrounds. It was also "inexpensive" because it was implemented on a timeshared minicomputer (Figure 10.1). The emphasis was on ease of access, and rudimentary communications with other systems, programs, and files were normally made readily available to others. Universities and defense con-tractors are alike in having common purpose and need to communicate among themselves (except when bidding on government contracts). The UNIX envi-ronment has been open in the best sense of the word.

At the present time, the most exciting thing happening in computing is the development of microprocessor-based workstations. It is now more eco-nomical to off-load certain types of research-and-development work from minicomputers to intelligent workstations. UNIX is an appropriate vehicle for such portability—it is an environment already familiar to those sitting at a SUN workstation. However, UNIX will not be termed easy to use by anyone who has grown up with PC-DOS, much less an Apple II or MAC. As a popular introduction to UNIX states: "Critics, on the other hand, charge that UNIX is 'cryptic, unfriendly, and lacking in key features.'" Just as IBM found out— ease of use means different things to different people.

The applications run in a research-and-development environment are generally more compute-intensive than I/O-intensive. This means they are essentially short jobs that do arithmetic on relatively small amounts of numerical data. Of course, there are exceptions, and some supercomputers are devoted to data reduction, but many supercomputers are front-ended with large mainframes to handle their I/O activity and data base management. Years ago, the differences between "scientific" and "commercial" applications were defined by the terms FEPAC (few executions per assembly or compile) and MEPAC (many executions per assembly or compile). There is no question that UNIX is essentially a FEPAC applications environment. (And please don't confuse applications with the tools used to develop them, such as UNIX filters.)

And as we have seen, when large projects develop in the UNIX environment, they are better centralized on mainframes where the complex I/O, data base management, and systems performance monitoring is left to more sophisticated operating systems. It is probable that the same data management problems encountered on the AT&T 5ESS project will surface in a UNIX environment where eight or nine IWSs are working together on the same project.

Even if we concede that the UNIX environment is narrowed down to the research-and-development environment described, the question becomes: How competitive is UNIX in that environment? Digital has had more experience selling minicomputers that run UNIX and VMS in the research and development environment than anyone, and Ken Olsen is never reluctant to express his opinion on controversial matters. Let's see what he had to say during an interview conducted by *Computerworld*.

As far as the portability of UNIX is concerned, Olsen pointed out that his earlier "snake oil" statement was carefully considered; you must have standards on every item used in developing the application. He told the press that they believed in "snake oil" because they never asked the right questions. For example, he suggested that the press should ask whether the same software would "play" on four Sun systems, and how much it costs to take something for "someone's UNIX to somebody else's UNIX." He concluded, "It costs a fortune." So as far as Ken Olsen is concerned, the portability of applications in the UNIX environment is "snake oil," and the press (and perhaps the Air Force) bought it.

When talking about RISC machines and UNIX, he makes the following points:

> It's clear that with certain applications which take a lot of high-speed computing and don't have an awful lot of communications going on, a UNIX-type machine or a RISC computer has enormous advantages.

However, when the speed required by the application system is "in the communications and the disk and memory, it gets to be a wash between the two." Then it becomes a question of "what the customer wants and where the best software is." And, as far as that is concerned:

> VMS will always be the best software, the best CASE (computer-aided software engineering) tools, the easiest to use—14 years will be awfully hard to catch up on.

Then he states that some people think that MIPS are the only things that count, and that if you get enough MIPS in a desktop machine "you're going to replace the mainframe." He then states that it should be pretty obvious this isn't going to happen because of the mainframe characteristics (I/O, disks, memory), and that reporters have to be pretty naive to believe this is going to occur. (I might add that not only reporters, but many "industry analysts" as well are naive enough to believe that everything can be "downsized.")

Olsen also stated that 10 percent of Digital's sales were Ultrix- (Digital's version of UNIX) related and were in "a category of somewhat simple things." So it appears that UNIX has a long way to go as far as Ken Olsen is concerned—even in the environment for which it was designed.

10.4   THE COMMERCIAL ENVIRONMENT

One of the first things that should be clarified about this environment is the meaning of the term "commercial." At the present time there is a great deal of emphasis on "systems integration." Major vendors are flocking to establish systems integration divisions; systems integrators are acquiring consulting firms; consulting firms are forming systems integration divisions; special supplements are being prepared for trade publications; and strategic alliances are being formed to take advantage of this potentially enormous market of $XX.X billion in 1992 (fill in any number you like). When systems integrators talk about the "commercial market," they mean everything except the federal government (including state and local government). That is not what I mean by the "commercial market."

By "commercial market," I refer to applications that fall outside the generally compute-intensive, research-and-development environment described above. What remains are the commercial or business applications; and in addition to the routine accounting and statistical applications, I include under that broad categorization "management information systems," "decision support systems," and emerging "expert systems." While some of these applications may be compute-intensive (in fact, some of the algorithms of operations research and artificial intelligence are so compute-intensive they may remain forever impractical), it is possible to characterize them as being primarily I/O-bound. Commercial applications can also be characterized by the fact that they depend heavily on data base management.

10.4.1 Data Base Management

The late Fritz Machlup in *The Study of Information* finally concluded that the term "data" had strayed far from its original meanings of "the givens" and now could more properly be defined as "anything that is stored in a computer." It is in that broad sense that I state that commercial applications are those that require data base management. Whether the data are text, relational tables, program libraries, images, graphics, voice messages, or full-color video, they require management. Otherwise, chaos is inevitable.

It does not require very much imagination to realize that file transfers of data rapidly become unmanageable in the commercial environment. I will not belabor the point here except to say that data base management systems (and data base administrators) came about out of necessity in the commercial world, not because of ascetic technical interests in data models. IDS, the foundation for the CODASYL model, was developed in the 1960s by General Electric to solve some very specific internal applications problems. Anyone who had ever developed a commercial application recognized its significance right out of the starting gate. However, systems programmers in a research-and-development environment were not very receptive. That is why IBM's initial reaction was, "Who needs this? We have ISAM."

I have demonstrated that UNIX is currently little more than a "subsystem supervisor" when it is ported to large mainframes for large projects such as the 5ESS. And Ken Olsen has pointed out that UNIX is far behind VMS in providing quality systems software. I would also point out that UNIX is also substantially behind in DBMSs despite the best efforts of independent software vendors, and this gap takes a quantum leap if I am correct in my assessment of IBM's SAA strategy. The tightly integrated hardware-software architecture of the IBM AS/400 is the key to IBM's distributed data base strategy, in my opinion. Let's look at what IBM had to say about UNIX at the time the AS/400 was announced.

10.4.2 UNIX and the AS/400

When the AS/400 was announced, Mr. William O. Grabe, IBM vice president and general manager of Applications Business Systems (ABS), was quite specific about his view of UNIX:

> We've said in the past that our AIX (IBM's version of UNIX) platform—which runs across the PS/2, the RT and the System/370—should be the primary choice where customers have UNIX requirements such as for federal government programs.
>
> And that still applies.
>
> But there's a really important point to consider in comparing the AIX operating system with the AS/400 Operating System. That is, they represent two totally different philosophies.
>
> AIX is the right choice for companies whose primary requirement is portability across multiple vendors, and who have an established base of UNIX programmers . . . programmers who are willing to build the systems themselves and to work with the operating system to customize their solutions.
>
> For those customers who don't want to get involved in the internals of an operating system . . . who don't have large, expert computer staffs . . . who operate in the commercial business world where immediate solutions provide the competitive edge . . . or who need to migrate System/36 and 38 programs . . . the high level of integration on the AS/400 makes it the solution that fits like it was made-to-order. It's just plain easier to learn and use.

These are reasonably straightforward statements. Few commercial customers will argue with Mr. Grabe when confronted with learning UNIX and some type of data base management system. UNIX is going to have a rough go in the commercial marketplace, regardless of the user interface that is provided.

At this point, it should be clear that the "demand" for UNIX is coming primarily from the federal government and from developers of IWSs and RISCs. The motivation of the various players in the UNIX struggle will be analyzed later, but now I would like to take a minor digression and discuss the importance of sorting in the commercial environment.

10.4.3   Sorting

In Chapter 8 of this book, I mentioned that 25 years ago, sorting represented 22 percent of the total computer usage among large IBM customers. (It was probably higher among the small customers.) I promised to come back to the question of sorting at an appropriate time. The appropriate time to discuss sorts is when discussing UNIX and RISCs in the commercial environment.

In 1986, IBM held a series of "road shows" around the country for its large users. At that time, improvements were announced in DF Sort, and the statement was made that large commercial installations devoted "between 15 percent and 30 percent of their CPU cycles and I/O activity on sorting." My company went back and reviewed the results of the ancient study and found the 22 percent number. Assuming a normal distribution within the current range, the total computer resource devoted to sorting in the commercial environment hasn't changed in the last 25 years! We thought this was amazing and called an ex-IBMer who developed some of the early sorts in the computer industry; he was amazed also. The basis for my amazement should be apparent.

In the early 1960s, installations were operating in a serial batch environment without the benefit of DASD (direct access storage device), multiprogramming, or data base management systems. These advances in storage hardware, process management (operating systems), and data management concepts (models) were supposed to decrease the amount of systems resources devoted to sequencing transactions for running against "master files," which frequently were redundant because they merely represented different arrangements of the same data.

The figures in the early study were based on wall clock measurements, which means that the percentage of the systems productive resource has actually increased rather than just remain the same. Consider the following:

- Not only has sorting resisted the efforts of the primary environmental changes (DASD, operating systems, and DBMSs) of the last two decades, but there have been significant improvements in channels and controllers for I/O.

- Sorting algorithms have been improved substantially since the early sort packages that were used in the early 1960s.

- Today's operating environment is substantially more complex (for example, interactive terminals), and yet sorting continues to absorb a comparable portion of the total systems capacity; therefore, the ratio of sort to problem program (production) must be much higher.

- For several reasons this apparent phenomenon is of more than idle interest and warrants analysis:

  - The relational model, which will be increasingly used in the distributed processing environment, specifically excludes sequential (ordered) files (tables); this will unquestionably play hob with all the sorting going on in the rest of the system (basically increasing it even more as relational tables are passed between and among systems).

  - Combining very large files, virtual storage and sorting can have disastrous performance impacts, and that pretty much describes the projected large host environment since they will serve primarily as enormous data base machines in a distributed data base environment. (This phenomenon, in turn, requires the distribution of data to lower levels in the processing hierarchy.)

The ramifications of this heavy emphasis on sorting in the commercial environment for the UNIX/RISC-based systems in a distributed data base environment should be apparent. One of the preliminary findings of the Japanese in their fifth-generation effort was to identify a "sort box" as the primary performance improvement necessary for artificial intelligence. The UNIX/RISC systems were not designed with efficient sorting as a primary design point and their "pipes and pipelines" are not amenable architectures. Since it is acknowledged that RISCs are not very good at floating-point arithmetic and that the solution is to add a floating-point processor, perhaps the solution is to provide a separate processor for sorting. We can then call it a RISC/CPC architecture for "reduced instruction set computer/complex processor complex" computer.

10.4.4 Pipes, Filters, and Valves

When personal computers began to appear in the corporate environment and users started to demand corporate data and micro-mainframe links, an embattled MIS vice president stated: "I will give them data if management tells me to give them data, but I know one thing: I am not going to let anything they send me get into my data bases if I don't process it." It is not difficult to understand why data-processing professionals feel that way—those in senior positions have been through the grubby work of building and maintaining those data bases. It isn't as glamourous as designing user interfaces or building expert systems, but the quality of commercial data-processing systems depends on them.

After reviewing UNIX, I expect that, in addition to pipes and filters, valves will have to be established at the point of interface between the UNIX world and major commercial environments (Figure 10.2). It is not difficult to imagine commercial information systems executives adopting an attitude that states very simply: "If I am responsible for the quality of data (in terms of synchronization, integrity, and security) in the organization, I must have control over the operating systems that are used on the network. I cannot be responsible for data and or applications that are developed in the UNIX environment, and I cannot be responsible for the quality of data that is distributed to UNIX systems. I will connect to UNIX systems if you tell me I must, but I demand

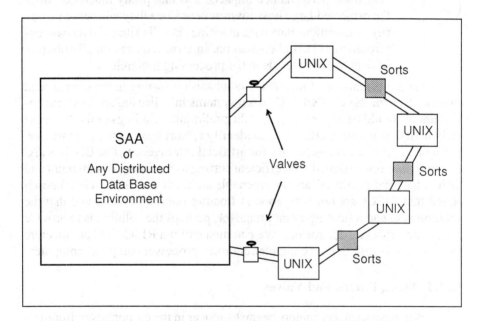

Figure 10.2 – Pipes, Filters, and Valves

the right to filter (process) all data (including programs) that enter my world (SAA), and the ultimate filter is a valve. You tell me to open it in either direction, and you take responsibility."

My analysis of UNIX indicates that UNIX has a limited role to play on even the level playing field, especially so in the commercial environment. Its pretensions of playing with the big boys are based more on bravado than common sense. However, UNIX has been a survivor, and there is no question that interest in UNIX is being manifested even by those who go to great lengths to point out its weaknesses. I will analyze this interest and the motivations of the players in the standards–open systems game in the following chapters of this book.

11

Foresight, Reality, and Hindsight

It is possible to get a "forecast" of enormous markets for practically any computer product or service. These forecasts have been uniformly inaccurate and have led to planning data that have neither validity nor reliability. On the basis of these data, computer industry "analysts" associated with the financial community reach conclusions about trends in the industry that are ludicrous. There are two primary reasons that classic market analysis and forecasting have not worked very well in the computer industry:

1. The inadequacy of current mathematics for modeling even the simplest supply-and-demand curve (much less the acceptance of complex interacting hardware-software technologies). The difficulties involved in mathematical modeling of any systems where the "human element" is involved have long been recognized. John von Neumann himself stated that it is "to be expected, or feared, that mathematical discoveries of a stature comparable to that of calculus will be necessary in order to progress in the field (game theory and economic behavior)." Considering that such mathematical discoveries have not been forthcoming, the inadequacy of practically all market research now being done is understandable (if not excusable).

2. The predominant role of IBM in exercising control over the acceptance of technology in the marketplace. While IBM cannot control the introduction of new technologies, it can and does exercise significant control over the acceptance of these technolo-

gies in its substantial customer base in the commercial market. This is tacitly acknowledged in the industry as IBM's "blessing" of new technologies and products. No private organization has ever established such a dominant technological position of control over a market this size.

It is significant that, while IBM is in a position of unparalleled control over the commercial data-processing market, its record of market analysis and forecasting is far from exemplary. After years of spending enormous amounts of money on market research and forecasting, IBM admitted that it took the emergence of Amdahl (with direct price-performance competition) to demonstrate that there was price-performance elasticity in the market for large mainframes. Apple learned this painful lesson with the MacIntosh.

More recently, IBM has acknowledged that computer networks developed substantially more rapidly than it anticipated (this being used as an excuse for the relatively poor network management facilities available within SNA), and that the market for personal computers in business was a complete surprise. It is difficult to think of two more significant developments during the last 15 years, and IBM has acknowledged that it miscalculated on both, despite the fact that it has substantial control over the acceptance of new technologies within its customer base.

Industry pundits aren't much better. In the early 1970s, the Diebold group sent out a technical bulletin on mass storage to its clients stating that magnetic disks would no longer be used by 1985 (optional media was supposed to replace it all).

The current struggles going on over "standards" and "openness" are obviously related to market analysis, forecasting, and competitive advantage. Since the outcome of these struggles will, in turn, have significant impact on future markets, Godel's incompleteness theorem comes into play—no one can "model" what is going to happen. Every published forecast I have seen should be labeled with the following warning: "Using this forecast for purposes of serious business planning or investment can be hazardous to your economic well-being." Think about this the next time you see those forecasts of UNIX or MCA market acceptance in the 1990s.

For the above reasons, I normally approach "crystal ball gazing" by using technological scenarios based on (1) technological forecasts that incorporate the fact that software always lags hardware, (2) the acceptance of IBM's dominant role, and (3) the fact that demonstrable cost savings will be the ultimate key to market size.

In the 1970s and 1980s, IBM had a business plan that was designed to maintain traditional growth. In 1980, the minimum growth plan (not including inflation) IBM was expected to be working against was depicted as shown in Figure 11.1. In order to achieve this growth IBM would be forced into new markets.

After analyzing what might threaten IBM's control of network development, I reached this conclusion:

- The potential threat of the explosive growth in personal computers should be of major concern to IBM for the following reasons:

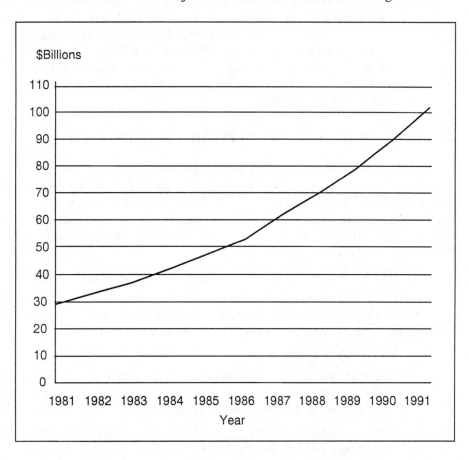

Figure 11.1 – IBM Minimum Growth Plan: 1981 to 1991

(*Source: Killen & Associates, Inc.*)

- It threatens a major shift forward in IBM's strategic plan.

- Personal computers are breaking out into business and professional areas; this represents a direct and specific threat to IBM markets.

- The lead times in establishing distribution channels in the consumer market are long, and consumer marketing represents a new marketing approach for IBM.

- Although personal computers represent only a remote revenue threat to IBM at this time, they present the single most significant management challenge IBM faces. Rather than the Bell System, Xerox, VANs (value-added networks), or minicomputer manufacturers, the biggest threat to IBM's control of future network development will come from what began as a cottage industry, and which was until recently disdained as the "hobby" industry.

11.1   STRATEGIC PERIODS—DEFINED AND REDEFINED

Having determined that a "reverse business plan" for IBM was the best model for projecting technological scenarios, my associates and I proceeded to do just that. We published a report in which we assumed that IBM's overall growth objectives for the 1980s and beyond (see Figure 11.2) would triple in revenue every 10 years. We made the following basic assumptions about IBM's plan to achieve its objectives:

- IBM would prefer to achieve its objectives by pursuing its traditional business.

- It is difficult to find new businesses that have the size, growth potential, and profit margins to satisfy IBM's management.

- IBM is not interested in pushing back technological horizons.

- IBM's planning process is designed to facilitate the controlled release of new technologies, products, and services. Management of technological change is a major IBM objective.

- IBM is not adverse to creating confusion in the marketplace, knowing that only IBM profits from such confusion.

These basic assumptions about the IBM planning process appear to remain valid, despite the turbulence and troubles of the 1980s.

We also described "four parallel market-product strategies" that were essential if IBM were to continue to grow at its traditional rate. We classified these strategies into strategic periods:

- The Distributed Data-Processing Strategic Period (DDP Period), described essentially as SNA-oriented and employing upgrades of current technology and products. It was projected to be the primary revenue generator through 1986. (Remember that the PC had been announced in 1981.)

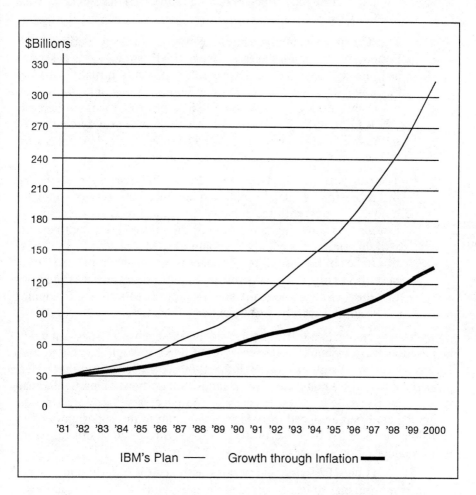

Figure 11.2 – A Reasonable IBM Plan?: 1981 to 2000 (*Source: Killen & Associates, Inc.*)

- The Office Automation/Electronic Office Strategic Period (OA/EO Period), described specifically in the report: "(it) will evolve from the current planned confusion in the IBM office automation product line. Starting with the loose integration of incompatible systems, it will proceed to the tight integration of hardware, communications and applications software. This integration will eventually lead to the totally integrated electronic office. This strategy of integrating people, software, and hardware will be the primary technological challenge during the 1986–1990 time frame." (That certainly is what SAA is all about.)

- The Computer-Communications Network Strategic Period (CCN Period), projected for the early 1990s. IBM's strategy was described as follows: "(it) will guide IBM's entry into the information services business. Starting with the fledgling IBM Information Systems Network, this strategy will become IBM's primary focus in the early 1990s (1991 through 1995), as it becomes increasingly challenged by AT&T." (IBM's fledgling has had a rough flight, but that is what "systems integration" and EDI are all about.)

- The Consumer Products Strategic Period (CP Period), described as the extension of the computer-communications services into the home. "Starting with the personal computer, IBM will continue to test the consumer market. Not until the mid-nineties (and beyond) will this strategy become paramount in IBM's plan." (I still believe this to be so; IBM's primary concern is personal computers in business. It is only as home computers are used for business purposes that they will become really significant to IBM's strategic planning — Prodigy is merely in anticipation of this time.)

We concluded that if IBM addressed the management issues that would be raised as these technological scenarios unfolded, it would be able to meet its growth objectives at least through the 1980s. By positioning themselves properly, competitors could carve out a significant portion of a particular market before IBM's "controlled release" of the necessary hardware-software technologies. Keeping ahead of IBM is tantamount to the opportunity of establishing de facto hardware-software price-performance standards for particular products and/or services (see Figure 11.3).

The original IBM strategic periods assumed an orderly and planned progression from one strategic period to the next. Once IBM really targeted a specific strategic period for its undivided attention, it was projected that only

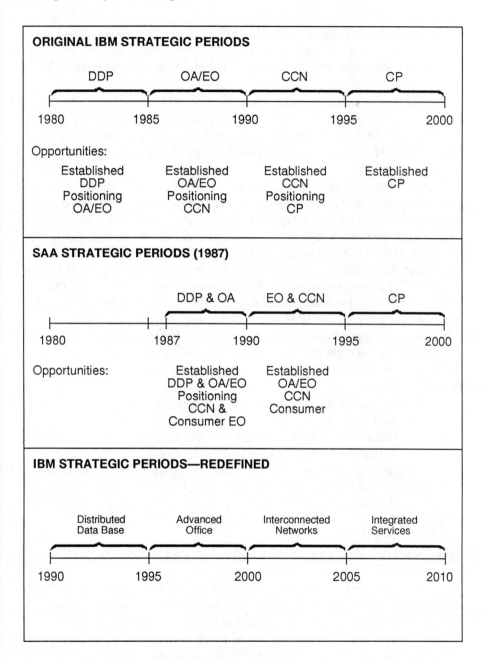

Figure 11.3 – Strategic Periods Defined and Redefined (*Source: Killen & Associates, Inc.*)

those vendors with a firmly established presence would have significant business opportunities in competition with IBM; other competitive vendors would do well to concentrate on establishing a leading-edge position for the following strategic period.

Remember that the strategic periods proceed in parallel, and IBM will react to even distant threats (for example, personal computers as consumer products) and will be engaged in activities to counter any significant long-term threats. However, major readjustments of IBM's plan will occur only when the plan fails.

IBM failed to address the primary issues of the DDP Strategic period during the early 1980s. (That failure and its impacts will be analyzed in the next section of this book.) Not until SAA was announced in 1987 did IBM provide its customers with any insight into its plan for distributed processing. By that time, IBM had to telescope the DDP and OA/EO periods together, and, obviously, the windows of opportunity have been kept open and will remain open into the 1990s. For example, the electronic office portion of the OA/EO Strategic Period implies substantial substitution of electronic for paper media, and it is now apparent that IBM will not have a significant impact on that market (with its own products) until the 1990s. In addition, the consumer market for personal computers and associated information services has developed rapidly enough that major opportunities have been telescoped in from the other end.

IBM really has its work cut out for it; everything is happening at once. SAA, the multi-billion-dollar answer IBM has been forced to invent, is designed to redefine the original strategic periods, and I have given them new names—Distributed Data Base Period, Advanced Office Period, Interconnected Network Period, and Integrated Services Period. They will be described in a later chapter. Essentially, they shift everything back 10 years. I will now explain why IBM had to build that big SAA mountain in the middle of the level playing field.

11.2   A BRIEF STRATEGIC REVIEW OF THE 1980s

The DDP scenario for the early 1980s was based on the "orderly distribution" of processing from mainframes to minicomputers and intelligent terminals. With computer power closer to end users, it was predicted that new applications would more than compensate for the leveling of mainframe revenues. Being mainframe-oriented, IBM saw fit to encourage the decentralization of mainframe technology in order to move processing power closer to end users. As one IBM old-timer stated early in 1982, "we have made a lot of money on big mainframes for a long time, and there are those who think it can go on forever."

During the early 1980s, IBM met its base plan with this strategy. Revenues for 1985 were $50 billion, which were right on target with the base plan I had projected. Predictably, as long as IBM can achieve its business objectives, it isn't going to provide new or innovative "solutions" to customers' problems (see the assumptions above).

Unfortunately for IBM, its traditional mainframe business could not support IBM's desired growth forever, and in 1985 it became obvious that revenues were peaking. 1986 revenues turned out to be "only" $51 billion, and 1987 revenues were $54 billion. IBM had dropped a full year behind its long-range plan in just 2 years!

Earnings were even worse. 1985 earnings dropped slightly from $6.5 billion to $6.3 billion, when adjusted for inflation (although IBM reported $6.6 in its financial statements). 1986 earnings dropped to $4.8 billion and modestly recovered to $5.26 billion in 1987, which is still less than IBM earned in 1983 ($5.5 billion). In 1988 IBM announced earnings of $5.8 billion —the struggle goes on.

It is difficult to generate much sympathy for IBM, since it was the most profitable private company in the world in 1987, but it is possible to get some perspective on the true costs of its strategic blunder in not addressing the DDP Strategic Period on a timely basis. Consider the following:

- IBM lost (or gave away) competitive advantage.
  - In 1979 Digital was the sixth largest company in the U.S. computer industry, with revenues of $2 billion. In 1985 they were the second largest, with revenues of $7 billion. Digital took advantage of an established position during the DDP Strategic Period, while IBM floundered with its sacred mainframes.
  - Wang went from $280 million and 23d place in 1979 to $2.4 billion and eighth place in 1985, while positioning itself as an established vendor for the OA/EO Strategic Period. (In early 1988, some IBM customers who needed image processing started calling in Wang, after hearing its radio and TV advertising.)
  - Despite the success of the IBM PC, Apple managed to grow from $75 million and 61st place to $1.8 billion and 11th place on the list of U.S. DP companies. In addition, Apple established a new

standard of computer ease of use during this period. (This doesn't refer exclusively to the vaunted Mac interface; Appleworks for the Apple II, with readily available desktop accessories, was way out ahead of the field—Apple also makes mistakes.)

• In addition, IBM's failure to recognize that the complexity (and cost) of its System/370 architecture systems would limit advanced applications development for the entire computer industry led to overlapping "solutions" at the departmental level. It wasn't until the 9370 failed that IBM was forced to invent (or reinvent) the AS/400. This allowed competitive solutions to proliferate in the midrange.

For once, confusion in the marketplace did not benefit IBM. Customers found out there were other vendors out there who had solutions that worked. A certain segment of IBM's customer base will never return to the days of blind faith in anything that wears the IBM logo. Therefore, IBM lost substantially more than a year's revenue growth and several billion in profits during the DDP Strategic Period.

However, perhaps the price was worth it if IBM management really learned something from the experience. And there are signs that this is the case. John Akers was interviewed by *Computerworld* in January 1989. When asked about the cost cutting and adjustments that had been made within IBM, he replied:

> For the past 25 years IBM has had a remarkable performance in business success. That success tends to have a management team that does not want to tamper with what's in place. As that success began to diminish a bit in the last three or four years, it's an awful lot easier to gain the attention of the management team and all the people.
>
> What had to happen for this enterprise is to have reality come in and hit us on the head.

After stating that IBM was now more interested in providing solutions for the customers' problems rather than just pushing iron, Mr. Akers was asked whether IBM solutions were "mainframe-oriented." He replied:

> Some of them will be 370, some will be AS/400, some will be PS/2, and some will be all of the above. When SAA gets fleshed out a bit more, it will go across all three.

When asked about fundamental market shifts in demand or market conditions that caused IBM to reassess its approach, he commented:

I don't think they were fundamental changes, other than the continuing changes toward easier to use, lower-priced computers and a plethora of workstations and networking. But I think all of us in the industry understood that that was going on." (And, IBM tried to control the rate of those changes during the entire DDP Strategic Period. It didn't work!)

Then, when asked about the two or three most significant technologies for large customers over the next 5 to 10 years, Akers responded:

I would say Systems Application Architecture is one.

Beyond that, I would expect that some of the things going on in image processing (will have a large impact). I went down to USAA Insurance in San Antonio to see what's going to happen there when they take the 25 million letters they get every year and eliminate all the paper; it's very exciting.

Perhaps expert systems will have a bigger impact, too.

It may have taken a "hit in the head," but SAA is going to be a technology that will have substantial impact on not only IBM customers but the computer-communications industry as a whole. As far as image processing and the elimination of paper is concerned, I couldn't agree with Mr. Akers more; and I even think he has put expert systems into proper perspective by saying "perhaps" they will have more significant impact in the next 10 years. But what does bother me about all this is that by staying with a highly centralized mainframe-oriented strategy in the 1980s, IBM has effectively delayed the potential benefits of available technologies to its customers (and the industry as a whole) by nearly a decade.

12

Technical Scenarios for the Competitive Jungle

The computer industry is burdened with ill-defined and constantly changing terminology. I believe that some of the fundamental terms I use, such as data, information, and knowledge, should be defined here so that we understand how they will be employed in the remainder of this book.

In describing what is happening in complex systems, such as computer-communications networks, it is convenient to employ the fundamental terminology of General System Theory described by Ludwig von Bertalanffy. Bertalanffy stated that as systems become more complex, they exhibit the following tendencies toward a natural hierarchical order:

- Progressive integration, in which the parts become more dependent on the whole
- Progressive differentiation, in which the parts become more specialized

These result in the system exhibiting a wider repertoire of behavior, which, in turn, results in:

- Progressive mechanization, which limits the parts to a specific function
- Progressive centralization, in which leading parts emerge which dominate the behavior of the system

When I use the terms *integration*, *differentiation*, *mechanization*, and *centralization*, they will refer to these tendencies toward a natural hierarchical order in artificial systems, such as computer-communications networks.

The terms *data*, *information*, and *knowledge* are not used with any precision within the computer-communications industry. This can lead to substantial confusion in determining or discussing technological scenarios. My definitions of these terms come from the late Fritz Machlup (*The Study of Information — Interdisciplinary Messages*, Wiley-Interscience, 1983, edited by Fritz Machlup and Una Mansfield).

- *Data* are "something given" and can be either "facts" or "assumptions" of varying quality. However, the distinction between data and information has become (according to Machlup) that data are stored in computers and are, therefore, processible. His position is (or was) that it did not make any difference whether data were numbers, text, graphics, etc., and that most distinctions between data and information represent quibbling. However, data can be characterized as being

  - Encoded
  - Structured
  - Defined
  - Qualified (either formal or informal)
  - Processible
  - Systems-oriented

- *Information* is the "telling of something," or "that which is being told." Information is distinguished from observation in that it requires at least two persons; one who tells (speaking, writing, imprinting, pointing, signaling) and one who listens, reads, watches. There is nothing in the definition of information that speaks to quality even in the sense of Shannon's information theory. Information can be anything from wisdom to deliberate lies. It can be characterized as

  - Piecemeal, fragmented, particular
  - Timely, transitory, ephemeral
  - A flow of messages
  - Not readily processible
  - Not structured

- *Knowledge* can be acquired without new information being received. Complexity is inherent because different individuals acquire different levels of knowledge from the same data and/or information. On the basis of their knowledge, they may take different actions in what are seemingly identical circumstances. This is what makes the stock market and forecasting so complex and fascinating. Knowledge can be characterized as

- Structured, coherent, universal (sometimes)

- Enduring, significant

- Stock

- Human (Data and Information contribute to human knowledge, and humans contribute their knowledge to data and information. Since humans are involved, it can also be stated that, by its very nature, knowledge is uncertain, inexact, partial, and intuitive.)

- A process that reduces uncertainty and/or changes beliefs

- Based on probabilities (statistical, logical, and subjectivist)

At the present time, *data* (by my definition) are stored on magnetic media ready for use by computers, most *information* continues to reside on paper, and *knowledge* remains the province of human beings. The application of computer-communications technology over the next 20 years promises (or threatens) to change this distribution. It would be possible to paint either a "best of all possible worlds" or a "worst of all possible worlds" scenario with equal confidence, but drastic change can be predicted without qualification.

Of all of the bastardization of terminology that has occurred recently, perhaps none rankles quite so much as the simple term *application*. The following definition of "applications program" is from the *Dictionary of Computing* (Oxford University Press, 1983):

> Any program that is specific to the particular role that a given computer performs within a given organization and makes a direct contribution to performing that role. For example, where a computer handles a company's finances a payroll program would be an applications program. By contrast, an operating system or a software tool may both be essential to the effective use of the computer system, but neither makes a direct contribution to meeting the end users eventual needs.

I comment:

- DBMSs, spreadsheet packages, and AI shells do not make a direct contribution to meeting the end user's eventual needs in a commercial environment.

- They are not *applications*, nor are they solutions (another horribly misused word) to the users' needs. A DBMS can best be classified as a subsystem of the operating system, and both spreadsheet packages and AI (artificial intelligence) shells are software tools.

- Users are beginning to understand this. Users also understand that even an applications program (by itself) won't solve problems. Without data of high quality, operating systems, software tools, and applications programs cannot meet end-user needs.

- IBM, in using the term *application* in both SAA and the AS/400, finally seems to have become aware of this basic truism. "Application-enabling" at least does not misrepresent the true state of the case.

- Users aren't buying nearly as much "snake oil" these days.

- The term *application*, in this book, refers to products and services that contribute directly to meeting the end user's needs.

12.1 IBM STRATEGIES AND TACTICS FOR THE FUTURE

While IBM may have delayed technological reality for its customers by one decade, it now appears to have an integrated strategic plan. That was previously lacking.

The importance of this plan (SAA) is not just its technical quality or its potential impact on the market. One of its primary benefits for IBM will be the manageability of the enterprise. For years, IBM was noted for "management by contention." With vast resources, IBM permitted competing hardware-software technologies to develop and compete within its planning process; and for a long time, this was a highly successful strategy. When new technology (such as virtual storage) was needed, someone could be found within the company who had a pet project that had been permitted to survive (either intentionally or through oversight).

Unfortunately for IBM, as competing technologies began to get out in the marketplace, they competed against each other. One of my favorite strategic maxims has long been "Go separately, but hit in unison." IBM appeared to be exhorting its troops to "Go separately and hit anything in sight (including each other)." The resulting chaos finally caught up with IBM, providing Armonk with the necessary "hit in the head." SAA is the strategic plan necessary to "hit in unison."

For purposes of strategic analysis, it is convenient to apply a template to the playing field. This template (Figure 12.1) will be used to generally analyze what SAA is currently to address.

SAA defines IBM's computer-communications networking strategy and addresses personal productivity and data management. It also has the stat-

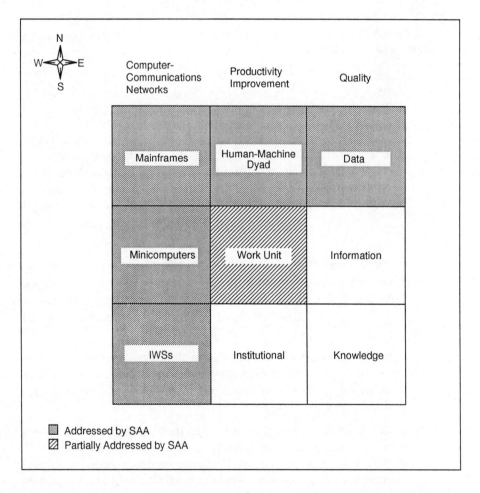

Figure 12.1 – The Playing Field Template (*Source: Killen & Associates, Inc.*)

ed objective of first addressing office systems (work unit productivity improvement) and then addressing integrated industry systems.

"Computer-communications networks" are broken down into the "proper" hierarchy of mainframes, minicomputers, and intelligent workstations that was mentioned earlier. SAA addresses this hierarchy by providing a framework for the development of applications that can move freely up and down this hierarchy.

"Productivity (or performance) improvement" is the stated objective of computer-communications technology, and it should be broken down for purposes of analysis (measurement) into four categories: hardware-software (computer-communications networks themselves), human-machine dyad, work unit, and institutional.

- Hardware-software productivity is simply price-performance— more bang for a buck. Today, we seem to be less sensitive to the complexity of hardware-software performance than we were 25 years ago. MIPS is a horribly misleading measure, and we are all beginning to see that benchmarks aren't much better. I will discuss hardware-software productivity and its measurement in more detail later. It will become increasingly important in an open environment—we are going to have a "horsepower race" to put the automobile manufacturers of the 1950s to shame.

- Practically all current office productivity improvement efforts (word processing, spreadsheets, etc.) are addressed primarily toward performance improvement at the human-machine dyad.

- SAA begins to address the work unit (by holding out the eventual integration of encoded data, image, voice, etc.), but most information in offices is still conveyed either on paper or directly between and among human beings.

- While SAA holds out the promise of "industry-specific" applications, the application of computer-communications technologies to improve institutional performance remains (and will continue to remain) the responsibility of users.

  There is no assurance that improved performance at other levels will necessarily improve performance at the institutional level; but there is every indication that inadequate or poorly designed information systems can adversely affect institutional performance.

The application of computer-communications technology to the improvement of office productivity is directly related to the quality and impact of data, information, and knowledge. SAA is intended to assure the quality and availability of data (remember my definition—data are anything stored in a computer). This is absolutely essential if information systems are to fulfill their promise. However, even the assurance of quality data does not necessarily improve the quality of information flow or assure the proper application of knowledge.

Essentially, SAA provides a general and flexible architecture, a comprehensive set of hardware-software tools, and some assurance of the availability of high-quality data. It addresses a lot of the fundamental issues and problems associated with building a high-quality information system in today's environment where most vendors market packaged "solutions" of questionable value. However, the responsibility for developing a specific information systems blueprint, the proper use of available tools, and the specific management of data, information, and knowledge have been left to the customer.

SAA is a clearly defined long-range strategy. Any mystery in it is due to either complexity or timing. This makes the concept of strategic periods especially important. Since one period logically follows another, by applying the assumptions I used to establish the original strategic periods (outlined in the previous section), we can distinguish between strategies and tactics in any specific period.

12.1.1 Distributed Data Base Period (1990–1994)

Figure 9.1 clearly shows the essence of the Distributed Data Base Period. IBM's strategy is to provide a tightly integrated network where the end user need not be concerned about where data (by my definition) reside. This improves individual productivity for both end user and the developer of applications. The following is implicit in IBM strategy during this period:

- IBM will focus attention on data and applications quality rather than on the hardware-software to support these applications. This is a significant change for IBM—to the benefit of its customers and the detriment of most of its competitors.

- The protection of intellectual property will be facilitated. While the user may not care whether SAA systems are implemented in hardware, software, or firmware, vendors jolly well have to care. Interfaces are going to more difficult for others to maintain as IBM distributes processing on both an architectural and geographic basis.

- An emphasis on distributed data bases puts IBM in a strong position to control the distribution of data over the computer-communications network and to extend the life (and revenues) of centralized mainframes. While the protection of mainframe revenues was IBM's primary strategy during the 1980s, the Distributed Data Base Period will be different because IBM's objective during this time will be to evolve an entirely new, tightly integrated, hardware-software infrastructure for commercial systems development. This infrastructure is proprietary from mainframe to desktop.

- The emphasis on "openness" and "connectivity" of competitive hardware is tactical. IBM's strategic objective is to use the Distributed Data Base Period to establish SAA as a proprietary architecture that will absorb anything connected to it.

12.1.2   Advanced Office Systems Period (1995–1999)

The major objective of the Advanced Office Systems Period is the integration of current paper-based information systems with data-processing systems—more specifically, to absorb paper information and documents into network data bases. The Distributed Data Base Strategic period is a necessary foundation on which to build advanced office systems; those distributed data bases will contain images as well as encoded data.

This period will be characterized by two significant parallel media shifts: (1) from paper to electronic media and (2) within electronic media, a shift from magnetic to optical media. Since IBM has dominated the large-scale, magnetic storage market and currently depends heavily on that market for growth, optical storage (of all kinds) represents a significant, potential threat to revenues. While IBM recognizes the importance of image processing (even Mr. Akers saw fit to mention that), the controlled release of the technology presents a real challenge. IBM's strategy appears to be as outlined below.

During the Distributed Data Base Period, IBM will be satisfied to establish a presence in advanced office systems (image processing). ImagePlus with hardware and software from multiple vendors is a delaying tactic at best. It creates the type of "controlled chaos" from which only IBM can benefit. In addition, IBM can be expected to do the following:

- Discourage its customers from entrusting "corporate data" on "unproven" optical technology

- Provide convincing arguments that some image processing applications can be cost-effectively implemented, at less risk, using magnetic storage devices

- Encourage careful analysis and test beds before embracing image processing for "strategic applications" (This probably isn't bad advice, but it can certainly be used to delay acceptance in the marketplace unnecessarily.)

In other words, IBM will do everything it can to keep optical storage from adversely affecting magnetic storage revenues and everything it can to see that magnetic storage remains the predominant storage media. From early work with State Farm Insurance (over a decade ago), IBM is fully aware of the considerations that inhibit customer acceptance of comprehensive image-processing systems. IBM will be able to employ a variety of tactics to discourage widespread acceptance of image-processing systems and optical storage until it is ready to enter the market with its own products.

IBM is no stranger to the technologies needed to support image processing, but it has always been extremely sensitive to the potential effect of optical storage on magnetic disk revenue. Unquestionably, IBM has products it could announce today—Scanmaster II, optical disk, etc.,—however, it is doubtful that IBM will announce its own products on a "mix-and-match" basis, which would be characteristic of an "open" system. IBM's strategy will be to enter the Advanced Office System Period with a tightly integrated hardware-software system under SAA. Then it will give its official blessing by actively marketing a proprietary system. (See *SAA: Image Processing* by Michael Killen, McGraw-Hill, 1991.)

During the 1990s (the Distributed Data Base and Advanced Office Systems Periods), IBM's challenge will be to control the acceptance, and therefore the impact, of hardware with dramatically improved price-performance—specifically, microprocessors and optical storage. It will accomplish this through value-added, tightly integrated, proprietary, hardware-software systems.

- One IBM executive was recently quoted as saying that the 1990s will be the decade of the "superserver" (IBM terminology for "large mainframes supporting enormous magnetic storage systems"). Perhaps it will be, but there won't be any lingering questions about when the dinosaurs started to die, or what killed them.

- At the same time, IBM executives in the Applications Systems Division know that in the 1990s their "servers" (primarily AS/400s) are going to surpass mainframes in revenue produced for the company.
- The 1990s will really be the decade that sees processing power go to the desktop, and data go to the work unit.
- It will also be the last decade when IBM can afford to remain so heavily dependent on hardware for revenue growth. Software and services are increasingly becoming the name of the game. SAA can be viewed as the master plan for what will follow.

12.1.3 Interconnected Networks Period (2000–2004)

Systems integration and electronic data interchange are not new ideas. Computer companies, some of which are no longer in existence, were talking about "integrated data processing" in 1959; and some railroads started exchanging magnetic tape (in lieu of punch cards) for freight car accounting at about the same time. We are now in a period, however, where these are being rediscovered.

We originally projected that if IBM were to grow beyond the $100 billion level projected for the 1990 to 1991 timeframe, it would have to start achieving substantial revenue growth through the sale of computer-communications services. I continue to believe that, regardless of when IBM hits the $100 billion level.

In *IBM — The Key Issues*, we pointed out that based on its track record in the services and communications areas, it would be difficult for IBM to make this strategic shift in emphasis. We specifically cited the dumping of the Service Bureau Corporation [as part of the CDC (Control Data Corporation) antitrust settlement] and the laboriously slow progress of SNA as indications of less-than-spectacular interest and/or progress in these areas. Since that time, IBM's experience with Information Network Services and its follow-on organizations cannot have been terribly encouraging to IBM management.

It now appears that IBM has pushed back the time to make this strategic shift. Furthermore, IBM will not be a $100 billion corporation until well into the 1990s and therefore will not "need" the revenue. IBM's strategy, clearly depicted in Figure 9.1, is to

- "Appear" to be open to competitive equipment so that competitive equipment can be "welcomed" (or at least tolerated) through gateways to SAA. The server depicted in that diagram, while it could be of System/370 architecture, will usually be an AS/400. There is every reason to support "standards" for connectivity and IBM did that even before SAA was announced.

- Standardize on UNIX as a means of connectivity. We should remember that IBM was committed to the support of UNIX and was well along with its implementation of AIX before the OSF came into being. IBM could not have asked for anything better than OSF to simplify its "connectivity" with the outside world—define a simple, agreed-upon data pipe to transfer files between SAA and competitive UNIX systems.

- Contrast this "pairwise" connectivity with the tightly integrated distributed data base environment of SAA. At the same time, the layered operating systems that will develop during the Distributed Data Base Period will complicate the interfaces necessary for tighter integration of competitive operating systems with those of SAA (except IBM's implementation of AIX on its own systems which will be tightly integrated with the AS/400 and, therefore, part of the distributed data base environment).

- Proceed aggressively with network management so there is no question about who is in charge of the interconnected network. It is practically inconceivable that any major networks that become interconnected will not run into an IBM "superserver" after a couple of hops; and regardless of terminology, there isn't going to be any question about who is going to be in charge— if for no other reason than IBM has a plan that effectively merges data base management and network management.

- Place a security "valve" in the data pipeline at the point of interconnection for electronic data interchange. It is doubtful that IBM would have much difficulty convincing commercial customers that UNIX (other than its own) should not be permitted to be incorporated into their business networks where vital corporate data reside. The acknowledged UNIX security problem is real, and it is not going to go away. Be sure that IBM will make any systems integration customer aware of the problems.

- Take advantage of industry reluctance to interconnect networks until IBM is ready to proceed on its own timeframe. IBM will probably have considerable help in this regard.

All of this can be taken as both a positive and a negative sign as far as EDI is concerned. Lawyers certainly do little to promote the use of new technology. On the other hand, when you see them swarming around a technology, you can be sure it has enough potential to warrant their "professional interest."

It is not very difficult to envision IBM taking advantage of such concerns when it turns the valve of UNIX connectivity off. IBM cannot, and I am sure will not, accept responsibility for the data base integrity (much less security) of data bases it cannot control. Commercial customers will both understand and sympathize with IBM on this issue, and IBM is certainly the preferred target for lawsuits if anything goes wrong.

One last thing, Figure 8.4 also shows that IBM is willing to support ISDN as the backbone for the follow-on period of integrated services into increasingly small businesses and into the home. The sale of its interest in ROLM is just another case of IBM floundering when it starts to invade the telephone companies' markets.

12.1.4 Integrated Services Period (2005–2009)

The extension of information services into every home is proceeding much slower than would have been anticipated given the availability of technology. Experiments in "telecommuting" clearly indicated that even current technology and services can be used to work effectively from home.

However, it is very difficult to convince some consulting clients that this is either possible or desirable. In two consulting contracts, one with a major computer manufacturer, the other with a telephone operating company, the computer manufacturer could not (or would not) arrange to transfer data directly to a home computer system for analysis, and the telephone company could not (or would not) permit the transmission of draft reports to their system for review. Both insisted on using Federal Express.

There has been great reluctance on the part of most independent consultants and small consulting firms to establish computer-to-computer communications from their homes. This is especially disconcerting when some of these consultants profess to be on the leading edge of computer-communications technology. Even simple file transmission seems to be beyond the capability of most personal computer users regardless of whether they work at home or in the office. The current interest in facsimile transmission (fax) will only delay the acceptance of transferring data in processible form.

For these reasons, it may be that IBM can do without substantial revenues from consumer products and services until the Integrated Services Period. However, IBM has lost ground and credibility in the consumer market. To correct this, IBM must do the following:

- Maintain and expand its presence in the computer market, regardless of how much revenue it contributes in the short term. Ease of use is the key to the integrated systems period, and IBM has acknowledged this with SAA and the promise of a common user interface. IBM is going to try to make network access sufficiently easy to use to attract the consumer as well as the very small-business user. It also wants to get a proprietary system out there. The PS/2s are going to be aimed directly at Apple, and the battle of the interfaces will be joined.

- Go proprietary with its Prodigy services offering; the MicroChannel architecture (or its follow-on) will be essential for integrated services in the home. This is true because home office computer users

  1. Would like to leave a computer on to receive data from other computers and an answering machine on to receive telephone messages. These two systems should be integrated.

  2. Want to be able to control and respond to call interrupts when on-line to an information service [even before ISDN (Integrated Services Digital Network) comes to home offices].

  3. May want business associates to be able to access and transmit data between systems while one of them is using a system.

  4. Want to receive or transmit images (fax) just like any other data (by my definition).

In other words, an integrated home system should be able to operate pretty much as a personal LAN, which is what it really will be. And in addition, that integrated system should provide all of the home services such as fire and intrusion alarms, and remote appliance control and monitoring.

These capabilities are precisely the ones that will make advanced services from commercial network services vendors all the more attractive. SAA can accommodate IBM's long-range plan to provide the types of hardware and services that will be attractive to those with offices in their homes. These in turn will evolve into the home information centers of the future.

In solving the data base management problems at the higher levels of the processor hierarchy, IBM will establish the framework for the management of personal data bases. As the use of personal computers expands to absorb these more integrated personal services (whether at home or in the office), we will all be confronted with being data base administrators. Many of us already are. Individuals and small businesses have the same problems of data base integrity, synchronization, and security that large businesses have. Many people will not want to be a "data base administrator," and can't afford to hire one, can't force a spouse to be one, and don't trust their children to perform the function. If they happen to have a secretary, they probably wouldn't be able to force or trust that person to perform the function, either.

Fundamentally, it will be data base (and network) management that will inhibit the use of personal computers for many of the possible products and/or services becoming available. IBM's strategy is to concentrate on solving these problems at all levels in the processing hierarchy.

IBM is going to apply expert systems technology first to solve the problems of data base and network management; it is probably to this area that Mr. Akers is referring when he states that "perhaps" expert systems will have major technological impact on IBM's customer base. It is also true that such systems will form the foundation for solving the personal data base management problem. In addition, expert systems will open up enormous opportunities for personal systems that can perform the data reduction needed as we enter the information age —screening news, phone calls, information sources, and on-line data bases of all kinds. This must be IBM's long-range strategy for the year 2000 and beyond if it is to have any chance of continued growth.

In writing some material for this book, I hit on the analogy of a "new watering hole in the jungle" for the emerging open systems environment. Lots of wild animals are eyeing this watering hole, and some of them have more than a drink of water on their minds. The laws of the jungle and the etiquette of dining around watering holes are quite complex, but two things I know: (1) the rights of discovery and current possession are ephemeral and (2) the lion's share is proprietary.

If you have any question about who the lion is, it is IBM, and SAA is a clear statement of a proprietary jungle that is loaded with de facto standards. Even if you respect the lion's share, you have to get a little nervous when the lion strolls down to the open systems watering hole.

13

Standards, Regulation, Litigation, and Free Enterprise

13.1 A NATIONAL COMPUTER-COMMUNICATIONS INFRASTRUCTURE

The technological scenarios presented in the preceding chapter represent the phased development of a national computer-communications network infrastructure. Beginning with the necessary integration of the computers (mainframes, minicomputers, and intelligent workstations) that are already out there during the Distributed Data Base Period; proceeding through the substitution of electronic media for paper communications during the Advanced Office Systems Period and the interconnection of public and private networks (both commercial and government) during the Interconnected Network Period; the network will be extended into private residences during the Integrated Services Period.

It is probable that this evolution will be tortuous. We do not have a national plan (much less standards) for such an infrastructure. To be in the preliminary stages of defining "open systems" and "standards" for such an infrastructure is indeed unfortunate, especially since it did not have to be that way. Projected advances in technology were sufficiently clear in the early 1970s to predict the need for a national computer-communications infrastructure comparable to that defined in the Integrated Services Period.

A general architectural and financial model for such a national infrastructure received wide circulation within the federal government in the mid-1970s. The study supporting the model was performed under contract for The National Bureau of Standards (NBS Contract Number 3-36006) and contained recommendations for standards that would ensure an open infrastructure. The fundamental conclusion was that the federal government should take the initiative in developing such an infrastructure for the following reasons:

- A national computer-communications network reaching into every residence would become at least as important as the Interstate Highway System.

- The cost of approximately $150 billion (in 1975 dollars) would require government incentive to the private sector.

- The services that would be provided from such a network would directly support major programs of national significance—education, medical, postal service, etc.—and therefore, it was in the best interest of the government to provide cost-effective services in those areas.

- Issues of privacy and security would have to be specified with extreme care if the negative impacts of such networks were to be avoided.

- The federal government had an obvious vested interest in seeing that the "information age" evolved in the best interest of all citizens.

The federal government did not assume a position of leadership in the development of such a national infrastructure for two primary reasons: (1) cost (even though the model identified revenue sources to pay for the network) and (2) lack of understanding—NBS was more interested in hardware standards than the "soft" standards identified as most important. That was extremely unfortunate.

While the federal government has chosen not to exercise a role of strategic leadership, it has used its position as the world's largest user of computer-communications equipment to influence the development of both hardware and software standards.

13.2   THE "UNLEVEL PLAYING FIELD"

Earlier in this book I mentioned the role the Department of Defense (DOD) played in getting COBOL established as a standard for commercial systems in both the government and industry. This particular effort was encouraged at the behest of the then Seven Dwarfs (Burroughs, Control Data, GE, NCR, Honeywell, Univac, and RCA) against Snow White (alias Big Blue), which was perceived to have something of an advantage in commercial data processing in the 1960s. DOD set out to level the commercial playing field and encourage good clean competition. COBOL promised software portability, automatic documentation, which would permit executives to read COBOL programs and find out what they were doing, and a lot of other nonsense.

In 1974, the same year of the NBS study, the National Science Foundation sponsored the "Computer Science and Engineering Research Study" (COSERS). It was intended to provide "a readily accessible record of past research in computer science and computer engineering, as well as some projections of future research directions." It had a steering committee of 14 well-known computer scientists including representatives from Bell Laboratories, DEC, IBM, Lawrence Livermore Laboratories, and several major universities. The supporting cast must have numbered in the thousands, and after 5 years of effort the magnum opus was finally completed in 1979. It had the following to say about language standardization:

> Standardization is both necessary and important. It makes software more reusable and allows competitive forces to produce more efficient processes. But standardization, particularly in older-generation programming languages such as FORTRAN and COBOL, can also freeze the United States into obsolete software practices. In short, maintaining standards at the lowest common denominator, in order to foster international cooperation and competition indeed contributes to a creeping paralysis in the country's inventory of software.
>
> Nowhere is this better illustrated than the current pervasive use of FORTRAN and COBOL. If software practices continue to drift, in 20 years the United States will have a national inventory of unstructured, hard-to-maintain, impossible-to-replace, programs written in FORTRAN and COBOL as the basis of its industrial and government activities.

The report then went on to state that this would give competitive advantage to the Soviets because "in fact, they plan to leapfrog FORTRAN and COBOL." COSERS concluded: "We could then face a software gap more serious than the missile gap of some years ago." (Those academic types really know how to get the government's attention.)

It doesn't seem that we are suffering from any great "software gap" with the Soviet Union. (When foreign rescue teams arrived in Armenia after the earthquakes, their work was hampered because there weren't any maps of the area, much less demographic and engineering data bases.) However, we have our national inventory of unstructured, hard-to-maintain, impossible-to-replace programs. These are now fondly referred to as the users' "investment in software." We have dug ourselves a big hole in the middle of the level playing field with government assistance and we might as well acknowledge that it is going to be extremely costly to climb out—CASE tools and C not withstanding.

The standards effort was a smashing success and COBOL has withstood the challenge of PL/1, which IBM intended as a replacement for both COBOL and FORTRAN. Nothing could better attest to the success of the COBOL standard than the fact that SAA mountain, looking down over the software quagmire, includes both COBOL and FORTRAN and not PL/1, a structured language.

The 1980 COSERS report published by MIT Press as "What Can Be Automated?" is 900 pages long, and its index does not contain a single reference to UNIX, although it has an entire section on operating systems, and MULTICS (the father of the illegitimate child) is referred to seven times.

If the parallel between the government's efforts in COBOL and UNIX are not sufficiently scary, I suggest you now go back and read the quotes from the COSERS report again, especially the part about "maintaining standards at the lowest common denominator, in order to foster international cooperation and competition." We ain't even got international cooperation on this one, we've got international conflict with offshore impetus coming from both directions and our native computer companies are split pretty much down the middle.

You say UNIX is not the lowest common denominator? Think about poor Herbert Zinn, Jr., an 18-year-old high-school dropout who was sentenced in 1989 to serve 9 months in prison, pay a $10,000 fine, and serve 2-1/2 years on probation for "breaking into AT&T computers in suburban Naperville and New Jersey, as well as into NATO computers run by AT&T in Burlington, NC, and at Robbins Air Force Base in Georgia." He reportedly stole 55 programs valued at $1.2 million, including "complex software relating to artificial intelligence and computers designs" and, as I understand it, some UNIX code as well. However, they weren't "classified," just "highly sensitive." Zinn is the first person convicted under the Computer Fraud and Abuse Act. There are some intriguing facts surrounding this simple case:

- Poor Herbert did not have the advantage of a Harvard education or graduate work in computer science at Cornell or Cal Berkeley or

Stanford. His father was not an expert on UNIX security working for the United States government, and he did not have friends who had worked on the UNIX mail system and left trap doors in the distributed version. No, he merely gained access to these computers through information obtained from "underground BBSes," and then was dumb enough to post his phone number and messages on the BBS. There must be thousands of hackers like Herbert who have browsed their way through government systems stealing a program here and there and screwing up a few data files. Just think of what those computer science grads who have been trained on UNIX could do. (We know they can "make a mistake" and bring 6000 UNIX computers down, but how many are prowling around undetected?)

- Herbert was intruding on the AT&T computers in 1987, when the Air Force was planning to tilt the playing field a little by requiring that AT&T UNIX be bid on its $1 billion order for minicomputers. We all know about that case. DEC wouldn't even bid because it thought the contract was wired, and it apparently was. Was that a level playing field? Is anyone in government questioning whether UNIX is an appropriate standard? Is this the way the government is compensating AT&T for breaking up the Bell System? Did anyone in government read the COSERS report? Has the government completely given up on privacy and security? Does anyone care? Hello . . . .

Of course, the quality of what the government contracts for may not be very important anyhow; there are cases where not much actually gets installed. That was reportedly the case on the large contract for UNIX-based systems for the National Security Agency. And software development still seems to be a problem. Consider a General Accounting Office analysis of nine U.S. Army software contracts which revealed that:

- 47 percent of the software delivered was not used.
- 29 percent was paid for, but not delivered.
- 19 percent was abandoned or reworked.
- 3 percent was used after changes.
- 2 percent was used as delivered.

That is certainly one way to level the playing field—just spread the money around whether anything delivered (or not delivered) is ever used or not. (The cancelled IRS project falls into the same category.)

Now that I have picked on two-thirds of the DOD, let's look at the Navy Department. About 2 years ago the Navy was placed under a 60-day restraining order during which it could not award new computer contracts in excess of $2.5 million dollars. This was a result of allegations by six competitors (Amdahl Corp., Vion Corp., NCR Comten, Storage Technology Corp., Memorex/Telex Corp., and PacifiCorp Capital, Inc.) that Navy procurement favored IBM. Among the accusations were the following comments:

- That the Navy "routinely draws up specifications that favor IBM."

- That EDS (the prime contractor on two Navy procurements totaling $1 billion) conducted "sham procurements" favoring IBM, and the Navy was responsible. (As a representative of PacifiCorp Capital reportedly said: "EDS is just doing what the Navy wants them to. If somebody hands you a billion dollars worth of business, you're going to do what they tell you to do. The prime contractor may be running the engine room, but we know who is running the damned ship.")

- That "the competitors make IBM-compatible equipment, usually at a lower price than IBM." (The importance of the IBM pricing umbrella when competing in the open systems market will be analyzed later.)

- That IBM "currently holds almost 55 percent of the Navy's large-scale computer base, compared with the company's 37 percent share government-wide." These numbers, supposedly government statistics, present other intriguing possibilities:

  - Since IBM has substantially more than 37 percent of the large-scale computer market outside the federal government, the Navy would seem to be more in line with the open commercial marketplace.

  - Since the Navy favors IBM so much, obviously there must be other federal organizations where IBM has substantially less than 37 percent of the large-scale computers installed. Is IBM being discriminated against in those cases?

  - Assuming that private enterprise is at least as sensitive to price and quality as is the federal government (a reasonably safe assumption), it would appear that overall government procurement policies should be brought under scrutiny, not just the Navy's.

The complaints against the Navy prompted me to recollect some past contract history. In the early 1960s, IBM received a request for reams of detailed technical information about all of its hardware and software. The request came from a fledgling organization that was developing something called SCERT, which was being proposed as a performance measurement system that could be used by the DOD (probably the Air Force) to automatically pick the best computer system based on a statement of requirements. The request stated that if IBM didn't provide the requested information, its products could never be recommended. To make a long story very short:

- The request was forwarded to those responsible for systems performance measurement, where the reaction was that it was "the most ludicrous idea we have seen in a long time." (This may have been a little severe; SCERT was certainly better than MIPS.)

- The inspiration for SCERT came from one Don Herman (the founder of COMRESS) who made a bundle of money on it.

- The same Don Herman left NCR COMTEN to become the first head of UNIX International. It's a small world.

It seems that no matter how you look at it, and regardless of its purpose, the federal government is trying to tilt the level playing field in one direction or another, frequently in directions that are at odds with each other.

13.3 SLAMMING OPEN DOORS AND WINDOWS

It's easy to kick the federal government around for what it has and has not done, but private enterprise can't feel very complacent, either.

13.3.1 Litigation

In the 1980s the computer news began to look like a court docket, with threats of more to come. IBM and Fujitsu accepted the arbiter's decision to the tune of $800 million for IBM, which is more than the total profits of the independent software industry since the time of its inception. The rich get richer, and the poor will not necessarily always be with us.

Then the Beatles' old company, Apple Corps, Ltd., sued Apple Computer over a secret agreement in which Apple Computer promised not to get in the music business!? That must have given Hewlett-Packard and Microsoft a few chuckles—first we have "look and feel," and then we have "the sound of music."

Along that line, Stanford University, trying to capitalize on the invention of a "talking glove" they believe was invented by a graduate student, was sued by VPL Research, Inc., which claims it got there first. The product was intended for either sight-impaired or hearing-impaired people. It could be classified as either a "feel and look," or a "feel and listen" device. Under any circumstances, it appeared to be a useful application of microprocessor technology.

Compaq dropped Businessland as a distribution channel because Businessland's Dave Norman had the audacity to state that IBM's MCA was an industry standard, and there was (or would be) no demand for the Compaq-sponsored Extended Industry Standard Architecture (EISA). Businessland thought about suing over that. IBM must have had a Mona Lisa smile—they know that large successful companies (Compaq hit $2 billion) don't treat their business associates or suppliers that way. If you do, not only are you a fat target for a lawsuit, but it makes your customers nervous. The rich get richer, and nouveau rich ain't got no class. Businessland, of course, had severe financial difficulties and was purchased.

And then, of course, there are those who even feel that icons and languages themselves should be protected. When you consider the foundation of some of these claims the next logical step may be to pay a licensing fee for the use of the digits 1-2-3 because they have become a proprietary "standard."

It would all be funny if it weren't so serious and unpredictable. In our litigious society, an enormous strain is being put on the referees. At least one of the players is demanding an instant replay after every down, creativity is being destroyed, there is no tempo left in the game, the very purpose of the game itself gets confused, and there is no end in sight. Meanwhile, the spectators are getting bored and frustrated with the whole spectacle.

13.3.2 Property, Protection, Ethics, and Crime

People have known for many years that the protection of intellectual property, as it pertains to software, was going to be a problem. Controversy over software copyrights and patents began about 25 years ago. Complexity gets added when firmware is introduced. Reverse engineering of hardware obscures the reality of the situation even more. Let's face it, we're still arguing about who invented modern computers in the first place. Aiken, Atanasoff, Bush, Eckert, Mauchly, Stibitz, Turing, and Wiener (and others) all had claims that are still being argued to this day.

Actually, despite all that, the industry managed to work reasonably well for a number of years. Major computer vendors had relatively simple cross-licensing agreements and went along their merry way. The major legal issues centered around antitrust and the announcement of phantom "fighting machines" to knock off competition. However, today there seems to be a new breed out there, and much of this change can be attributed to the personal computer.

What started as a hippie commune, with the avowed purpose of computer power to the people, has grown into a yuppie resort hotel where everyone wants to impress the rabble with their conspicuous achievement represented by earnings and stock prices. From an attitude of share and share alike, we have progressed to the general attitude of "what's mine is mine," and "what's yours is fair game." This attitude manifests in many ways pertinent to this book:

- The trends in the industry are not toward openness. The trend is toward protection and acquisition of property (intellectual, market-share, etc.). Only a few examples are necessary to prove the point.

- IBM is staking out its territory with SAA, and in the process is closing the open doors and windows of opportunity that permitted software-compatible mainframes and plug-compatible peripherals to proliferate. There is no question what the PS/2, MCA, and OS/2 EE are designed to do. Designing the AS/400 as the first "real SAA system" (and a sign of things to come) is about as closed as you can get. The only door being opened by IBM is one way—it leads to new territory and business opportunity.

- While Apple didn't exactly slam the door on the Apple II, the open standard of the commune, it has certainly shut down the window of opportunity by
  - Establishing Claris as an independent software vendor
  - Restricting, more effectively than any competitor possibly could, the market for the Apple II in favor of the Macintosh, a proprietary system
  - Attempting to inhibit the progress of the industry by what can, at best, be classified as a frivolous "look-and-feel" lawsuit

- AT&T attempted to establish proprietary rights and control over UNIX development, only to find that it was but one of a herd of poor little lambs that had gone astray and wandered in the wilderness. Regardless of the outcome of the shepherd's efforts, AT&T's original and unquestionable intent was to get all those little lost critters penned so they could be sheared but good. However, the faithful UNIX sheep got a little nervous when one of their number started howling at the moon about SPARC being a standard and about open systems. That is how the OSF and UNIX International got started. Now that AT&T has sold its interest in Sun and turned over most of its computer systems business to NCR, industry participants are a somewhat happier bunch.

With even the hint of success, all vendors of "open systems" exhibit a common propensity to make their own house secure. However, those who grew up during the "commune" days exhibit varying degrees of sensitivity to the property of others. Somewhere along the spectrum between using specific commands and icons, reverse engineering, and the actual lifting of source code, there are ethical as well as legal questions. Many of the new breed fail to demonstrate awareness, much less sensitivity, to the former, and willingly ignore the latter if the potential gain is sufficient. There seems to be an inability to discriminate between the following:

- The difference between sharing someone's food and their toothbrush in an open communal environment.

- The difference between sharing food in a communal environment and breaking into someone's house to raid the refrigerator.

- And we aren't just talking about hackers here, we are talking about "businessmen." It is little wonder that the trend is not only toward closing and locking the doors and windows, but buying an assault rifle to protect one's turf.

Vaporware has been around the computer industry practically since its inception, but we have now reached the point where it isn't just advertising and hype that are the problem; real products are being mislabeled and misrepresented. It is definitely "buyer beware" time. Some "relational" data base systems are more relational than others, and some aren't relational at all. Recently we have been treated to conflicting systems performance comparisons that remind me of the old cigarette advertisements about tar and nicotine.

You wouldn't keep going to a supermarket if it sold rice in cornmeal boxes; you wouldn't keep using a tailor who measured you for a suit and upon delivery told you it was necessary to make it larger (and charge you more) when you hadn't gained weight; you wouldn't pay a plumber $150 (much less $120 million) if the toilet still didn't flush; you wouldn't believe you were gaining competitive advantage by spending more money on computer equipment if your competitors (who spend less) consistently make more money than you do—would you?

However, the computer industry expects its customers to accept such practices (and more) on a routine basis. The credibility gap among vendors, information systems personnel, and users continues to widen.

Government, computer-communications vendors, and information systems "professionals" are afflicted with a lack of vision about the potential of emerging technologies and a lack of understanding of the limitations of these technologies (or at the very least, an unwillingness to acknowledge the limitations). This is indeed a very bad combination.

At the first IBM Programming Symposium in the late 1960s, Dr. Jerome Weisner of MIT spoke about the possible economic, sociological, cultural, and political consequences of the application of computer technology. He stated that to talk about controlling the application of technology was like talking about controlling a jet plane when it has reached the point of no return on takeoff—the only options are to take off or crash; there is no turning back!

Since Dr. Weisner's speech, more than 20 years ago, there has been both good and bad news. The good news is that the plane is still in the air—computers have become so much a part of daily lives that practically all the passengers recognize it is too late to change their minds about going for the ride. The bad news is that no one knows where we are going or who is flying the plane. Vague talk about heading toward the "information age" and "open systems" isn't very comforting to nervous passengers, whether they are the Fortune 500 jet-set ensconced in first class or the ordinary citizens crammed in the rear.

13.4 ISSUES

It is important to have some awareness of a few simple, but very important, issues.

At the present time, no one knows where our flight into the information age is going to land (Figure 13.1). It could be Sir Thomas More's *Utopia*; there are certainly indications that computer-communications networks have enormous potential for correcting many of the social, economic, legal, and even political injustices of modern society. It could be Aldous Huxley's *Brave New World*. Even setting genetic engineering aside, the increased stratification of society made possible by the computer is much worse than that of Henry Ford's "mass production," which is what inspired Huxley. Norbert Wiener recognized early on that the industrial revolution devalued human muscle, whereas "cybernetics" could devalue the human brain. Clerks, engineers, doctors, teachers, voters, and "experts" of all types can become slaves to computer-communications networks.

Our destination could also be George Orwell's *1984*. There were legitimate reasons for concern about the community-wide networks portrayed in the NBS Study. Those networks have the inherent ability to track where individuals are and what they are doing. Winston would find that even time away from the TV tube could be tracked, and an IRS audit is like "Room 101" for an ever-increasing number of Americans.

Wiener was right when he stated: "This new development (cybernetics) has unbounded possibilities for good or for evil." It has now been more than

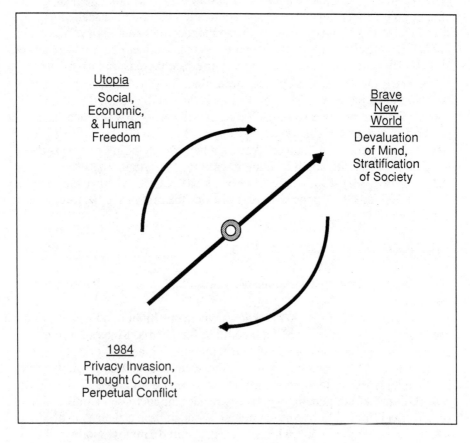

Figure 13.1– The Information Age—More, Huxley, or Orwell?

40 years since this observation, and it remains the central issue that should concern all of us.

Assuming that the majority of those on board would vote in favor of Utopia, or at least against the other two destinations, the question then becomes: Who has the responsibility for laying out a course to get there? Simply stated, the issue is over what role the government should play in encouraging and/or providing the national computer-communications infrastructure which must inevitably develop. Perhaps the government's role should be determined by comparisons with

- The U.S. Postal Service (and the Post Office Department before it)
- Interstate highway development
- Incentives given to railroads
- Incentives given to airlines
- Just how important a national computer-communications infrastructure is to the nation's and its citizens' well-being

Regardless of the federal government's role in encouraging and/or developing such an infrastructure, what is its regulatory role over such networks as they evolve?

The role of the federal government in establishing standards, ensuring openness (at a certain level), and ensuring a reasonably level playing field becomes an issue regardless of the degree of leadership or other involvement. If private enterprise is to be responsible for the development of the national computer-communications infrastructure, where does "cooperation" among vendors end and restraint of trade begin?

While there are numerous other issues that should be addressed, the above list should be enough to keep us all busy for at least a little while.

13.5 OPINIONS

In summary, the federal government has not seen fit to provide what I consider to be essential leadership in the following areas:

- The development of a national computer-communications infrastructure to take advantage of emerging technologies in solving social and economic problems of national importance
- The establishment of security and privacy safeguards, which are required to assure the well-being of the nation and its citizens, and the education of the general populace about the nature of these dangers

- The encouragement of a healthy and competitive computer-communications industry, through the intelligent use of advanced technology within the government itself

On the other hand, the computer-communications industry has contributed substantially to a credibility gap between itself and its customers by consistently overrating technology and consistently underestimating the problems in implementing its "solutions."

Despite all this, there is reason for hope. I have found that leaders within the computer industry are confronting their mutual problems and are willing to cooperate in solving these problems. They have stood up to present their points of view on complex and sometimes controversial topics. Nowhere has this been more clearly demonstrated than in their availability to be interviewed on Killen & Class Productions' "High Technology with Killen & Class" television program. I believe that such openness is good for the industry, and I believe it will provide a framework of understanding that can help us all on our flight into the information age.

14

Infrastructures, Architectures, and Standards

Unlike the interstate highway system, the federal government has not attempted to define a national computer-communications infrastructure or provided leadership to define the technology and standards for the development of such a network. The tendency has been to depend on the fallout from military programs to advance the state of computer-communications technology. This hasn't worked very well in recent years.

Two things resulted from this failure:

1. The continuing plea for government support for research and development in the computer industry. These research requests for specific technical assistance range from research on basic technology to high-definition TV (HDTV) and seem to be based on the virtual panic that has been generated by "Japan, Inc." (The problem is not so much with technology, but the application of the technology in product development.)

2. Since the government has not been specifically asked to assist or provide leadership in the development of a national computer-communications infrastructure, the commercial application of computer and communications technologies has been left up to private industry. Essentially, this means that IBM will have substantial control of the base architecture of any national infrastructure that develops. This is indeed unfortunate, and it is necessary to look at the realities of the commercial market.

14.1   COMMUNICATIONS NETWORKS

The big news in networking during the early 1970s was ARPANET (a network established by the Advanced Research Projects Agency—packet switching was supposed to solve all the world's problems); it was well suited to a timesharing environment. Some of the creators of ARPANET started Telenet to extend the wonders of packet switching to the commercial environment. All of this should begin to sound familiar, because as ARPANET grew into a national research and development network of government agencies, universities, and private research organizations, UNIX flourished. Now, various vendors arc trying to cxtcnd UNIX into the commercial environment.

Let's look at an actual case study of the economics of networking in the commercial environment at that time. It will explain a lot of what has happened since then and provide some guidance for the future.

14.1.1   The "Upsizing" Case Study

There is a great deal of talk today about "downsizing," from mainframes to minicomputers, and from minicomputers to intelligent workstations, which of course is anathema to any vendor being downsized by a competitor. This case study will present the economics of "upsizing" and shed some light on some possible impacts of downsizing.

Figure 14.1 presents the actual experience of a diversified international company that decided to replace its stand-alone computers throughout the United States and Europe with centralized mainframes in a single location.

The economics were impressive. Before the consolidation began (in 1970-71), computer hardware costs were rising much more rapidly than were company revenues. By replacing 18 smaller IBM systems, ranging from a System/3 to System/370 Model 158, with a then top-of-the-line IBM System/370 Model 165/8, the company was able to cut annual hardware costs from a high of $9.1 million in 1970 to $2.8 million in 1976. This type of networking was obviously not very attractive to IBM.

Of course, this reduction in the cost of computer hardware was somewhat offset by increased costs of terminals (some of which were really minicomputers used for remote job entry) and communications costs. At that time, the increased communications costs were especially noticeable. Comparing the cost distribution of the subject company with other industries revealed that 31 percent of its network costs were for communications (primarily leased lines ranging from 1200 baud to 50 kilobaud, although a couple thousand in-

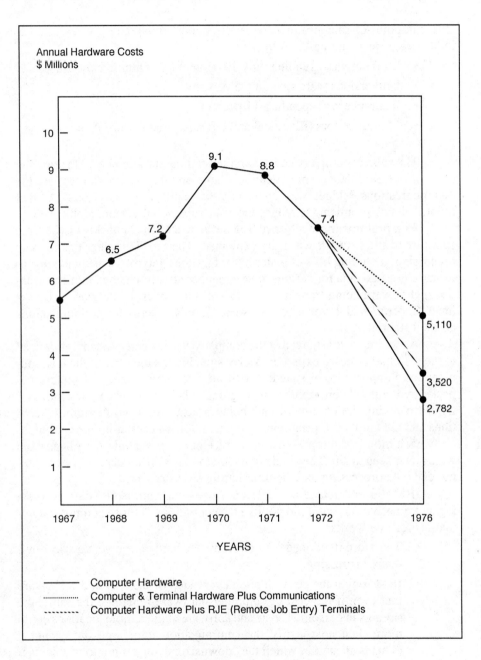

Figure 14.1 – Impact of a "Sensible" Network

telligent, point-of-sale terminals were also being polled daily), whereas other industries were spending the following:

- Banking was spending only 13 percent on communications.
- Universities were spending 5 percent.
- Insurance was spending 11 percent.
- Manufacturers (Electrical and DP Equipment) were spending 7 percent.

The subject company had a communications staff dedicated to reducing costs of not only data communications, but also telephone and telex, but the communications budget was constantly scrutinized by corporate. At that point, Telenet, promising to reduce the costs substantially, entered the picture.

At a preliminary meeting at Telenet's offices in Cambridge (MA), the structure of the network was fully explained. They made it clear that all data processing, including bills of material for factories, payroll, worldwide inventories, classified data for various government contracts, batched retail transactions, etc., were being transmitted back and forth over the network. The Telenet "experts" said it would be "no sweat" to reduce network communications cost substantially.

A meeting was arranged at the company's data center. When introduced to the nationally known expert on packet switching, a member of the Communications Support Group stated: "With all due respect, sir, if I understand packet switching, I don't think you are going to be able to save us any money." After reviewing the volume of data being transmitted from the remote locations and the number of print lines being transmitted back from the central facility each month, the representatives of Telenet left shaking their heads and were never seen again. They had not understood the differences between commercial data processing and the timesharing environment.

IBM did understand the difference between commercial data processing and timesharing, but it did not like the economics of those computer-communications networks:

- The aforementioned loss of computer hardware revenue was obviously distressing.
- IBM fought the consolidation every step of the way and was aware that even if the cost of computer hardware remained the same, the savings in personnel costs and software at the remote locations could more than cost-justify the centralization into large data centers. (This is an area in which the "downsizers" may run into problems if they ever decide to do a true cost analysis.)

- In addition, IBM knew the subject company was a strong advocate of distributed processing. The plan was to consolidate and standardize hardware-software systems and then proceed with the "orderly distribution of processing back to the using organizations." "Orderly distribution" refers to balancing the reduced communications costs against potential increased operating costs at the remote node.
- Finally, and this has continuing significance for the "downsizers" at all levels, large mainframes could replace twice as many smaller stand-alone systems than anticipated by their performance ratios (by "performance" I am referring to throughput, not MIPS), because smaller systems were not used as effectively as large systems and peak loads are naturally smoothed across time zones.

IBM had to do something about the potential threats of computer networking epitomized by this case study. Its answer was to provide an IBM preferred network architecture. Thus, SNA was born.

14.1.2 Architectures—SNA and SAA

The name of the whole game IBM has played and continues to play with "architectures" is "control the distribution of function over the processing hierarchy" (see Figure 11.1). As the standard-bearer of mainframe computing, IBM has been waging a 20-year war against minicomputers assuming their proper place in the processing hierarchy. First, IBM established mainframes as host computers under SNA, then, when personal computers entered the corporate environment, it attacked the other flank of minicomputers with microprocessor technology.

Now, high-performance RISC-based intelligent workstations are fighting a fierce border war, threatening (with more bravado than common sense) to wipe out not only minicomputers, but mainframes as well. While IBM doesn't take this too seriously, it does see UNIX-based IWSs as an opportunity to defeat minicomputers in their traditional areas of strength—interactive timesharing.

The primary problems of this war have as much to do with terminology as technology and computer architecture. I rejected the idea of classifying mainframes, minicomputers, and microprocessors based on architecture very early on, even though, in the early 1970s, the simple rule was 32-bit mainframes, 16-bit minicomputers, and 8-bit microprocessors. A more lasting and practical classification is cost. Therefore, I adopt the general rule of thumb that anything over $200,000 is a mainframe, anything more than $20,000 is classified as a minicomputer, and anything less than $20,000 is classified as a personal computer (intelligent terminal or workstation).

This classification has stood the test of time rather well. Therefore, when Pyramid Technology Corp. announces an "MIServer" (as it did in February, 1989) promising a "massive boost in computing power" with systems up to 140 MIPS—"power equal to that of the largest mainframe systems,"— I look at the price ($700,000 to $1.8 million) and dump them in the mainframe category. It doesn't matter whether they are RISC machines, whether Pyramid has always considered itself a UNIX-based minicomputer vendor, or even whether the whole thing is packaged as a portable; as far as I am concerned, it is a mainframe. The corporate controller and IS department are going to be involved in its purchase, and it can't be hidden in a departmental (much less personal) budget. When coming under such scrutiny, the hardware will not be evaluated on promised MIPS, and UNIX will not avoid questions about robustness and security.

14.1.3 SNA

SNA, regardless of its extended gestation period, has been enormously successful from IBM's perspective. It is the networking architecture for the business environment; it is real; it is installed in tens of thousands of locations; it is not going to go away. More importantly, SNA has been highly successful in controlling the distribution of function and data over the processor hierarchy. Let's briefly look at how effective IBM's SNA strategy has been and look at what IBM is planning (see Figure 14.2).

The "proper hierarchy" used by the company in the networking case study presented above was an obvious solution in 1971. The purpose of consolidating into these large data centers was to replace stand-alone batch systems, paving the way for the "orderly distribution of processing" back to the appropriate level in the hierarchy. It is this hierarchy that IBM was attempting to control. What was a proper distribution of function in 1971 has remained remarkably stable in practice since that time. Below, I will review the proper hierarchy shown in Figure 14.2.

Level I—Truly heavy computation, whether done on a vector, array processor, or supercomputer, normally will be channeled through a mainframe node on a network, if for no other reason than a mainframe has proven to be necessary as a "front end" for the supercomputer. Large central mainframes have literally evolved into enormous "data base machines" (or superservers by IBM's latest definition). For those who have decentralized and continue to

LEVEL	Proper Hierarchy (1971)	Original SNA (1974)	IBM Hierarchy (1983)	IBM's "End-User Software Environment" (1986)
I Mainframes > $200,000 (Processor)	**Large Mainframes** 1. Heavy Computation 2. Transaction Processing (large data bases) 3. RJE Replacement of Stand-alone Batch	**Large Mainframes** 1. Heavy Computation 2. Transaction Processing (all data bases) 3. Timesharing 4. Program Development & Maintenance 5. Collection & Editing of Data 6. Network Control	**Mainframes** 1. Heavy Computation 2. Transaction Processing (central data bases) 3. Timesharing 4. Program Development & Maintenance 5. Network Management	**Central Hosts** 1. Operational Applications 2. Operational Data Bases 3. Central Library 4. Network Management
II Minicomputers > $20,000 (Processor)	**Minicomputers** 1. Network Control 2. Scientific Timesharing 3. Program Development & Maintenance 4. Simple Transaction Processing (work unit DBMS)	**3705 Controller** 1. Limited Network Control	**3725 Controller** **43xx, System/3X** 1. Limited Network Control 2. Limited Local Transaction Processing (departmental) 3. Replacement of Competitive Minicomputers	**Departmental Processor** 1. Professional Office System 2. Electronic Mail 3. Document Library 4. Departmental Data Base 5. Financial Modeling & Analysis 6. Data Extraction Program
III IWSs < $20,000 (System)	**Intelligent Terminals** 1. Collection, Editing, & Display of Data 2. Terminal Control	**3790 Controller** 1. Terminal Control	**Series/1, 8100s, PC-based** 1. Collection, Editing, & Display of Data 2. Personal Data Bases 3. Personal Calculations 4. Limited Program Development 5. Terminal Control	**IWS** 1. Dialog Manager 2. Professional Office System 3. Integrated Decision Support Tools 4. Application Dev. Tools 5. Word Processor 6. Instructional System 7. Com. & File Transfer to Host
IV Variable	**Terminals** 1. Data Entry & Display 2. Sensing & Control Devices	**Terminals** 1. Data Entry & Display 2. Sensing & Control Devices	**Terminals** 1. Data Entry & Display 2. Sensing & Control Devices	**Terminals**

Figure 14.2 – Processing Hierarchy and "Architecture"

have what is essentially batch processing on smaller mainframes, the economics in the "upsizing" case study still apply.

Level II—I still believe that network management should be off-loaded from the mainframe onto an appropriate minicomputer (more on that later). I still think that the most economical solution for most scientific and engineering work is at the work unit (minicomputer) level, and this will generally remain true regardless of how many MIPS are packaged in an IWS that sells for less than $20,000. This applies to program development and maintenance also. And, it remains true that as much processing as possible should be done as close to the point of transaction (work unit) as possible for both cost (communications) and quality control (data base management).

Level III—It is remarkable that the functional definition of an IWS (or intelligent terminal, as I defined it in 1971) has remained so appropriate for 18 years. Certainly, there can be little question that the primary application of microprocessors is word and text processing; however, "collection, editing, and display of data" has broad applicability when my definition of data is used, and if "editing" is viewed in its broadest sense (changing a formula in a spreadsheet can be viewed as editing), it is not difficult to see that the functional distribution applies to

- Use of spreadsheet packages
- Personal data bases
- A design engineer working on a three-dimensional model
- The control of "less intelligent" terminals

Level IV—When this definition was first established, it applied to 2260-type displays, remote card readers, printers and keyboards of all types, "dumb" point-of-sale terminals, plotters, etc. Today, the fact that we have laser printers, scanners, and high-resolution displays only makes the proper role of the IWS more clear. Indeed, the "new peripherals" will require all of the MIPS the IWS can offer if they are to be effectively "controlled." (Visualize an operator sitting at an IWS that is "editing" scanned documents by applying pattern recognition to update encoded data bases, building a full-text index of the document, and compressing any images that must be stored. Even the fastest IWS will have plenty to do at its proper level.)

I won't belabor the fact that SNA was not originally designed to support the proper hierarchy. I will belabor the fact that SNA's primary observed purpose was to delay acceptance of the reality of existing and new technologies at Levels II and III, this despite the avowed purpose of leading its customers toward distributed processing. It is wise to remember this as IBM now talks about "connectivity" and "openness."

It is also wise to remember that IBM was remarkably competent at achieving its objectives for nearly a decade. Only after the PC was announced in 1981 and became successful did IBM begin to lose its stranglehold on the hearts and minds of the commercial data-processing community.

By 1983, the IBM hierarchy was so confused that no one could make sense out of it. The allocation of IBM products across Levels II and III in Figure 14.2 doesn't seem to make sense because it *didn't* make sense. Semi-intelligent "controllers" like the 37XX and the 8100 became intermixed with minicomputers, mainframes, small-business systems, and "office products" (not shown). Even IBM customers came to realize that text processing was most cost-effectively done on PCs, and the revolution was under way.

By 1986, IBM finally established a recommended "software environment" for its users, which implied that certain functions were most effectively addressed at the various processing levels. Unfortunately, by being related to IBM software, it had a certain natural bias. However, it did recognize that there were three distinct levels in the processing hierarchy. IBM's depiction of the hierarchy showed two arrows: one indicating "information extraction" from mainframes to departmental processors and IWSs, and the other showing "information archiving" going in the opposite direction.

All this "progress" took more than 15 years from the time IBM recognized that a hierarchy of mainframe (System/360, Model 65), minicomputer (IBM 1130), and IWS (IBM 2250 Display) systems was the only cost-effective solution for IBM's internal planning departments. That, friends, is control of the acceptance of technological reality in the marketplace.

In 1978, Dr. A. L. Scherr published an article called "Distributed Data Processing" *(IBM Systems Journal*, vol. 17, no. 4), which addressed the general problems of distributed processing and properly concluded that if the advantages of distributed processing were to be achieved, the following would be necessary:

- Centralized design of the system data base and control over its content, level of usage (by particular elements of the application programs), synchronization, recovery, and distribution

- Structuring the application program into distributable pieces and defining the unit of distribution

- And, once a distributed application is up and running, centrally controlling the level of the programs, the data bases, and the operating systems themselves (which would require at least a central library control and distribution package that operated in the central node of the system)

Dr. Scherr then concluded:

Distributed processing offers an unprecedented level of flexibility in the design of applications systems. Because flexibility is inevitability a two-edged sword, however, it is more necessary than ever before to proceed with understanding and with deliberate, manageable plans. It is for this reason more than any other that the cornerstone of any effective distributed processing system must be the ability to implement a high degree of centralized control.

That was a sound conclusion, and it remains true to this day. IBM's problem has been that, in attempting to solve the general problems of distributed processing, it has essentially "protected" its customers by putting them on such a short hardware-software leash that precious little processing has ever been distributed from the large central mainframes. A highly centralized, "star-type" network has been the result. This is the de facto standard in the commercial market at the present time.

14.1.4 SAA

In 1987, Dr. Scherr published another article on distributed processing—"Structures for Networks of Systems" (*IBM Systems Journal*, vol. 26, no. 1)—in which he points out that, with the introduction of minicomputers and especially with the advent of personal computers there has been increasing debate about the proper role of mainframes, departmental processors, and the desktop personal computer, and that there have been arguments that "one or more of these classes of machine and/or usage will disappear."

After a well-reasoned review of both the history and potential of distributed data processing, Dr. Scherr concludes:

In this paper, we have looked at a full spectrum of possibilities. It is difficult to escape the conclusion that each type of system has a significant role to play, and it is difficult to imagine technology changes that would eliminate any of the types. Each type of system represents unique advantages that argue strongly for its usage. Thus, we conclude that multiple-tier systems will be in general use, particularly in large corporations, for many years to come.

Shortly after this article appeared, IBM announced SAA and clearly signaled its direction for the 1990s. At that time, IBM reaffirmed its support for certain OSI standards and presented a status report on "connectivity" (see Figure 14.3). Then, as we all know, IBM joined OSF in 1988, committing to work on not only UNIX, but standard interfaces and connectivity with the SAA environment. IBM is giving its customers what they want, or, I might say, what some of them have demanded. It makes a pretty picture of openness, but what are things like in the real world?

IBM Vice President Ellen Hancock had quite a bit to say about that. When I met her in late 1990 and asked her about OSI and SNA, she stated: "It will be years and years before OSI will have the equivalent" of what SNA has now. While OSI standards exist to connect devices, they are not complete enough to define a full network.

She also stated that it was improbable that OSI would ever catch up. To support this contention, she cited the rejection and argument that surrounded the eventual acceptance of LU6.2 into the OSI draft standard, just because it was an IBM proprietary protocol, pointing out that the industry now has to wait for OSI to have peer-to-peer capability. I agree.

On the subject of network management systems, she observed the following:

- That, while she liked the OSI/Network Management Forum's linking of network management systems with a standardized protocol, the problems of interfacing NetView/PC with the Common Management Information Protocol were moot points because "NetView/PC is there now and already has strong existing vendor support."

- As far as IBM supporting AT&T's Unified Network Management Architecture, she pointedly stated that, "NetView doesn't work well as a subsystem."

She then promised the early release of an "explosion of network management capabilities."

The other message that came across from Ms. Hancock was that demand for ISDN was growing and IBM would announce enhanced capabilities later in the year through its partnership with Siemens AG. However, she expressed concern that ISDN differed from switch vendor to switch vendor, and

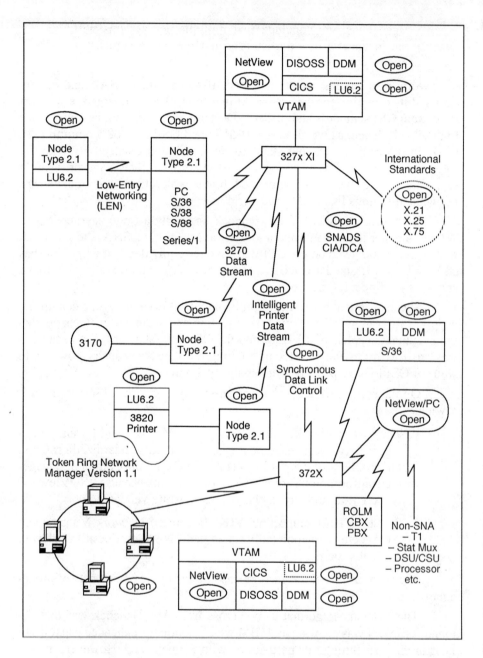

Figure 14.3 – The Status of "Connectivity" at SNA Announcement (*Source: IBM*)

promised that IBM would also announce voice-data integration products independent of ISDN. The two companies have done what she said they would do.

The message is clear. SNA is out there, OSI is only promised. In the meantime, if you want to build a network, you've got the de facto industry standard, and the promise that open industry standards will be supported when and if the functional specifications are ever refined; by which time, SNA/SAA will probably be at a substantially more advanced level.

For example, IBM already has advanced peer-to-peer networking (APPN) for the AS/400s and S/3Xs. Both APPN and APPC (LU6.2) are an integral part of OS/400, the AS/400 operating system. IBM has incorporated APPN under SAA and is opening it up by offering it to OSI.

IBM's "architectures" (SNA/SAA) must become the basis for any national infrastructure for business data processing. This is reality. It is also reality that the System/3X and AS/400 have always been more successful in Europe than they have been in the United States, despite the standards activities of X/Open. No other proprietary or open architecture will be able to exist independent of this reality as we progress through the 1990s. It will be impossible to take very many hops on the "open, network playing field" without bumping into the existing SAA mountain.

IBM's SNA/SAA strategy will make it easy to bump into the mountain. When SAA was announced, IBM published a diagram depicting the status of "connectivity" (Figure 14.3). My only comment is that all of those open doors swing in both directions. Competitors, including partners in OSF, may view them as a way to simplify penetration of the commercial market; IBM views them as open doors to markets in which it has never been especially successful. UNIX and OSF are the nicest presents IBM could have wished for. It is as if everyone got together and decided to wear "tennies" to play the game on the level playing field—IBM knows you aren't going to do very much mountain climbing with that equipment.

SNA is currently the de facto standard. IBM is investing billions of dollars in SAA, substantially more than the combined investment of the open systems efforts. The objective is to make the SAA-supported operating environments into a single, tightly integrated, distributed operating system. It is against this probable de facto standard that UNIX-based open systems must compete if they are to penetrate the commercial market.

14.2 OPERATING SYSTEMS AND DBMSs

14.2.1 UNIX versus OS/400

When the AS/400 was announced in the summer of 1988, IBM put on the biggest announcement in its history. Since most IBM customers would not settle for the simple statement that the AS/400 was the first real SAA system, William O. Grabe, assistant general manager of IBM's Applications Business Systems, was called on the explain how things fit together within IBM's still confused midrange (minicomputer) product line. This led to the following comments about the IBM 9370 and UNIX:

> As for the 9370, its strengths play best in large accounts supported by staffs with strong System/370-based skills . . . or where the primary requirements include the distribution of System/370 host applications . . . or where support exists for applications such as CAD/CAM or numeric intensive computing . . . or where there's a need to coexist or communicate with other vendors in the network . . . or where there are UNIX applications.

> We've said in the past that our AIX (IBM's version of UNIX) platform–which runs across the PS/2, the RT, and the System/370–should be the primary choice where customers have UNIX requirements such as for federal government programs. And that still applies.

> But there's a really important point to consider in comparing the AIX operating system with the AS/400 Operating System: they represent two totally different philosophies.

> AIX is the right choice for companies whose primary requirement is portability across multiple vendors, and who have an established base of UNIX programmers . . . programmers who are willing to build the systems themselves and to work with the operating system to customize their solutions.

> For those customers who don't want to get involved in the internals of an operating system . . . who don't have large expert computer staffs . . . who operate in

> the commercial business world where immediate solutions provide the competitive edge . . . or who need to migrate System/36 and 38 programs, the high level of integration on the AS/400 makes it the solution that fits like it was made-to-order. It's just plain easier to learn and use.

The initial reaction in the marketplace has confirmed IBM's assessment of ease of use. The AS/400, announced with over 1000 applications packages available (a figure that has now grown to 7000), has been well received and has sold well. Many systems go into businesses without any systems personnel; there is reason to believe that this will continue. The AS/400 established a standard of usability for real-world business applications. It is extremely doubtful that UNIX, for commercial applications, will gain very much market share at the expense of OS/400, despite our best prognostications.

14.2.2 UNIX versus IBM/370 Operating Systems

UNIX is easier to use than IBM/370 mainstream operating systems—MVS, VM, and DOS/VSE—and in a classic timesharing environment is also substantially more cost-effective. However, UNIX does not currently have the functionality and robustness required for large commercial applications, and all vendors have extended versions of UNIX when competing in that environment. It may be possible to create a UNIX that will compete directly with MVS/ESA, but it will no longer be UNIX, and it will not come out of any of the standards or cooperative efforts. As functionality and robustness increase, ease of use and performance will decease. Just as Bell Labs noted about security, adding necessary security destroys the very ease of access that made the system so attractive. That also applies to ease of use.

At the present time, a great deal of work needs to be done on standard UNIX to make it competitive or even acceptable in the large-scale commercial market. Such things as virtual memory, large file handling, record locking, security, the management of complex I/O subsystems consisting of multiplexed channels and highly intelligent controllers, performance statistics, and that old bugaboo, security, are all beyond the basic capabilities of UNIX. It is difficult not to agree with Omri Serlin, president of Itom International and a leader in attempting to establish performance standards for on-line transaction processing, when he states: "It's hard to take UNIX seriously as a tool in the multiprocessing transaction-oriented environments when the basic file system isn't very robust and doesn't understand things like record indexing."

In fact, security alone is enough to rule UNIX out of the large-scale commercial environment. Am I beating a dead horse on this one? Not really, the darn critter keeps raising its ugly head. After the Morris affair and the sentencing of Zinn to jail under the 1986 Computer Fraud and Abuse Act, the West German Government began arresting members of the Chaos Computer Club for espionage because they wandered around through sensitive systems and sold classified data and access codes to the Russians, who probably are hacking around right now. These events have one thing in common—UNIX. This has all the makings of a national scandal and obviously has been going on for a long time. If I were to recommend systems to a business right now, I would be hard put to recommend a UNIX-based system for any applications of significance (from routine accounting to strategic planning) in which security is a significant factor. On the other hand, I would recommend UNIX systems for many other business applications and for most computer-aided workstation applications.

One of the "solutions" to some of these problems is to ride a DBMS on the shaky UNIX platform and let that handle some of the deficiencies. This is not a very satisfactory solution for either the DBMS vendor or the user— it is expensive and complicated for both of them. However, some vendors of proprietary systems are doing just that. Vendors of proprietary systems—somewhat of a dying breed—have the advantage: they have designed hardware, operating system, and DBMS to work together. In addition, the dependence on various DBMSs destroys applications portability.

It does not appear that UNIX will gain significant market share against large-scale proprietary systems (mainframes, by my definition).

14.2.3   UNIX versus OS/2, MS-DOS, etc.

UNIX is not easier to use than personal computer operating systems, and the addition of graphic interfaces will not hide this fact. Because MS-DOS is "out there" and people have been trained on it, it will exist for a long, long time. Remember IBM's experience trying to get rid of DOS on the System/360-370. After nearly 25 years of concerted effort, DOS/VSE is still the operating system of choice for about 50 percent of the System/370 installations—all this after IBM has tried to convince "data-processing professionals" of the benefits of progress and new technology. End users are not going to flock to *any* new operating system, let alone one that is more complex.

Most personal computer users use only a small percent of the capabilities of their operating systems now; not many of them are going to change to something more complex. In fact, not many of them will change to something simpler. UNIX will not gain a great deal of market share from current MS-DOS, ProDos, Apple Mac, or any other personal computer operating system being used for general business (office) purposes. And those who are going to graduate to OS/2 (whatever flavor) will want to make the transition as easy as possible.

To compare the shift from DOS to UNIX to the switch from CP/M to DOS is absurd. The personal computer explosion was just beginning then, and DOS had IBM and the PC behind that shift. Now UNIX is battling against both the old and entrenched and a new operating system(s). The individual personal computer users are going to stick with what they have when they are in stand-alone mode, and when on a network, there are better and more secure ways of communicating with others than by using UNIX.

14.2.4 Will the Real UNIX Market Stand Up?

It seems obvious that

- UNIX-based systems will probably not grow to 20 percent of the total computer market.
- UNIX is not robust or secure enough to serve as the centralized host in a large network.
- UNIX is not suited for, nor will it be accepted as, a departmental processor in the tightly integrated distributed data base environment.
- It is neither needed by, nor will it be accepted by, the great mass of clerical and accounting types who are using spreadsheets and word processing on stand-alone PCs.
- It is unlikely that the traditional UNIX applications (scientific and engineering) and markets (federal government, higher educational institutions, and private research laboratories) will grow sufficiently in relation to the overall computer market to obtain 20 percent market share. This is true despite the best efforts of the federal government to extend UNIX beyond its capabilities.

There is a possibility that the shift in operating systems usage could occur without the scientific and engineering market having to grow all that much. How is this for a real-life horror story?:

- IBM decides that UNIX is going to be a standard for scientific and engineering work, which it appears they have. It has very little to lose since its track record hasn't been all that great.

- If IBM now becomes successful in the scientific and engineering market with the RS/6000 and 9370s at the expense of its traditional minicomputer competitors, there could be a significant shift away from its proprietary systems. The old lion of the proprietary jungle isn't sniffing around that new open watering hole just to see whether the water is safe to drink—it may have dinner on its mind as well.

While the above scenario could possibly result in dramatic shifts in operating systems usage just within traditional applications and markets, I anticipate that there are appropriate opportunities for UNIX growth on the leading edge of hardware-software development.

14.3 HARDWARE SYSTEMS

It is entirely appropriate that RISCs are inextricably connected with the surge of interest in UNIX. Microprocessor technology, in terms of both cost and application, has the capability of freeing us from the dull gray world of the general-purpose computer.

Today, microprocessor technology is inexpensive enough to permit us to differentiate processors by performance and application. A RISC is substantially more cost-effective at doing the integer arithmetic necessary for driving high-resolution displays and laser printers, and for image processing and graphics applications. Vector and array processors are more cost-effective for scientific applications; data base engines with associative memory will be more cost-effective for data base applications; symbol processing engines for the cognitive scientists, and list processors for artificial intelligence applications. This is not the time to standardize on processors; this is the time to differentiate and mechanize hardware, and we can use the CAD/CAM (computer-aided design and manufacturing) tools of the technology itself to permit variety, not standardization.

At this point, programming raises its ugly head. All of these specialized engines depend on software to be effectively integrated with other applications and environments. For even though it may not be wise to drive specialized engines too far beyond their bounds (in terms of thinking that RISCs will replace all general-purpose CISCs), they will inevitably be networked and have to talk with each other. Compilers and program development tools must be able to take advantage of the hardware technology effectively, and relatively inexpensive operating systems are necessary. It is here that UNIX becomes important. An easily transportable operating system is necessary to facilitate the differentiation and mechanization of new hardware products, both as a development platform for the system itself and also for the end product. The portability of UNIX is substantially more important than the promised portability of applications across the various UNIX-based platforms. (And it's a good thing, because applications portability will remain pretty much "snake oil" anyhow.)

UNIX, or some relatively clean, unencumbered, portable operating system, is desirable right where it is being accepted (and demanded), straddling the border between IWS and minicomputers. With this understanding, it is possible to draw at least a rough map of the level playing field (see Figure 14.4).

These specialized UNIX-based systems are appropriate as professional workstations (and small minicomputers, by my definition) for individuals and/or small works units. I believe that these UNIX-based systems should be integrated with office systems (departmental processor-servers) at a relatively low level for data base and network management. This does not preclude a geographically distributed UNIX-based network for the work unit interpersonal communication and file transfer. However, it does preclude the idea that UNIX will be used for organizational and management control of the distributed data base environment as I described it earlier in this book. (If tails had brains, they might think they wagged dogs, but general system theory says that progressive centralization dictates the development of a "leading part" that controls the whole organism. UNIX-based systems are intelligent appendages; they are not that leading part.)

As far as productivity is concerned, these specialized professional systems are specifically designed to improve productivity at the human-machine dyad, not only in their interface, but in their applications as well. These UNIX-based systems are partially appropriate for addressing work unit productivity. They provide the processing power at the interface, while a distributed data base engine will provide the necessary centralization and control that Dr. Scherr outlined in his "Distributed Data Processing" paper.

To be cost-justified, these professional IWSs must demonstrate that they affect institutional performance. It is one thing to substitute a personal computer for an adding machine and hope it helps old Harry do his spreadsheets. It is quite another to put a $20,000+ workstation on someone's desk. Such a machine must demonstrate institutional performance improvement or at least appear to contribute to the organization's success.

Finally, these systems, by definition, will be the knowledge nodes on the network. Professional employees (and their systems) are the repositories of knowledge. Professional workstations will eventually evolve into the

"knowledge capture" systems for the distributed network, and by my definition, knowledge becomes data once it is stored on the artificial system (computer network).

It can be clearly seen that UNIX-based systems operating on the level
playing field can both complement and supplement proprietary systems as defined by SAA (see Figure 12.1). The interesting and challenging work for the
1990s will be in developing specific applications solutions (in the true sense

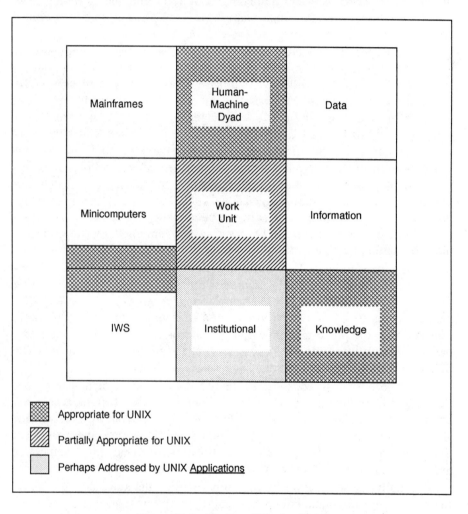

Figure 14.4 – The Level Playing Field

of the word) on appropriate hardware-software platforms. Progressive differentiation will be accompanied by progressive mechanization of increasingly complex aspects of human endeavor (that is what expert systems domains are all about). There is sufficient challenge here for all of our human resources. The interesting work is out in the open, on the level playing field. UNIX has a significant role to play—it would be unfortunate if it were diverted into areas where it is currently not appropriate.

Let's summarize briefly what we have covered to this point in this section:

1. There is no effective leadership from government to provide an open national computer-communications infrastructure.

2. The efforts to create open systems interfaces and standards lags the development of SNA by several years and is unlikely to catch up in the foreseeable future. Therefore, SNA will remain a de facto networking standard for business and will continue to coexist with open networks as they develop.

3. The functional economics of computer-communications networks will continue to dictate a proper hierarchy of mainframes, minicomputers, and microprocessor-based systems. This "proper" distribution of processing power and data can be anticipated (predicted) and will change relatively slowly regardless of the rapid advances of technology.

4. Appropriate operating systems to support the functional distribution of processing and data over the network are determined by ease of use, functionality, and performance.

5. UNIX-based systems, as they currently exist, are appropriate for a relatively narrow band of the processing spectrum (mainframe, minicomputer, microprocessor) outside the scientific and engineering community. The constraints that limit UNIX are

   • Functionality on the high end, where it will continue to be behind accepted standards in the industry for business applications

   • Ease of use for small business and work unit (departmental) applications

   • Ease of use for a substantial portion of personal computer users (This applies to practically any operating system change, including the migration to OS/2, but it will be especially troubling for UNIX if it attempts to "be all things to all people.")

- Performance in I/O-intensive business applications (this is a problem with system structure that will not be easily solved)

- Lack of system, network, or data base management (accounting), and the control functions that permit it to operate effectively in the emerging interconnected business environment

- Security

6. Extending UNIX to break through these constraints will mean that it is literally no longer UNIX. (It would certainly be possible to have MULTICS rise like Phoenix out of the ashes. Or UNIX could ignore its DNA and evolve in the image of MVS, but under neither circumstance would it be UNIX.) This would be unfortunate since UNIX has an important role to play on the leading edge of professional workstations and work units.

7. I conclude that the major business computer-communications architecture will be predominantly proprietary (specifically SAA) for the foreseeable future and that the open architecture will evolve around the proprietary foundation of SAA and coexist with it.

14.4 STANDARDS AS REALITY

There are two realities: (1) IBM has defined SAA, and it, in turn, will define the de facto standards of the IBM customer base; and (2) IBM, in its involvement in OSF, has committed to support the standards which that organization will define for the open environment, and they, in turn, will tend to dictate the de facto standards of the open environment. After all, what we are really talking about here are the interfaces between the open environment and SAA, and how UNIX will coexist with SNA in the real world. The question then becomes: Where will the line be drawn between the proprietary de facto standard and the open de facto standard?

There is also one other reality—IBM's vision of where that line will be drawn is entirely different from that of the rest of the open systems advocates, especially in terms of timing. IBM is still in the business of controlling the distribution of processing and data over the processing hierarchy. The best way to predict where the line will actually be drawn is to review the "proper hierarchical network" (see Figure 14.5) against the strategic periods that were defined earlier.

The left-hand column of Figure 14.5 represents my upgrade of the proper functional distribution over the computer systems hierarchy. Significant revisions have been marked by asterisks and will be explained below. However, some new terminology clarifies the functional distribution defined in 1971.

"Centralized Network Management" has been added under Level I mainframes. I have steadfastly maintained for 15 years that Network Management should properly be done at Level II because I stubbornly resist those 37XX controllers that have consistently had less bang for a buck than any box IBM has ever developed (and that is saying something). This change is not capitulation—it has been inserted for the following reasons:

- The reality is that IBM has managed to win with SNA, but more important is the fact of the personal computer revolution which has literally distributed processing power so rapidly that some highly centralized control has been necessary.

- I have redefined network management so that certain functions remain centralized and some get distributed. This is due primarily to the merging of data base and network management during the 1990s, something that was not as readily apparent in 1971.

I have made another significant change in terminology (although the meaning remains the same) at Level I. Rather than say "replacement of decentralized (or stand-alone batch)," I now say that Level I mainframes properly "replace isolated systems and networks." This terminology should be clearer, especially when I describe the "Interconnected Networks" Strategic Period.

At Level II (Minicomputers), I have expanded some of the data base management functions that were previously implied in "simple transaction processing." Nothing is simple these days, but I always intended that transaction processing against local data bases should cover both office and operations support systems.

At Level II, Distributed Network/Data Base Management and Control replaces the simple "Network Management" that was previously used, for the same reasons mentioned at Level I.

"Scientific Timesharing," the primary initial minicomputer function, has been dropped from Level II. It is now possible to satisfy the demands for sufficient processing power on the desktop more economically. (Project control and work unit processing will still go on but the classic timesharing has dropped to the IWS.)

At Level III, the general catch-all term "Collection, Editing, and Display of Data" has been clarified by adding "Point-of-Transaction Processing"

LEVEL	Proper Functional Distribution	Distributed Data Base Present → 1994	Advanced Office Systems 1995 → 1999	Interconnected Networks 2000 → 2004	Interconnected Services 2005 →
I Mainframes > $200,000	Transaction Processing— Large Data Bases / Secured Central Storage / Centralized Network Mgmt.* / Replacement of Isolated Systems/Networks / Large-Scale Scientific Processing	Multiple Operating Sys.– SAA / Centralized Data Base Management / Centralized Network Management / Orderly Distribution of Processing & DBs?	The Centralization Engine / Tightly Integrated OS/ DBMS/Comm. / Archives, Information/ Knowledge Libraries, incl. Dict., Directories / Accounting, Auditing – / Security	The Centralization Engine / Tightly Integrated OS/ DBMS/Comm. / Archives, Information/ Knowledge Libraries, incl. Dict., Directories / Accounting, Auditing – / Security / Replace Isolated UNIX and Proprietary Nets	Community-wide Utilities / ISDN & Broadband
II Minicomputers > $20,000	Transaction Processing— Local Data Bases / Operational Data Bases / Image Processing & Storage / Dist. Network/Data Base / Mgmt. & Control* / Program & Systems Dev. & Maintenance	Tightly Integrated OS/2, DBMS, Comm., OS/400 / Distributed Data Base Management / Sub-net Oper. Control – APPN / Gateway to Open World – X/Open / Voice-Data Integration Office Services / UNIX Open	The Integration Engine / Voice, Data, Images / Video – Operating Sys. / Network Control – / Virtual Nets / ISDN & Wideband – / Fiber Optics / UNIX	The Integration Engine / Voice, Data, Images / Video – Operating Sys. / Network Control – / Virtual Nets / ISDN & Wideband – / Fiber Optics / UNIX / Knowledge to Data Acq. / Import-Export Control / (Filter & Valve)	Neighborhood Service / ISDN & Broadband
III IWS < $20,000	Collection, Editing, & Display of Data / Point-of-Transaction Proc. / Personal Data Bases* / Personal Processing* / Human-Machine Knowledge Bases* / Support of Lower-Level Terminals	Multiple Operating Systems / OS/2 EE for DDBM / UNIX – Open – Differentiation Engines / Controlled from Levels I & II	Multiple Operating Systems / OS/2 EE for DDBM / UNIX – Open – Differentiation Engines / Controlled from Levels I & II / UNIX-based Prof. IWSs Become de facto Std. / Knowledge Nets Develop	Multiple Operating Systems / OS/2 EE for DDBM / UNIX – Open – Differentiation Engines / Controlled from Levels I & II / De facto Standards by Application / Knowledge Nets Subord.	Personal Castle? / Personal Prison? / ISDN & Broadband
IV Terminals, Variable	Mechanization of Function				

Figure 14.5 – A Framework for the Future (Characteristics by Level)

(which was implicit in the original description). However, the power of personal computers has reached the point where the following must be considered new functions (even though the general catch-all category did imply limited functions in all areas).

- Personal Data Bases (the lowest level of distribution)
- Personal Processing (for scientific and engineering work)
- Human-Machine Knowledge Bases (the anticipated set of differentiated professional workstations described above)

Level IV, originally defined as "dumb" terminals, is now described as having "limited intelligence and providing for mechanization of specific functions with microprocessor technology." The opportunities for creativity at this area are virtually unlimited, and the opportunities for establishing de facto industry standards and obtaining competitive advantage are substantial throughout all the strategic periods.

If my assessment of SAA is correct, IBM's primary purpose is to maintain and extend control over data base and network management. This is an extension of an SNA strategy that was hideously successful in delaying the proper distribution of processing during the 1970s and early 1980s. As mentioned earlier, IBM's current plan is approximately 10 years behind that which could have been possible with existing technologies.

The darkly shaded cells in Figure 14.5 show the inexorable extension of IBM control over data network management, from controlling its mainframe domain to what amounts to a veritable computer utility of the next century. The lighter shading indicates points of vulnerability (from IBM's perspective). The clear borders indicate "openness," but the following should be pointed out in that regard:

- There are elements of all the strategic periods operating in parallel at all times, just as progressive centralization, integration, differentiation, and mechanization occur in all systems.
- The dark shading merely indicates where IBM may have established de facto standards for data network management; open systems will exist in parallel. In fact, even if IBM is "successful," the resulting system will, of necessity, be open (either that, or we will be confronted with a very unpleasant reality).

My comments on the characteristics of the Strategic Periods will be limited to defining the interplay with open systems.

14.4.1 Distributed Data Base Period (1989–1994)

IBM will remain firmly in control of mainframe technology—Level I. UNIX-based open systems may make some progress against DOS/VSE systems (as IBM continues the battle to convert them to MVS and/or VM), but there will be no question that the de facto standard will be SAA. IBM DBMSs are firmly in place, and NetView will not be subordinated to other vendors' network management systems. The one big question for mainframes is whether, even now, IBM will encourage the "orderly distribution" of processing and data bases to its own SAA systems at Level II.

- The AS/400, emphasized throughout this book, is the key to the Distributed Data Base Period. This is the system that UNIX-based systems must both compete against and interface with. The merging of data base and network management at Level II is the reality of the early 1990s; this is where the battles between (and among) proprietary and open systems will be fought. The major question is whether IBM will diligently proceed toward placing the AS/400 in its proper place in the SAA environment. The role that APPN will (or won't) be assigned is critically important—SAA or open?

At Level III, the battle line will be clearly drawn between distributed data bases and file transfer. Regardless, UNIX is going to be there on the professional workstations.

14.4.2 Advanced Office Systems Period (1995–1999)

Level I will clearly remain the "leading part" of the network, and it will have evolved into the "superserver" that IBM is beginning to talk about. Complexity is going to increase substantially as IBM plays with hardware-firmware-software. (Fujitsu can inspect all the MVS code it wants to; most of it will be obsoleted during this period.) UNIX-based systems will not gain on mainframe systems software.

How UNIX will fare in the continuing battle at Level II will be determined by how effectively UNIX-based systems (at all levels) can be interfaced with the AS/400. This is the most critical square in the whole mosaic. Systems integration is the name of the game in the 1990s, and commercial companies (unlike the government) cannot afford to spend hundreds of millions of dollars for systems of questionable value. This is where "solutions" are required.

At Level III, the importance of professional workstations will be easily recognized by this time, and UNIX-like systems will be prominent in the high end of the market. The horsepower race will be over and individualized solutions will predominate; however, Level III will continue to support great variety, just as it should.

14.4.3 Interconnected Networks Period (2000–2004)

Electronic data interchange through file transfer is going to be found wanting before this period, but this is the time when it will really become intolerable. Everyone will finally understand what data entropy is all about (at last). It will be apparent that something must be done about it, and Level I will serve as the focal point for absorbing "isolated networks" under the greater SAA umbrella, just as stand-alone batch systems were absorbed during earlier "consolidations." Computer-communications utilities will begin to develop.

Knowledge capture will become a practical reality during this period. As old Charlie gets ready to retire, the network is going to know an awful lot about how Charlie really did his job.

The knowledge nets that developed among professionals during the previous strategic period will become more specialized and will be subordinated to the Level II knowledge capture systems described above. Intelligent computer systems will be colleagues in the networks. (If you feel this will be something like having someone read over your shoulder or open your mail, you are right. The manner in which such systems are implemented will be of major importance, but develop they shall.)

14.4.4 Integrated Services Period (2005–2009)

The Integrated Services Period will see the beginning of the open, national (and perhaps international) computer-communications infrastructure. It will have all of the potential and problems that were outlined in the NBS study of the 1970s.

The "information age" will be upon us. I assume it will be "open" in the sense that it is available to everyone. It truly will have infinite capacity for good or evil. In order to assure a new freedom and a new happiness, the concept of "open" may have to be refined, but at least we have a chance.

If the system is "closed" in any sense, dramatic changes must take place in government, business, and the commonwealth. It does not take much imagination to predict that we will not like most of these changes. The electronic prison will surround us unless we continue to have freedom to choose the extent of our participation.

14.5 PERFORMANCE MEASUREMENT AND COMPETITION

Presumably, if everything is open and equal (compatible hardware and systems software), the selection of computer systems will be made on the basis of price-performance. However, if experience tells us anything, it is the fact that everything is seldom equal.

For example, it is well established that IBM is more equal than others in the corporate world. When Amdahl was getting started as the first truly IBM "plug-compatible" mainframe (I prefer the term "software-compatible"), performance and market analyses of the system were conducted. Results concluded that Amdahl would have to clearly demonstrate price-performance improvement of at least 25 percent before most IBM customers would consider installing anything other than a "blue box." Since Amdahl has survived as a viable alternative to IBM (thanks to no small degree to AT&T, which has always sought alternatives to IBM), there are some customers who will settle for savings of less than 25 percent, but NAS and Amdahl have only been able to capture 10 to 12 percent of the IBM mainframe market. There has been accommodation under the IBM pricing umbrella over the last 15 years, which seems acceptable to both IBM and its competitors.

Even in the less-than-competitive environment in Japan, Japanese manufacturers have found it impossible to dislodge IBM with their own products. And it is probable that the settlement reached in the Fujitsu/IBM operating system dispute represented more net income to IBM than its competitors in the software-compatible mainframe market have generated since Amdahl started the whole business in the mid-1970s.

There is, of course, the case of personal computers in which operating systems were "open," but the same facts must be faced—IBM will establish the price-performance umbrella under which others will succeed or fail as viable businesses. Given the fact that IBM has a built-in markup in direct head-to-head competition with identical products, the advantage becomes even more pronounced when there are questions concerning the quality (performance or function) of the product. That leads us to the fuzzy area of performance measurement.

While it is beyond the scope of this book to go into detail about the complexity of performance measurement, I can provide a frame of reference (see

Figure 14.6) that may help maintain some sanity in an environment where both vendors and "experts" have a propensity toward the irrational.

The first thing to state about performance measurement is that we have not made a lot of progress in the last 25 years. We knew then that average instruction times (MIPS) were not meaningful measures across architectures. We knew about instruction mixes, thanks to Jack Gibson. We knew about kernels and benchmarks and their relative merits or lack thereof. We knew about the enormous impact of compilers and operating systems. We knew about "quick and dirty" systems software, and we knew how to cheat on practically any performance measurement used (either that, or we knew how to confuse the issue enough so that the results would be suspect). Therefore, it is with

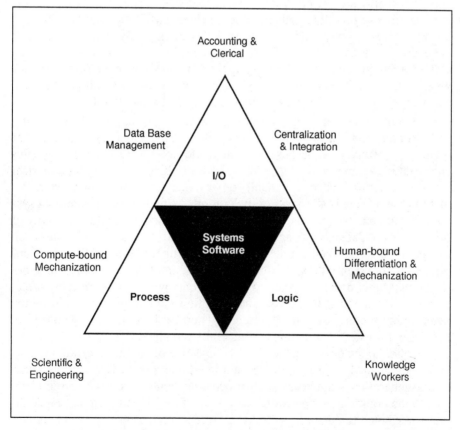

Figure 14.6 – Performance Measurement Triangles

some trepidation that I watch the industry heading toward another horsepower race. However, let's walk around the Performance Measurement Triangle.

The MIPS and megaflops war is already on at the IWS level where compute-bound work exists (see Figure 14.6). This issue is complicated by the fact that there aren't going to be standard processors at this level, and RISC technology dictates that performance competition will center around the quality of the software. Compiler and operating system implementations vary tremendously in terms of their performance, and RISCs are especially susceptible to wide variation. It will soon be obvious to even the most naive user that MIPS can be very misleading as a performance measure, depending on hardware architecture, systems software implementation, and your particular application.

A whole new set of programmers is going to learn why some of those crazy instructions exist in CISCs. Where really high-speed arithmetic is required, specific functions will become mechanized in coprocessors (or embedded processors in devices), but from the user perspective performance will depend on systems software. Computer architects and engineers have complained about programmers "lousing up their engines" since the first computer was invented, but they continue to place themselves in the position where the survival of their products is based on the quality of systems software.

Commercial computing can be described very simply as "accounting and clerical," and it is becoming more so all the time. Data base management systems were invented because humans could not ensure integrity and synchronization among computer generated files (which is essentially a clerical function, whether it is done manually or written by a simple program to reformat the files). This is a process of integration. As data base management systems developed, data base administrators were needed to ensure the quality of the centralized data bases (once again, a clerical function for which it has been extremely difficult to attract the quality of personnel required). Data base applications are essentially an I/O-bound process, and for a long time, some believed that the programs written to massage data would not noticeably affect system performance (the DBMS and operating system quality would be the determining factor, and the object code generated by compilers would have only trivial impact). While this has generally remained true, our penchant for ever-higher languages (with the ultimate objective of talking with our computers) has managed to pile interfaces and interpreters upon CASE tools, upon fourth-generation languages, upon procedural languages, upon assemblers, etc., to the point that the performance failure of developed systems can be directly attributed to the tools being used. Once again, performance and competition will be directly dependent on the entire range of systems software.

Just in case the remarkable progress in hardware technology provides enough arithmetic and I/O power to satisfy the scientists and the clerks (which it probably never will), waiting in the wings is the unfulfilled promise of the "giant electronic brains" of 30 years ago. We have not yet been able to create our systems in our own image from a logical point of view, much less from a creative and intuitive point of view. If we are to succeed in even a rough emulation, we must consider the following:

- Expert system domains must remain narrow. This process of differentiation will continue even within the domains themselves, for it will be found that things that work well in one organization (or environment) do not work well in others. It is not a question of modeling a single human expert; it is a question of modeling the human expert's functioning within the specific information structure of a particular organization. That will require all the processing, logic, and I/O capability we will ever have.

- The mechanization of human sensory functions so that our computers can "read" and/or "listen" and record information from the outside world (with minimal understanding) is even more demanding on current technology.

- Providing even relatively simple functions to improve the performance of knowledge workers will absorb all of our wonderful technology for the foreseeable future. The application of technology in this area is "human-bound"—artificial intelligence has absorbed some of the best minds in the world (and many of questionable quality as well) for several decades and precious little progress has been made.

  There is one very good reason for this—the performance of hardware-software systems for knowledge workers has a clear standard of performance; it can be compared with human performance for the same tasks. It is not a question of how fast a forecaster can generate forecasts using the spreadsheet package; it is how good those forecasts are. [Apple's decisions to stockpile DRAMs (dynamic RAMs) and raise prices were probably based on some beautiful graphics that were generated quite easily on the MAC. The performance of the knowledge workers involved in these decisions, at all levels, was not enhanced by the improved performance at the human-machine dyad—quite the contrary.]

- Knowledge-based systems will not be evaluated against MIPS, response time, how fast a spreadsheet can be recalculated, how many pretty reports can be generated, or how much data can be managed. None of these will be sufficient. It will be a question of how the system performs compared to old Charlene, who has actually run the company for years. In other words, we will start measuring our systems on the results of applications rather than on the "solutions" that are being peddled.

In the meantime, the industry is about to embark on a round of rediscovery in computer systems performance measurement. Even vendors realize that they are losing credibility with some of the published and unpublished benchmarks being advertised. Fortunately, there are signs of progress. The Transaction Processing Performance Council (TPPC) and vendors seem to be willing to cooperate in establishing a standard OLTP (on-line transaction processing) benchmark. It is good work, but it will inevitably lead us into all the complexity of software performance measurement. We will learn the lesson of just how difficult performance measurement and prediction are when there are massive failures of complex systems that passed benchmarks and even simulations with flying colors.

This is only by way of saying that in an open environment in which operating systems are theoretically equal in function, you need to establish some standards of performance and quality against which to compare competing systems.

Given all the complexity of performance measurement, I predict the following:

- The MIPS war must settle down. Some vendors will die, some will surrender, and the survivors will sign an armistice.

- The raw price performance standard that is finally agreed on will be the perceived (or measured) performance of IBM systems. The normal "umbrella effect" will apply; competitors will settle in under the IBM pricing umbrella, and accommodation will be reached.

- Assuming that all systems will "look and feel" much the same at the human interface, which seems to be inevitable regardless of the litigation we have seen, the focus of competition must then turn to actual applications, and the measure is going to be institutional performance. No more lists of a "Premier 100" based solely on how much money the companies spend on information systems technology, and no ignoring profitability. As we proceed through the strategic periods, "performance" of information systems will increasingly be based on demonstrable results rather than on vague promises. It is about time.

15

Conclusions

15.1 WHAT IT WILL TAKE TO WIN

To the degree that there is competition between OSF and UNIX International, the deck started out stacked against the latter. Consider the following.

Regardless of how much distance AT&T and Sun put between themselves and UNIX International, in 1988 and 1989 there wasn't any question of what they started out to do—they attempted to seize control of an open standard and use it for competitive advantage to the detriment of major licensees. I did not think this would be forgotten.

OSF seemed to be committed to addressing the real concerns of the marketplace—interfaces between and among network and applications architectures— whereas UNIX International seemed to be operating under the mistaken impression that UNIX alone would solve all the world's problems.

Assuming that interfacing is the real name of the game, the OSF members controlled the two primary architectures everyone must be concerned about—SNA and DECnet were here and were not going to go away. It is also true that IBM, DEC, and HP had and still have the largest share of the mainframe and minicomputer installed base of applications and exercise some account control over their respective customer bases. UNIX systems will continue to interface with these installed bases in the foreseeable future, and these customers are likely to follow the guidance of the current major vendors. No operating system is an island today—the predominant trend is integration.

In addition, IBM, DEC, and HP were and are still well-known, well-established organizations outside the United States; AT&T and Sun are not.

253

Enrollment in the two organizations originally showed that the OSF probably would prevail also:

- As of March 31, 1989, OSF had 96 members while UNIX International had 58.

- Of these, 24 members belonged to both organizations.

- If the dual enrollments were eliminated, OSF was attracting twice as many members as UNIX International (72 to 23).

By the summer and fall of 1989, the membership rolls had changed somewhat:

- The OSF had 112 members on July 31, 1989. UNIX International listed 98 members on September 15, 1989 and stated that applications under consideration, if approved, would bring the total to 106.

- Of these, 37 members belonged to both organizations. I viewed this as bet-hedging or acknowledgment that both "standards" would have to be supported.

In August 1991, the membership had changed as follows:

- The OSF lists 173 "formally announced" members and states that its current membership is more than 300 (Figure 6.1).

- UNIX International lists 240 members (Figure 5.1).

- The number of members enrolled in both organizations is 42.

There is a certain philosophy that states one should "stick with the winners." A lot has happened since 1988, and it appears that the organizations interested in an open software environment are fairly evenly divided over who the winner is or should be.

Regardless of which side is picked, team play breaks down practically immediately—the name of the game is one-on-one competition. DEC, IBM, Wang, and Data General aren't going to stop competing against each other just because they have all put a little money into OSF. In any given competitive situation, these competitors are at least 10 times as likely to be competing against each other as they are against such stellar members of the UNIX International team as AT&T, Amdahl, Unisys, Prime, or Sun. The most important thing that will separate the winners from the losers is a good healthy sense of the reality of the game that is being played.

The first and perhaps most important thing to understand is the reality of UNIX. For example:

- It will not ensure applications portability across competitive platforms, and customers are going to find this out soon.

- UNIX will never replace the proprietary operating systems that have become de facto standards (among the IBM, DEC, and HP customer bases).

- UNIX will not be standardized; specialized versions will continue on their own course despite the best efforts of management to control them.

- "Standard UNIX" will never catch up with proprietary systems in terms of functional capability and robustness.

You can't sell hardware and give away software; you can't sell service and give away hardware; and you can't sell software and give away hardware. You can't depend on outside sources for systems software and expect to control your own destiny for very long. While the above may sound somewhat foolish, some major vendors have adopted business strategies that ignore these realities. Loss leaders have a way of getting out of control in the computer industry. Not knowing whether you have a profitable strategy is an even more serious problem.

What this means, fundamentally, is that winners will have very good product measurement accounting systems—they will know their hardware-software development costs, manufacturing costs, and S&A expenses; and they will have effective planning systems (and data bases) to support their business. The reality of the computer industry is that vendors have consistently had problems with their own administrative systems. Some companies (such as IBM and DEC) have survived major problems caused by inadequate internal systems. The list of companies that have failed for this reason is lengthy indeed.

The movers and shakers who were analyzed above represent a small portion of the current membership in OSF and UNIX International. Even a cursory look at that membership indicates that the following categories are represented:

- Systems vendors who will provide complete hardware software systems with their own stamp on it (the movers and shakers already mentioned).

- Hardware vendors who are looking to UNIX as a standard operating system for their hardware product, thus saving development and maintenance expense for software development.

- Systems integrators who are obviously interested in promoting standard interfaces. They are all too aware of the complexity of the problems they are being called on to solve.

- Then, of course, we have users (although this subset is represented primarily by universities) who have practical, academic, and perhaps even business reasons for being interested in standards.

A rough analysis of the membership of OSF and UNIX International reveals the following:

- While some hardware and systems vendors belong to both organizations, there is a clear split between the have's and the have-not's. UNIX International is loaded with systems and hardware vendors who are intent on "redistributing the wealth." Their targets are IBM (naturally), DEC, and HP, who currently have the lion's share of the markets they are trying to penetrate. These systems and hardware vendors want to level the proprietary mountains (and hills) that arise around the currently limited level playing field.

- DBMS vendors tend to be hedging their bets by joining both organizations or betting on OSF (Software AG). Most applications software vendors seem to be patient and are waiting to see whether this UNIX thing is for real. In the meantime, they have more than enough to do by keeping busy with traditional proprietary operating systems from major vendors and the emerging OS/2 and OS/400 systems. Let's face it, SAA is closer to being a reality than a standard UNIX system is at the present time.

- To the degree that systems integrators and users (universities) are being attracted to the organizations, there is no question about their choice—OSF. This tells us something. The work of OSF, broader than the single-mindedness of UNIX International, is perceived as more important to success on the level playing field.

- One additional factor about the UNIX International membership list may have something to say about what it takes to succeed on the "level playing field." Three members of UNIX International have been in the penalty box within the last few years because of rules violations—I refer to Unisys's past problems in dealing with government procurement officials, Fujitsu's problems with IBM over lifted operating systems code, and the 1989 story that a representative of Gould had been paying off a Navy Department procurement official for 5 years. Things get tough down there in the trenches.

If UNIX and open systems are to have a bright future in the commercial market, it is necessary to understand the critical integration factors with which an applications developer is confronted. The term "platform" is not appropriate in the open environment. A more descriptive term would be "raft." The applications developer is going to be confronted with a bunch of floating logs and will have to build a raft from scratch. The quality and performance of the raft will depend on the logs that are selected and how they are tied together:

- There will be a variety of processor "logs" from which a raft can be built; these will become more diverse as RISC technology progresses.

- Performance of the log selected will be determined by the quality of the compiler logs available and/or selected.

- The DBMSs, while they may all be roughly described as "relational," will vary tremendously in terms of the quality of their implementation. Their ultimate performance will depend on the processor selected, the quality of the compilers in which they are written (I assume C), and the quality of implementation of the operating system logs to which they are lashed.

- Network architecture (and management) logs will, in turn, be interdependent with all of the above before the physical network ties the whole raft together. The quality of the raft on which an application must be built depends on the quality of all the logs from which it is constructed, and it doesn't make any difference which log one starts with. As the logs are selected, each one must be evaluated, and making a mistake is literally as "easy as rolling off a log." Sometimes perfectly good logs won't fit together very well, and water-logged logs can cause the whole raft to founder. Thus go the problems of bottom-up systems development. Proprietary systems will look like yachts when it comes time to build applications of any significance on some of the possible "open" rafts.

Those who win will be those who know what the raft is expected to carry and those who carefully collect the right logs ahead of time. Increasingly, the raft as a whole, not the individual logs, will be evaluated. Serious competitors will not be able to depend on others to provide proper-sized logs of good quality. While one-on-one competition may be the name of the game on the level playing field, teams will first have to be formed to even enter the competition with the big boys.

The winners in the long term will be those who can provide applications systems solutions to specific customer problems. This implies detailed knowledge of what those particular problems are – including the peculiarities of the particular industry and/or organization. The days of buying technology for the sake of technology are rapidly coming to a close.

15.2 HOW THE GAME CAN BE LOST

The open systems game can be lost in any number of ways, but three scenarios are especially important.

- The game can be lost by those who do not understand that the name of the game in the 1990s is data base management, specifically, distributed data base management. This implies sensitivity to considerations of data base integrity, synchronization, privacy, security, and the general quality of information.
- The game can be lost by concentrating on the development of tools (hardware, software, CASE, etc.) and by labeling (and selling) such tools as "solutions" to applications sets for which they are not suited. This refers specifically to the action of extending UNIX into markets for which it is not well suited.
- The game can be lost by concentrating on a horsepower race without regard for or understanding of the consequences. Turning computer power into a commodity does not ensure that anyone will make any money, and it certainly does not ensure demand. Ask any farmer.

15.3 HOW A PRISONER CAN BE A SURVIVOR

Having selected UNIX as the name of the game on the open playing field, those who depend exclusively on UNIX will find themselves prisoner of proprietary mountains on two sides and a swamp of limitations on the other two sides. The level playing field with its open watering hole is literally surrounded (see Figure 15.1).

While SAA has been used as an example, other proprietary systems are not going to go away, either. UNIX is firmly established only in the classic timesharing environment represented by the process-dependent work unit. One does not escape this situation by striking off blindly into the mountains or the swamp.

COMPUTER-COMMUNICATIONS NETWORKS	PRODUCTIVITY (PERFORMANCE)	DATA/ INFORMATION/ KNOWLEDGE
Mainframes	Human-Machine Dyad	Data
Proprietary Superior Function Superior Structure Network Management Transaction Processing	First-time Users Small Business Installed PCs All Easier to Use	Security Integrity Control
Minicomputers	Work Unit	Information

Business –
  Predominantly
  Proprietary (90+%)
Superior Function
Easier to Use
Hardware-Software
  Integration (OS/400)
	Data-Dependent
	
	?
	
	Process Dependent
	(UNIX)
		Data-Dependent
		Security
		Privacy

Personal Computers/ Workstations	Institutional	Knowledge
DOS Standard Ease of Use OS/2 Hardware/Software Integration (OS/2 EE)	Data & Accounting Dependent Failure of "Scientific Management"	Differentiation Limited Results Data-Dependent Highly Sensitive Highly Specialized

Figure 15.1 – The Playing Field Prison

I have suggested in this book that there is a passage through the mountains between the minicomputers and the workstations. This passage is not merely the scientific workstations where UNIX has already been successful, but an entire spectrum of professional workstations that will be used by knowledge workers.

There is also the possibility of establishing some firm ground in the swamp. The swamp is composed of data dependencies on large central mainframes which currently have control of centralized data bases and network management. UNIX is ill-equipped to drain this swamp. However, there is an increasingly important element of data—the capture of knowledge. The professional workstation is the place where knowledge becomes data, and information contributes to knowledge. Emerging expert systems and the tools of artificial intelligence, operations research, and "scientific management" are process-intensive. UNIX is well suited to the knowledge area, which is the most important challenge confronting the computer industry. It is the ground on which institutional performance improvement must be built. A "prisoner" who leaves the rest of the data swamp to others will not only survive, but prosper.

15.4 CONCLUSIONS

The development of "soft" standards in the computer industry (from ASCII to networking) has been fraught with politics and the desire to "level the playing field." Any vendor with perceived competitive advantage at the time a standard is being developed can be reasonably certain that the "official" standard will deviate from any de facto standard. This has resulted in the following:

- IBM, the company normally perceived to have competitive advantage, has largely ignored industry standards in favor of proprietary products. IBM has been largely successful with this strategy, and the result has been IBM-related de facto standards which are the practical realities of the marketplace. IBM supports standards in order to penetrate market areas that would otherwise be closed to it.

- The federal government, the world's largest computer user (and with influence going beyond its actual usage), avows that it will maintain both a level playing field for vendors and alternate sources of supply. This results in the installation of a great variety of computer hardware in the government with the concomitant problems of compatibility and expense. Over the years, the government has attempted to standardize the software with the hope that the problem would go away. This strategy has not been successful in terms of either implementation or results. The cost of integrating these diverse systems, while viewed as a business opportunity by vendors, has been unbelievably difficult and expensive.

- These strategies on the part of the world's largest computer vendor and the world's largest computer user have both tended to slow the practical application of advanced computer technology in the marketplace. IBM has a vested interest in "managing" the release and application of technology to avoid affecting existing products, and the federal government has tended to standardize and maintain software (both systems and applications) at the "lowest common denominator." Integrating such obsolete hardware-software systems is extremely expensive and dangerous, not only to an individual organization, but to the economy and competitive position of the nation.

The fact that computer systems and communications systems would merge into computer-communications networks has been apparent since computers were first applied to business applications (as opposed to engineering and scientific work). For the last 15 to 20 years, it has also been apparent that a hierarchy of mainframes, minicomputers, and microprocessor technologies would be employed in such networks. The proper distribution and application of these technologies over the network is based on economics that is so compelling that not even IBM has been able to control the acceptance of new and diverse technologies by its customer base. The result has been

- A demand for integration (connectivity) of diverse minicomputers and microprocessor-based systems. This demand is based on the perceived cost-effectiveness of the new technologies and the need for access to data which are stored on mainframes.
- Well-known and very real problems associated with the distribution of data over computer-communications networks. These problems have to do with
  - Data base integrity and synchronization
  - Data base security
  - Data and information quality

All of the above can be summarized by the fact that distributed data have high entropy with the potential for adverse effects at the institutional level.

IBM has been forced to acknowledge the need for "connectivity" of competitive products, which has led to the endorsement of "openness" and "standards" at the communications interface level. (This commitment has recently been verified by IBM's announcement that it will provide OSI support for SAA's Common Programming Interface for Communications.) IBM also understands both the complexity of distributed data base management and its importance in the commercial environment.

A good case can be made that IBM's highly centralized control of data bases on large mainframes is not only prudent, but necessary, until the problems of distributed data base management have been solved.

Control of the central data resource and the distribution of data over the network will determine how applications will be run at various levels on the network. Classic top-down design of systems will normally result in this type of applications architecture. That is the reality of current in-place commercial systems.

Bottom-up systems development (evolution) immediately runs into problems of system integration if for no other reason than data and/or reporting dependencies. This, of necessity, means that such systems will be subordinated to the more robust central systems.

At the present time, there is every indication that any open systems at the mini and micro levels will be controlled by proprietary mainframe systems. The mainframe systems have the data, they have professional systems personnel, and until the problems of distributed data bases are solved, they are the only way to keep data and information entropy from increasing.

Distributed data base management lies at the heart of IBM's SAA. Various components of SAA are already de facto standards (e.g., SNA), and it is safe to assume that SAA will establish the general environment around (and within) which open systems will compete. It is, therefore, important to understand several important conclusions about SAA.

Hardware, operating systems, data base management, and network management functions will all become more tightly integrated under SAA as it evolves in the 1990s. OS/400 and OS/2 EE are better models for the future SAA "operating system" than are the loosely integrated software systems on System/370 architecture mainframes.

Distributed data base management and network management will become inextricably connected as SAA unfolds. The AS/400 is the key system in the distributed data base environment, and APPN is obviously going to become increasingly important.

It appears there are still many within IBM who do not understand (or who will not accept) the key role of the AS/400 in SAA. The longer it takes IBM to properly position the AS/400 in the network hierarchy, the more opportunities will exist for competitive vendors. (It is possible that the very success of the AS/400 in a more conventional role could delay IBM's progress over the Distributed Data Base Period.)

The role of UNIX in the open environment is assured. There are two distinct, and diametrically opposed, views of that role. Vendors other than IBM perceive it as the door that will open the commercial data-processing world (as defined by SAA) to them. IBM considers it the door through which it will penetrate the markets in which it has never been very successful. It is possible that the UNIX gate swings both ways, but it is doubtful it will fulfill expectations in either direction for the following reasons:

- UNIX is years (one might even say decades) behind standard operating systems in the mainframe environment, and it will never catch up. It is fine and good to say that UNIX can be improved to the point where it has the capabilities of MVS/XA or ESA, but that doesn't address when, or the fact that MVS will have evolved into a tightly integrated hardware-software system by that time, or that if UNIX did reach the level of MVS, it would no longer be UNIX (in the best sense of the word).

- Where functionality and robustness limit UNIX at the high end of the processing spectrum, ease of use will tend to limit its use against minicomputers (such as the AS/400) and against personal computers which are being used for most commercial applications.

- There is also the issue of security. It is real. Hackers from all over the world have penetrated UNIX systems. It is discovered that access codes to classified UNIX-based systems have been sold to the Soviet KGB. A high-school dropout is put in jail for penetrating Department of Defense computer systems and "stealing UNIX code." (You can't put the KGB in jail, but you sure have to wonder whether they aren't capable of making more sophisticated penetrations.) A "playful" graduate student makes a "mistake" while penetrating a whole network (for purposes which have yet to be disclosed) and brings down 6000 UNIX systems – his father is a government expert on UNIX security. The FBI declined to investigate the penetrations that led to sale of access codes to the KGB. The Air Force standardizes on UNIX and lets what is potentially a multi-billion-dollar contract to AT&T despite the fact that the high-school dropout penetrated UNIX-based computer systems being run for it by AT&T. If this doesn't have all the makings of a national scandal, I don't know what does.

In summary, I quote once again from AT&T's *Bell Laboratories Technical Journal* (vol. 63, no. 8, October 1984; "UNIX Operating Systems Security):"

> All but a few of their files (UNIX-based systems) are at least readable by anybody, and most such systems have access to thousands of other systems via remote mail and file transfer facilities. That is, they use the UNIX system as its creators intended it to be used.
>
> Such open systems cannot ever be made secure in any strong sense; that is, they are unfit for applications involving classified government information, corporate accounting, records relating to individual privacy, and the like.

And, later in the same article:

> Most UNIX systems are far less secure than they can and should be. This unwarranted insecurity is largely caused by complacency and the use of concealment as a security measure. The administrators do not want word of security problems to be circulated.

The wisdom of this internal analysis of UNIX security has been amply demonstrated. I deplore the fact that a perfectly good system has been, and is being, promoted beyond its intended use. It is apparent that UNIX still has a long way to go before it can be made "fit" for many commercial uses. To the degree that concealment is still being practiced as a security measure, it could have drastic consequences for vendors, users, government agencies, and the individuals involved.

As far as IBM's use of UNIX to penetrate markets in which it has not been traditionally strong (government, scientific and engineering, education, development workbench), I base my conclusion solely on past performance – any organization that could establish ease of use as a primary design point for an operating system and then develop what has evolved into MVS/ESA will find some way to ruin UNIX also. The current method is to put it under VM; in the future, they will probably enhance it to death.

In the entire spectrum of computing, UNIX (and its primary language, C) is best suited for a relatively narrow, but important segment—that of high-performance professional workstations, which will be highly differentiated (personalized) by hardware and applications software. UNIX is a relatively easy to use and understandable operating system and is easily portable. It will be the operating system of choice to support the development of RISC and the other specialized processors that will be used to drive intelligent new peripherals (advanced scanners, displays, optical disk, etc.), and the operating system of choice for advanced applications (such as expert systems in all their variety).

UNIX will remain primarily a file transfer system with all the limitations the term implies. For purposes of data base and network management, it will be buffered through more robust and secure proprietary systems—specifically, SAA. I believe that the AS/400 will serve as the "buffering server" by providing tight integration with UNIX-based intelligent workstations and minicomputers (both IBM and OEM). While IBM is committed to support both AIX and OSF/1, it is possible that AIX will always remain ahead of OSF/1 in terms of its "connectivity" with SAA. Nevertheless, both will be superior to the connectivity that can be anticipated for competitive proprietary systems.

The federal government's endorsement of UNIX, combined with its failure to exercise leadership in the development of a national computer-communications network infrastructure in the 1970s, virtually assures that IBM's SAA will become the backbone network for business applications. It also means that the development of an open national infrastructure will essentially be left to vendor organizations.

I conclude that UNIX International (as its name implies) may still be obsessed with UNIX, whereas OSF (as its name implies) is also concerned with the interfaces necessary for the connectivity of various public and private networks. It appears that OSF has been able to move at least a little above proprietary interests and traditional competitive instincts to pursue its charter with some degree of objectivity. I sincerely hope that this is the case.

IBM, in its attempts to control the development of computer-communications networks, has succeeded in delaying the development of such networks to the point where customers are leading vendors in their demands. I now conclude that, while SAA may not be too little in terms of concept, it is too late in terms of being able to satisfy specific demands of the marketplace. This means that there are unparalleled opportunities for vendors who are willing to compete on that part of playing field that is truly level and open.

15.5 RECOMMENDATIONS

- Accept the reality of SAA and that IBM is likely to succeed in controlling the distribution of data bases during the Distributed Data Base Period, and recognize that integration with IBM proprietary systems is inevitable.

- Do not push UNIX-based systems into applications areas for which they are "unfit." (It is as important to know what *not* to do, as it is to know *what* to do.)

- Concentrate on how UNIX-based systems will interface with proprietary mainframe systems and use those systems to compensate for current weaknesses in UNIX. If the 1990s are going to be the decade of the "superserver," make sure they can be of maximum service without enslaving their patrons.

- More importantly, look ahead to the AS/400 and determine how it will serve UNIX-based systems. Use OSF to clarify the role of the AS/400 and how it will interface with UNIX-based systems. Place special emphasis on
  - When C will be available (it is committed)
  - Whether a UNIX-based operating system (or shell) will be available
  - Determining what the future of APPN will be

- Depending on answers, get OSF to consider taking the initiative on "opening up" the AS/400 in terms of assuring good interfaces for UNIX-based systems. Have OSF request that APPN be declared an open standard, and see what IBM has to say to that.

- After defining the SAA mountain on the level playing field as clearly as possible, turn away from the mountain (it isn't going to move very much) and look beyond the Distributed Data Base Period to the Advanced Office Systems Period. Surround those proprietary servers with UNIX-based, differentiated office systems. Specifically, I see image processing as a particularly attractive opportunity. In addition to Intelligent Workstations, we need to be able to drive the next generation of peripherals:
  - High-speed intelligent scanners
  - Hi-res (high-resolution) displays, laser printers, fax, and HDTV when it comes

- Process-intensive engines for pattern recognition to encode and classify documents for data base update
- Logic-intensive engines to provide individualized expert systems for screening the vast amounts of information that will be available, and for other expert systems which are coming.

- Concentrate application systems and their cost justification on the basis of reducing paper communications and documents. This strategy not only supports cost savings in clerical personnel, but ensures that the systems are properly designed and frees the professional employees for additional functions.
- Support the development of industry measures of price performance, but compete on demonstrable value added.
- Price products and services carefully, and be sure that the prices reflect true value added.
- Concentrate on applications, not hardware and tools.

I do not know what the precise market breakdown is going to be between the general-purpose "data base servers" and the specialized professional workstations of tomorrow; however, I do know that the opportunities for creative solutions to real business problems are unlimited.

Appendix:
IBM Programming Announcement –
March 17, 1987

IBM Systems Application Architecture

Today, IBM announces IBM Systems Application Architecture, a collection of selected software interfaces, conventions, and protocols that will be published in 1987.

IBM Systems Application Architecture will be the framework for development of consistent applications across the future offerings of the major IBM computing environments—System/370, System/3X, and Personal Computer.

Highlights

Systems Application Architecture provides the foundation for IBM to enhance the consistency of IBM software products by

- Providing a common programming interface
- Providing common communications support
- Providing a common user access
- Offering common applications
- Enhancing the availability and consistency of National Language implementation

Description

IBM offers systems based on several different hardware architectures and system control programs. By pursuing a multiple-architecture strategy, IBM has been able to provide products with outstanding price-performance to meet our customers' requirements. Today, IBM's products support the information processing needs of people in very different environments.

IBM Systems Application Architecture makes it easier for IBM's broad product line to solve customer information processing needs by providing the framework for the development and delivery of IBM products that address consistency requirements across the major IBM systems. Systems Application Architecture provides the foundation for IBM

- To enhance the consistency of IBM software products

- To define a common programming interface with which customers, independent software vendors, and IBM can productively develop applications that can be integrated with each other and ported to run in multiple IBM Systems Application Architecture environments

- To define common communications support that will provide interconnection of systems and programs and cross-system data access

- To define a common user access, including screen layout, menu presentation and selection techniques, keyboard layout and use, and display options

- To offer common IBM applications that run in each of the major computing environments.

Delivery of the IBM Systems Application Architecture will be evolutionary, beginning this year and continuing on an ongoing basis. This is the beginning of a long-term strategy similar to the process that has implemented IBM Systems Network Architecture (SNA). SNA started as a framework for consistency in the communications environment and has continued to be enhanced and extended. Today, SNA is the basis of communications for IBM's products and for many other vendors' products. In addition, IBM will continue to invest in applications and systems software that is specific to particular computing environments.

Elements of the Architecture

IBM Systems Application Architecture consists of four related elements—two of which are new (Common User Access and Common Programming Interface). The third is based on extensions to today's existing communication architectures (Common Communications Support). These three establish the basis for the fourth, Common Applications, developed by IBM to be consistent across systems. Independent software vendors and customers developing applications for IBM's major systems will also be encouraged to use IBM Systems Application Architecture products.

In addition, Systems Application Architecture provides IBM with the foundation to enhance the availability and consistency of National Language implementation in software products.

Common User Access: The Common User Access defines the basic elements of the end user interface and how to use them. The primary goal is to achieve (through consistency of user interface) transfer of learning, ease of learning, and ease of use across the range of IBM Systems Application Architecture applications and environments.

The Common User Access is a definition for IBM-developed software to adhere to over time and will be published so that customers and independent software vendors can develop programs that follow this definition.

Common Programming Interface: The Common Programming Interface is the application programming interface to the Systems Application Architecture systems. This interface consists of the languages and services used to productively develop applications that can be integrated with other applications and ported to run in multiple IBM Systems Application Architecture environments.

IBM is defining a Common Programming Interface that enables an application to be developed using IBM Systems Application Architecture products in one environment and then ported to another Systems Application Architecture environment with minimal changes to the application. This can result in increased programmer productivity and wider applicability of applications.

The initial elements of the Common Programming Interface are

- COBOL

  Based on ANS (American National Standard) Programming Language COBOL, X3.23–1985 Intermediate Level

- FORTRAN

  Based on ANS Programming Language FORTRAN, 77 level
- C

  Based on the draft proposed ANS Standard (X3J11)
- Application Generator

  Based on elements of the interfaces found in the existing cross-system product
- Procedures Language

  Based on the existing REXX language
- Database Interface

  Based on the ANS Database Language SQL, X3.135–1986, and IBM's SQL (Structured Query Language)
- Query Interface

  Based on an extension of the interfaces found in today's Query Management Facility (QMF) product
- Presentation Interface

  Based on extensions to the interface found in key elements of today's Graphical Data Display Manager (GDDM) product, provides services to present textual and graphic information on displays, printers, and plotters
- Dialog Interface

  Based on extensions to the interface found in today's EZ-VU product, provides for the definition, display, and management of textual information and menus, and for the control of screen flow within applications

This Common Programming Interface provides a basis for customers and independent software vendors to use IBM Systems Application Architecture products to develop portable applications. Additional elements will be defined, and the elements named above will be extended. The long-range goal is to define a comprehensive and productive set of IBM programming development languages and services.

Common Communications Support: Common Communications Support is used to interconnect Systems Application Architecture applications, Systems Application Architecture systems, and communication networks and devices. This will be achieved by the consistent implementation of designated communication architectures in each of the Systems Application Architecture environments. The architectures announced here are the building blocks for distributed function to be detailed in future announcements of Common Programming Interfaces and IBM Systems Application Architecture applications.

The architectures selected have been chosen largely from Systems Network Architecture (SNA) and international standards. Each was also included in the Open Communications Architectures announcement of September 16, 1986 (Programming Announcement 286-410), thus reaffirming IBM's commitment to openness.

As IBM expands the Systems Application Architecture, additional communications architectures will be evaluated for inclusion in Common Communications Support.

Included in Common Communications Support at this time are the following:

Data Streams

- 3270 Data Stream

  The 3270 Data Stream consists of user-provided data and commands, as well as control information that governs the way data are handled and formatted by IBM displays and printers. The Systems Application Architecture computing environments will all support the 3270 Data Stream. In addition, the System/3X family will continue to support the 5250 Data Stream. The 3270 Data Stream is documented in the IBM 3270 *Information Display System Data Stream Programmers's Reference* (GA23-0059).

- Document Content Architecture

  Document Content Architecture defines the rules for specifying the form and meaning of a text document. It provides for uniform interchange of textual information in the office environment and consists of format elements optimized for document revision. This is documented in *Document Content Architecture: Revisable-Form-Text Reference* (SC23-0758).

- Intelligent Printer Data Stream (IPDS)

  IPDS is the high function data stream intended for use with all points addressable page printers. Planned availability for documentation of this data stream is third quarter of 1987.

Application Services

- SNA Distribution Services (SNADS)

  SNADS provides an asynchronous distribution capability in an SNA network, thereby avoiding the need for active sessions between the endpoints. SNADS is documented in *Systems Network Architecture Format and Protocol Reference Manual: Distribution Services* (SC30-3098).

- Document Interchange Architecture (DIA)

  DIA provides a set of protocols that define several common office functions performed cooperatively by IBM products. This is documented in *Document Interchange Architecture: Technical Reference* (SC23-0781).

- SNA Network Management Architecture

  SNA Network Management Architecture describes IBM's approach to managing communication networks. The protocols of problem management offer a vehicle for monitoring network operations from a central location. This is documented in *Format and Protocol Reference Manual: Management Services* (SC30-3346).

Session Services

- LU Type 6.2

  LU (logical unit) Type 6.2 is a program-to-program communication protocol. It defines a rich set of interprogram communication services including a base subset and optional supplementary services. Support of the base is included in IBM LU6.2 products that expose an LU6.2 application programming interface. This ensures compatibility of communication functions across systems. LU6.2 is documented in *Systems Network Architecture: Format and Protocol Reference Manual, Architecture Logic for LU Type 6.2* (SC30-3269).

Network

- Low-Entry Networking Node

  A SNA *Low-Entry Networking Node* (Type 2.1 node) supports peer-to-peer communication. Type 2.1 nodes can be either programmable or fixed function systems. SNA Low-Entry Networking allows, through a common set of protocols, multiple and parallel SNA sessions to be established between Type 2.1 nodes that are directly attached to each other. Low-Entry Networking is documented in *Systems Network Architecture Format and Protocol Reference Manual: Architecture Logic for Type 2.1 Nodes* (SC30-3422).

- X.25

  X.25 defines a packet-mode interface for attaching data terminal equipment (DTE) such as host computers, communication controllers, and terminals to packet-switched data networks. An IBM-defined external specification, *The X.25 Interface for Attaching SNA Nodes to Packet-Switched Data Networks General Information Manual* (GA27-3345), and the 1984 version of this interface (GA27-3761) describe the elements of CCITT X.25 that are applicable to IBM SNA products that can attach to X.25 networks.

Data Link Controls

- Synchronous Data Link Control (SDLC)

  SDLC is a discipline for managing synchronous, code-transparent, serial-by-bit information transfer between nodes that are joined by telecommunication links. This is documented in *IBM Synchronous Data Link Control Concepts* (GA27-3093).

- IBM Token Ring Network

  The *IBM Token Ring Network* consists of a wiring system (the IBM Cabling System), a set of communication adapters (stations), and an access protocol that controls the sharing of the physical medium by the stations attached to the LAN. The IBM Token Ring Architecture is based on the IEEE 802.2 and 802.5 standards. This is documented in *Token Ring Network Architecture Reference* (part number 6165877).

Common Applications: It is IBM's intent to develop common applications across the Systems Application Architecture environments. The initial focus is on office applications and, later, industry-specific applications. With the publications that define the IBM Systems Application Architecture and the availability of products, IBM is encouraging independent software vendors and customers to develop applications based on IBM Systems Application Architecture products.

As with the Common Programming Interface, elements are being defined for office applications. The elements being defined include:

- Document Creation
- Document Library
- Personal Services, Mail
- Decision Support

Summary

IBM Systems Application Architecture is a set of software interfaces, conventions, and protocols—a framework for productively designing and developing applications with cross-system consistency. Systems Application Architecture defines the foundation to build portable, consistent application systems for the future with IBM hardware, control programs, and IBM Systems Application Architecture products.

Publications

The following publications are the primary deliverables planned for the Systems Application Architecture in 1987:

- *Systems Application Architecture Overview* (GA26-4341)

  This publication introduces Systems Application Architecture concepts and provides the initial designation of the systems and products participating in Systems Application Architecture. Planned availability is second quarter of 1987[1].

- Common User Access Publication

  A reference manual is planned to be available in the third quarter of 1987[2] (3Q87). It will specify the common user access

---

1. Publication became available on June 30, 1987.
2. Publication became available on September 30, 1987.

interfaces for intelligent workstations. Specifications for common user access interfaces for mainframe interactive terminals is planned to be added to this specification in the fourth quarter of $198/^3$ (4Q87). The elements to be specified include screen layout, menu presentation and selection techniques, keyboard layout and use, and display options.

- Common Programming Interface Publications

Reference manuals are planned to describe each interface that participates in application enabling for Systems Application Architecture. These reference manuals will provide the grammar and syntax (supplemented by the programming guidance provided by the products that implement the interface) needed to develop applications for the Systems Application Architecture environments. The publications and their planned availability dates follow:

Title	Available
Common Programming Interface COBOL Reference	$3Q87^4$
Common Programming Interface FORTRAN Reference	3Q87
Common Programming Interface C Reference	3Q87
Common Programming Interface Procedures Language Reference	3Q87
Common Programming Interface Application Generator Reference	3Q87
Common Programming Interface Query Reference	3Q87
Common Programming Interface Database Reference	3Q87

3. Updated publication became available on December 31, 1987.
4. All publications in this section with the availability date of 3Q87 were published on September 30, 1987.

Common Programming Interface
Presentation Reference   3Q87

Common Programming Interface
Dialog Reference   3Q87

- Writing Portable Programs

  This publication provides guidance on developing application programs that are consistent and portable among Systems Application Architecture systems. These applications will use the common Programming Interfaces and implement the Systems Application Architecture Common User Access specification. Planned availability is third quarter of 1987[5].

- Common Communications Support Publication

  The section Common Communications Support names the publications that define Systems Application Architecture communications protocols and standards.

---

5. This publication became available on September 30, 1987.

Index

About the Author

Michael Killen is founder and president of Killen & Associates, Inc., a company which specializes in helping large users and suppliers of information technology to manage the complex and accelerating pace of the integration of the boundaries of information systems technology and humans, within companies. He heads the firm's technology market programs, which analyze the impact of information systems technology on management and the implications for business strategies. With an expanded management consulting staff, Killen works with users and suppliers to develop information systems strategies that improve bottom-line performance and to formulate market policies.

Killen, based in Silicon Valley, is internationally known for writing the industry's first book on Systems Application Architecture—*IBM: The Making of the Common View* (Harcourt Brace Jovanovich, 1988). Killen contends that SAA provides the computing infrastructure that will take us through the 1990s and beyond.

Michael Killen is the author of *SAA: Managing Distributed Data* (McGraw–Hill, 1991), an important new book that analyzes IBM's approach to the development of distributed data base infrastructure under SAA. He is also the author of *SAA: Image Processing* (McGraw–Hill, 1991), which addresses IBM's approach to the replacement of paper-based computer systems with electronic-based systems.

Killen is a principal member of the editorial board of the United Kingdom's *SAA Spectrum*, the leading technical journal on SAA. His credits include several articles on technology trends and the impact of information systems performance in the SAA- and UNIX-based environments. He has also served as a columnist for *Business Communication Review (BCR),* a computer industry newspaper, a California business journal, and a major Japanese Daily.

Widely known as a speaker at AT&T, IBM, NEC, and NTT events, he has shared his insights of the codependence of the organization and information systems technology to improve performance.

Killen began his computer science career at Wang Laboratories in the early 1970s. He established Wang's Applications Programming and Field Programmers departments. He managed Wang's southern district sales and service organization, wrote two books on mathematics and programming, and helped to develop and implement Wang's initial strategy into the word processing and small business computer markets. Six years later, he joined Rockwell International as director of Market Research and Development. In 1980, the People's Republic of China invited him to tour major universities to report on the status of the teaching of computer science.

In conjunction with Killen & Class Productions of San Jose, California, an innovative TV and development organization, Killen has created a unique forum through the television broadcast medium to further his current areas of research on information systems and management innovation with CEOs, CIOs, and computer experts, discussing and publicly airing what has been learned from the integration of information systems technology into the business arena. His TV talk show, *High Technology with Killen & Class,* airs each week in California, Massachusetts, Michigan, Minnesota, and Texas.

Guests on the program have included CEOs, VPs, and CIOs from the following organizations: AT&T, Digital Equipment Corporation, Hewlett-Packard, Unisys, McKesson Corporation, Network Equipment Corporation, Network General, Silicon Graphics, Sun Microsystems, UNIX International, and many others.

Each month, Killen & Class Productions publishes two 30-minute videos that address management and technology trends.